AFRICA AFTER THE COLD WAR

AFRICA AFTER THE COLD WAR

THE CHANGING PERSPECTIVES ON SECURITY

EDITED BY

ADEBAYO OYEBADE

&

ABIODUN ALAO

Africa World Press, Inc.

P.O. Box 1892
Trenton, NJ 08607

P.O. Box 48
Asmara, ERITREA

Africa World Press, Inc.

P.O. Box 1892
Trenton, NJ 08607

P.O. Box 48
Asmara, ERITREA

Cover design: Jonathan Gullery
Book design: Wanjiku Ngugi

Library of Congress Cataloging-in-Publication Data

Africa after the Cold War : the changing perspectives on security / edited by Adebayo Oyebade and Abiodun Alao.
    p.   cm.
   Includes bibliographical references and index.
   ISBN 0-86543-650-9 (hardbound) . -- ISBN 0-86543-651-7 (pbk .)
   1. Africa--Politics and government--1960- 2. National security--Africa--History--20th century. 3. Africa--Economic conditions--1960-   I. Oyebade, Adebayo. II. Alao, Abiodun.
DT30.5. A3495 1998
960.3' 2--dc21   98-14115
                CIP

CONTENTS

LIST OF TABLES

ACRONYMS

AAF-SAP	African Alternative Framework-Structural Adjustment Program
ADB	African Development Bank
AID	Agency for International Development
ANC	African National Congress
ARMSCOR	Armament Corporation of South Africa
CD	Campaign for Democracy
CEEAC	Economic Community of Central African States
CIA	Central Intelligence Agency
CONSAS	Constellation of Southern African States
ECA	Economic Commission for Africa
ECOMOG	ECOWAS Monitoring Group.
ECOWAS	Economic Community of West African States
FIS	Front Islamique du Salut
FLAM	Force de Liberation Africaine de Mauritanians
FRELIMO	Frente de Libertacao de Mocambique
FRUIDEM	Front for Unity Independence and Democracy in Mauritania
FURAM	United Front for Mauritanian Armed Resistance
GDP	Gross Domestic Product
GIA	Group Islamique Armee
GNP	Gross National Product
GUNT	Government d'Union Nationale de Transition
IAEA	International Atomic Energy Agency
IFIs	International Financial Institutions
IFP	Inkhata Freedom Party
IGADD	Inter-governmental Authority on Drought and Development
IGNU	Interim Government of National Unity (Liberia)
IMF	International Monetary Fund
INPFL	Independent National Patriotic Front for Liberia
LNTG	Liberian National Transitional Government
LPA	Lagos Plan of Action
LPC	Liberian Peace Council
MIA	Mouvement Islamique Armee
MNR	Resistencia Nacional Mozambicana
MOSOP	Movement for the Survival of the Ogoni People
MPLA	Movimento Popular de Libertacao de Angola

NAACP	National Association for the Advancement of Colored People
NAM	Non-Aligned Movement
NATO	North Atlantic Treaty Organization
NIF	National Islamic Front
NPFL	National Patriotic Front of Liberia
NPRC	National Provisional Ruling Council (Sierra Leone)
NPT	Non-Proliferation Treaty
NRM	National Resistance Movement (Uganda)
OAU	Organization of African Unity
PAC	Pan African Congress
PLO	Palestinian Liberation Organization
RENAMO	Resistance de Nacionale de Mocambique
RPF	Rwandan Patriotic Front
RUF	Revolutionary United Front
SADC	Southern African Development Community
SADCC	Southern African Development Coordination Conference
SANDF	South African National Defence Force
SAP	Structural Adjustment Program
SPLA	Sudan Peoples Liberation Army
SPLM	Sudan People's Liberation Movement
TNCs	Trans-National Corporations
ULIMO	United Liberation Movement of Liberia
UN	United Nations
UNAMIR	United Nations Assistance Mission in Rwanda
UNAMO	United Nations Supervisory Mission on Mozambique
UNAVEM	United Nations Angola Verification Mission
UNEP	United Nations Environment Program
UNHCR	United Nations Office of High Commissioner for Refugees
UNITA	Uniao Nacional Para a Independencia Total de Angola
UNITAF	United Nations Interim Task Force (Somalia)
UNOMIL	United Nations Observer Mission in Liberia
UNOMOZ	United Nations Operation in Mozambique
UNOSOM	United Nations Operation in Somalia

PREFACE

Abiodun Alao

Adebayo Oyebade

In 1991, both of us were independently researching African security in the post-Cold War era. At Temple University, Philadelphia, in the United States, Adebayo had identified some themes in this area, and had started collecting materials for the possible publication of a treatise. At King's College, University of London, Abiodun had embarked on a similar venture. In mid 1992, Professor Toyin Falola of the University of Texas at Austin thoughtfully suggested we combine our research efforts. Thereafter, efforts to edit this book began in earnest. Trying to coordinate the work from either side of the Atlantic created an immediate problem; but Abiodun's two month visit to the United States in early 1993 removed the difficulty and we mapped out the conceptual and analytical frameworks. We created chapters and contacted contributors on three continents: America, Europe, and Africa. We began what seemed an endless stream of correspondence over the telephone and through the mail. However, we smoothed some of the rough edges in our position and approach during a 1993 meeting of the editors in Nigeria and during Adebayo's subsequent visit to London. Abiodun's research trip to the United States in February 1995 finally afforded the editors the opportunity to give definite direction to the book.

The motivation for this book is our concern about the African perspective of the numerous security problems plaguing the continent, especially at a period when the world stands at the doorstep of a new era. The demise of the Cold War and the prospects for security on the continent demand the attention of students of African security. This becomes particularly necessary because the end of the Cold War has introduced fundamental changes to the global perception of security. Some of the security issues undergoing this change in perception are identified and discussed in this book. The dynamic nature of security issues and limited space preclude the inclusion of all the topics we would have wished to discuss.

We are grateful to all the people who have assisted us in creating this book. First, we thank our contributors for enduring the hardship of having, at our insistence, to rewrite, and sometimes rewrite again. We also thank Professor Toyin Falola for writing the forward to the book. Our colleagues and friends at Temple University, and King's College, London, deserve special thanks. We have been fortunate to be members of two institutions that have devoted considerable attention to Africa and global security. We have, in particular, benefitted from various seminars presented by the staff and graduate students of both universities. In particular, we want to thank Professor Lawrence Freedman, of the War Studies Department, King's College, London; Professor Michael Clarke, and Dr. Chris Smith, both at the Centre for Defence Studies, King's College; Dr Teshale Tibebu, and Professor Matthew Sadiku, of Temple University's History and Electrical Engineering Departments respectively; and finally Dr. Olusola Akinrinade, of the Department of History, Obafemi Awolowo University, Ile-Ife, Nigeria.

The convention of acknowledgment places last a gratitude, which in the sincerity of the author's mind, comes first—that is to the author's immediate family. Adebayo wants to thank his wife Folashade, and his children, Olufemi Jr. and Oyebola, for bearing, with remarkable understanding, his continued absence from home while editing this book. Abiodun wishes to thank Oyeronke, who put up with far less attention than she is entitled to so soon after their wedding.

FOREWORD

With crises of monumental proportion in such places as Liberia, the Sudan, Nigeria, and Algeria; conflict-inducing politics in other places, and a myriad of problems everywhere, this book is timely, relevant, and significant. It is a thoughtful project, executed with genuine intention, brilliance, and originality.

The background for the analyses in all the contributions is the end of the Cold War and its implications for global politics and security. How can African countries prevent wars, external domination, internal troubles, and a pervasive atmosphere of fear? This book answers all these important questions with confidence, skill, honesty and diligence. In addition, the authors emphasize that in the African context, citizens' needs for food, employment, water, shelter, and health must be considered in addressing security issues. It is true that poverty has engendered political instability. Integrating the broad terrain of economic development in this study is very useful indeed.

As on other continents, the determinants of security concerns in Africa have changed from time to time, adjusting to economic and political exigencies. In the 1960s, when African countries were just freeing themselves from the yoke of colonial rule, Africa's security agenda focused on decolonization, the avoidance of involvement in superpower rivalries, and the maintenance of territorial integrity of its boundaries. Since the end of the Cold War, concerns have changed to reflect the marginalization of the continent and the increasing poverty on the continent.

This is an important book that will surely enhance the status of security studies in Africa, a fledgling field of inquiry. It is a nuanced, matured, and detailed understanding of the history and issues involved in the domestic and external stability of the continent. The stress on the link between economic development and security is wise, because the threat to the majority of the African countries is not external invasion, but the inability to ensure sustainable development. Food scarcity, environmental degradation, and ethno-religious nationalism are the real dangers to stability and survival.

This is the first major post-Cold War era book to examine in a comprehensive manner the various dimensions of African security. The book points attention to early warning signals that can be used to prevent major wars and political dislocations. It is useful both as an academic and a public-policy oriented project.

All the contributors are respectable scholars, in their mid-careers and with the definite assurance that they will in future become famous intellectuals and perhaps, play prominent role in shaping events and advising policy makers. The editors are talented scholars, and one of them has published a highly reputable book on Southern Africa.

Here is a book to gauge both the present mood of serious African scholars and to anticipate the future of the continent. If the political class can be as concerned and passionate as the contributors to this volume, the future of Africa will certainly be bright.

Toyin Falola
Professor of History
University of Texas, Austin

Chapter 1

INTRODUCTION: REDEFINING AFRICAN SECURITY

Adebayo Oyebade and Abiodun Alao

While the emergence of nation-states in the international political system first occasioned concern for state security among decision makers, it was not until the post-Second World War period that the study of security issues assumed a subject of popular discourse among scholars. In the West, particularly in the United States, the idea of security studies gained ground in academic circles with the advent of the Cold War and the consequent creation of a bi-polar world armed with a weapon system of mass destruction. As the physical preservation of the United States expressed through national security policies became the vital interest of America in the nuclear age, security studies became intellectualized.

Although security studies have been an integral part of academic study in the West for almost a century, it was only in the last couple of years that the 'third world' focused on this subject.[1] The inspiration for security studies and the driving force behind them may partly be attributed to the bi-polar international political system. National security became of considerable importance to many African states as they found themselves, overtly or covertly, in one ideological camp or the other. Apart from the expansion of the Cold War to Africa, the South African nuclear threat also provided a major security concern for the continent as a whole.

THE CONCEPT OF SECURITY

The term *security* has been used in such a plethora of ways
that, as Barry Buzan puts it, it is a "contested concept."[2]
Indeed, the term is vulnerable to ambiguity. Buzan also notes
that it "combines a powerful emotional and political appeal
with an enormous possible range of substantive meanings".[3]
The elasticity of the concept is such that it is even used to
justify policies with contradictory tendencies. For example,
used by states, national security has been employed to justify both respect for human rights and its violation, for "free
trade and protectionism", for "arms [race] and arms control," etc.[4] However, the desirability of the concept may be
the reason why the term is used in so many and at times,
contradictory ways. The huge sums of money that have been
spent, and the many conferences that have been held to ensure that individual countries or groups of countries are "secure" from external military attacks bear excellent testimony
to the importance of the concept. It is certainly this indis-
pensability that underlines the "traditional" definition of security, exemplified by Walter Lippmann's famous contention that:

> security is about the possession by a state of a
> level of military capability sufficient enough to
> avert the danger of having to sacrifice core val-
> ues, if it wishes to avoid war, and is able, if chal-
> lenged, to maintain them by victory in such a
> war.[5]

Arnold Wolfer further reinforces this line of thought. According to him:

> security, in an objective sense, measures the ab-
> sence of threats to acquired values [and] in a
> subjective sense, absence of fear that such val-
> ues will be attacked.[6]

This line of thinking dominated the interpretation of secu-
rity for more than two centuries. It was popularized in the
West especially in the United States. At the end of World
War II when the Cold War became the primary force gov-

erning East-West relations, the concept of national security in the U.S. became the physical preservation of America in the event of a possible Soviet confrontation. The U.S. strategies particularly to counter the perceived Soviet threat to its security, and generally to prevent the Kremlin from its supposed grand design to expand the frontiers of communism, have been referred to as 'containment.'[7] The core component of this definition of security is the preservation of the state through the ability to prevent or contain external attack.

During the early part of the Cold War, the military threat to national security was unduly overplayed. For example, the conceptualization of the national security ideology in Latin America was derived, in part, from the military consideration of defense against an external foe. The origins of the Doctrine of National Security and Development in Brazil have been traced to the Cold War theory of total war and superpower confrontation.[8] One of the basic concepts of the national security doctrine was resistance to possible external communist aggression. Under the doctrine, national security involved a commitment to the Western sphere of influence in the Cold War power configuration. The doctrine assumed that Latin America had a duty to take sides with the West because of its geographical contiguity. Latin America was thus thought of as having a role to play in the general defense of the Western Hemisphere against the threat of communist incursion.

By the second half of the twentieth century, however, opposition to the "traditional" notion of security had emerged. A school of thought began to challenge the preoccupation of the traditionalists with military threat as the sole determinant of state security. Scholars began to insist that the concept of security must go beyond the guarantee of territorial integrity; that it must include a whole range of internal factors far beyond the narrow confines of external aggression. Norman Myers captures this essence of security when he contends that it

> amounts to...protection from harm and injury but [also] access to water, food, shelter, health, employment, and other basic requisites that are the due of every person on Earth. It is the col-

lectivity of these citizens needs—overall safety and quality of life—that should figure prominently in the nation's view of security.[9]

Thus, the concept of security significantly widened in scope from the 1960s to encompass factors as diverse as the economy, the socio-political state, the citizens' well-being, and even the environmental situation. For the developing or the underdeveloped world in particular, the economic component of the problem of security is, perhaps, the most fundamental. Several scholars have underscored this important attribute of security. For instance, Muthiah Alagappa sees "economic health" as "inextricable part of national security."[10] Alagappa concludes:

> It is a prerequisite to the pursuit of national security—both in its internal and external dimensions. It provides the means to neutralize some of the domestic sources of conflict, makes the state less vulnerable to external pressure and penetration, and makes possible the allocation of necessary resources to counter internal and external threats.[11]

Africa, Latin America, and Asia have attested to the fact that a poor economy is a constant threat to security. South America has, indeed, incorporated economic development as one of the basic components of the national security doctrine. This aspect of the Latin American ideology of security rested on the premise that national security is dependent on the nation's economic development. To quote Alagappa further:

> Insofar as the developing countries are concerned, the economic well-being of their citizens is certainly a goal that has national security implications.[12]

THE EVOLUTION OF AFRICAN SECURITY STRATEGIES

The African conception of continental security came directly out of the historical experience of African peoples. When most of the countries obtained their political independence in the early 1960s after years of colonial subjugation and exploitation, their utmost security concern was to protect their newly won freedom. The document establishing the Organization of African Unity (OAU) best expresses the importance the states attached to this task. At the Ethiopian capital, Addis Ababa, in May 1963, African leaders expressed their determination at the maiden summit conference of the pan-African organization.

> to safeguard and consolidate the hard-won independence as well as the sovereignty and territorial integrity of our states, and to fight against neo-colonialism in all its forms.[13]

Accordingly, for the African states that gathered at the Ethiopian capital for the founding summit of the OAU, the concrete element of African security was safeguarding the continent's integrity by protecting the sovereignty of the independent states. To most African leaders, this was the definition of African security. The idea was further expressed in the purpose statement of the organization—"to defend their (African states) sovereignty, their territorial integrity and independence."[14]

Strategies to pursue this basic desire were created. Four of these are important because of their long term relevance to security on the continent. The first was the determination to ensure that other African states still under colonial domination became free. The charter of the OAU called for "absolute dedication to the total emancipation of African territories which are still dependent."[15] Many African leaders, indeed, believed that until the continent was totally free from foreign rule, its security was threatened. These dependent countries fell into two categories. First, there were the territories under European colonial regimes. Second, there were the territories under racist minority regimes in southern Africa. The later was to attract greater attention from African states. Indeed, the fervent desire to free the continent from all forms of foreign domination was an issue which, according to Zdenek Cervenka, dominated the proceedings of the OAU's founding summit. Cervenka described the resolution on decolonization as thus:

> It ranks first both in importance and effectiveness. In many ways it surpasses the Charter itself in its straightforward language and the urge for action. All delegates were unanimously convinced of the "imperious and urgent necessity of co-ordinating and intensifying their efforts to accelerate the unconditional attainment of national independence by all African territories still under foreign domination.[16]

Subsequent OAU summits were to devote considerable attention to this objective.

The second strategy for preserving African independence was the continent's declared policy of non-involvement in the East-West ideological struggle. To be committed to either of the two power blocs, in the view of the African states, was to give foreign powers an opportunity to create a neo-colonial relationship with them which would eventually jeopardize their independence. Kwame Nkrumah succinctly expressed the dangers of neo-colonialism when he wrote:

> Neo-colonialism acts covertly, maneuvering men and governments, free of [the] stigma attached to political rule. It creates client states, independent in name but in point of fact pawns of the very colonial power which is supposed to have given them independence.[17]

Thus, African states thought that their sovereignty would best be preserved by not taking sides in the superpower conflicts. This was a factor that influenced their adoption of a non-aligned foreign policy which, they hoped, would shield the continent against becoming a Cold War battle ground. Already, the Congo political crisis at the heels of the country's independence in 1960 was an indication of how foreign intervention in African affairs could be detrimental to African security.[18] In line with their non-aligned policy, African states also expressed through an OAU disarmament resolution, their determination to make the continent a nuclear weapons free zone and, at least theoretically, they hoped to end all forms of military arrangements with former colonial powers, since such entanglements were not considered to be in the best interest of African independence.

A third strategy was the provision of "non-interference" in the "internal affairs" of other African countries. This again found enshrinement in the OAU charter. African countries believed that if the social and political issues considered "internal" were addressed by those states themselves, the sovereignty, territorial integrity, and the principle of good neighborliness would be ensured. It was felt that if interference from non African powers was condemned, no less objection should be given to similar tendency from other African states. Thus, the provision of any form of support for internal rebel movements by other African countries was condemned.

Finally, African countries aspired to protect their newly won independence by respecting the inherited colonial boundaries. Apart from the charter, the sanctity of these boundaries was further endorsed by the resolution of the 1964 OAU summit conference held in Cairo, Egypt. Although African countries acknowledged the irrationality of the inherited colonial division, they decided to accept those boundaries because they felt that any attempt to redraw them would create more problems than it would solve.

A close look at some of the strategies African countries tried to adopt in order to defend their independence reveals the origins of some of the security problems that later engulfed the continent. Where these strategies were not half baked or ill-conceived, they fell into the neo-colonial traps that they aspired to fight. For instance, the principle of non-alignment became compromised in its execution. Although all African states remained members of the non-aligned movement throughout the Cold War era, the meaning of the movement soon became subject to independent interpretation by respective African countries. For example, Kenya did not see the provision for British military bases as being antithetical to its non-aligned stance. Angola's "Treaty of Friendship" with Moscow, was not, in the MPLA government's view, incompatible with non-alignment. It was also the case that most Francophone African countries had some form of security and defense arrangement with France. In short, the extent to which a country was non-aligned was not determined by the original intent to stay out of Cold War politics, but more by the vicissitudes of its internal and sub-regional politics.

The issue of "non-interference in the internal affairs" of other states also became problematic. Nosakhare Obaseki rightly noted that "well known pleas such as `leave African problems to Africans' are constantly countered by statements in the vein of Africa does not exist in a vacuum".[19] The actual meaning of the key phrases, "non-interference" and "internal affairs," was at the root of this controversy. Conflict over haphazardly drawn political boundaries made the definitions of interference and internal affairs confusing. Again, under the OAU arrangement, the discretion of seeking foreign assistance to address internal political difficulties was left entirely to each member state, and any assistance given to internal dissident movements, no matter the extent of the repression they had suffered or the justification of their cause, was seen as interference. However, many African countries that felt obliged to support armed insurrections against their neighbors argued that respect for human rights and justifications for the cause of the oppressed transcended the legal clause of "non-interference". This was particularly the case in southern Africa.

But what created the greatest problem was the issue of colonial boundaries. Almost immediately after this clause was put into the OAU charter, some African states saw the need to redraw their boundaries with neighbors, while many ethnic groups anticipating or experiencing oppression in the national framework in which they belonged soon started clamoring for secession. This has resulted in civil wars and in border clashes with neighboring states. The border clashes were more intense in regions that are potentially rich in mineral resources. Also, the desire to preserve the "territorial integrity" of the country soon became confused with the desperate bid to preserve the incumbent leaders in power. This grand self-preservation desire, in turn, created security problems which still remain in some African countries. For example, because of their desire to stay in office, some

African leaders committed gross human rights violations and resorted to repressive measures. They used arms and ammunition acquired from foreign sources mainly to suppress internal opposition, not to ward off external aggression. The primary motive of preserving territorial integrity thus became confused with self-preservation.

One of the greatest criticisms of OAU's attitude towards security during the Cold War is its "state-centric" nature. Because of this tendency, the organization unwittingly endorsed human rights abuses, economic mismanagement, and the undemocratic practices of some of the members under the guise of non-interference in the internal affairs of member states. Despite the enormity of human rights abuses by former Presidents Idi Amin of Uganda, Emperor Jean-Bedel Bokassa of Central African Republic, and Macias Nguema of Equatorial Guinea, the OAU did not offer a concerted policy response. The only issue on which African countries seemed close to consensus was the stand against minority and apartheid regimes in Southern Africa. But even on this issue, the "consensus" had its limitations, as differences over the methods of discouraging it were sources of major conflict. While Nigeria and some members of the Frontline States advocated a militant policy against South Africa, countries like Malawi and Cote d'Ivoire believed that apartheid could be reformed through some form of accommodation with the Pretoria regime. Also the creation of an African High Command, which could have enhanced the achievement of the OAU's goal of liberating colonial territories and defending the independence of African states, never took off. This was largely because of mutual suspicion and differences in perception of member states.

During the late 1970s, the independence of Angola, Mozambique, and Zimbabwe resulted in the subtle radicalization of views on some of the issues the OAU held sacrosanct. In fact, almost immediately after the independence of Angola and Mozambique, some African countries had begun to reconsider issues like the non-interference in the internal affairs of other states, and the non-violation of inherited borders. For example, in 1979, former President Julius Nyerere of Tanzania had ordered the invasion of Uganda and the overthrow of Idi Amin. In 1980, when Zimbabwe made its first appearance at the OAU summit, Prime

Minister Robert Mugabe, in language uncommonly used at the OAU summit, condemned the claim of King Hassan of Morocco to the Western Sahara.[20]

At the 1978 OAU summit in Khartoum, Sudan, the fundamental issue of foreign intervention in African affairs underwent major redefinition. The organization made a distinction between foreign "neo-colonial" intervention and "progressive interference" in the aid of specific African objectives. The summit:

> upheld the right of every independent state to call upon friendly countries outside the continent to come to their assistance if they perceived that their security and sovereignty are under threat.[21]

This distinction between "neo-colonial" and "progressive" interference was made specifically to provide a cover for the Cuban intervention on the side of the MPLA government against the UNITA rebels in Angola.

Other possible threats to the security of the continent were viewed as peripheral. For instance, the poor state of African economies was not expressly considered a threat to the security of the continent. Although an OAU resolution addressed the question of Africa's economic problems, it was not of primary goal for the attainment of African security. This was amply expressed at the Addis Ababa summit of 1963, when President Kwame Nkrumah's proposal for an African Common Market was unenthusiastically received.

African states began to recognize the link between the economy and security in the decades following the 1960s. Indeed, by the late 1970s, African security was no longer seen exclusively in strategic terms of fear of external aggression. From this time on, economic underdevelopment was percieved as a dominant issue in the threat to African security. This was to assume even greater priority in the post-Cold War era.

On the whole, it could be said that for the most part of the Cold War, Africa was confused about the management of its security. Also, there were few issues on which everyone agreed.

MOTIVATION OF STUDY AND OVERVIEW OF CHAPTERS

For nearly half a century, global politics were based on the Cold War premise. However, after the collapse of communist rule in the Soviet Union, the Cold War ended. This event has produced significant changes in international relations. It has fueled the reform movement in Africa, contributing to the popular demand for democracy on the continent.

However, in Africa, as in the whole global village, the march toward a new world order is bedeviled with old problems and emerging ones. Extreme ethno-religious nationalism still underscore intra-African conflicts. The continent is sunk, more than ever before, in the deep abyss of economic stagnation. Catastrophic wars are still going on. Environmental degradation is becoming a major problem, and in some states, the search for a democratic political system has turned into civil violence which threatens the very foundation of national sovereignty. These are fundamental problems that collectively pose a threat to the security of the continent, establishing a new basis on which to assess security problems.

Although it is widely recognized that Africa's security problems are acute, few scholars have studied the subject. Indeed, prior to the publication of Aforka Nweke's *African Security in the Nuclear Age* in 1985, no significant work has comprehensively addressed the increasingly varied problem of African security. Likewise, since the publication of this book more than a decade ago, no further in-depth study has appeared. This lack of scholarly discourse on the many dimensions of the African security problems is the major consideration for this book. The scanty literature available on African security problems has failed to underscore the totality of issues that make up security problems. Therefore, beyond such traditional themes as extra-African intervention in African affairs, this book raises, and attempts to find answers to new questions within the framework of the emerging post-Cold War order.

The nine chapters in this volume deal with some aspects of the security question in Africa. The contributors come from different disciplinary backgrounds including African Studies, International Relations, History, Economics, and Strategic Studies. This difference in intellectual orientation precludes a uniformity in the conceptual approach to the subject. Nonetheless, the volume provides some of the broad range of issues necessary for the understanding of the changing perspective on African security.

The present chapter by Adebayo Oyebade and Abiodun Alao provides an introductory framework for the book. The link between Africa's economic problems and the continent's security is addressed by Victor Okafor and Sheriffdeen Tella in chapter two. The chapter shows the extent of Africa's economic problems and considers security related issues like the implications of the debt burden on security; the economic recovery problems of African countries that have just emerged out of wars; and the issue of defense expenditure in the post-Cold War era. In their conclusion, the authors argue that Africa would not attain a sustainable and dependable security until the basic issue of economic development is effectively addressed.

In chapter three, Abiodun Alao and Amadu Sesay attempt an investigation of the security issues emerging from democratic pressure that followed the end of the Cold War. The authors discuss the manifestations of the democratic desires and the security concerns that came with them. Particularly, the chapter examines the security implications of continued suppression of democratic demands and the prospects for sustenance of democracy in war torn countries.

In chapter four, Abiodun Alao takes a critical look at the issue of environment. He considers environmental issues that may affect defense on the continent in the future and the environmental implications of some defense actions and/or inactions. Some of the issues discussed include the alarming increase in Africa's population, the problem of water resources, the refugee problem; the security consequences of excessive environmental exploitation; and the issue of toxic waste disposal. The author argues that if environmental issues are not given due attention, they may in due course be a source of major security problem.

Adebayo Oyebade takes another look at the issue of nuclear weapons and African security in chapter five. The chapter discusses Africa's history with nuclear weapons, and traces how perceptions have changed with the end of the Cold War and the end of the apartheid policy in South Africa.

Oyebade also considers the efforts being made by South Africa, the only known African nuclear power, to divert the use of its nuclear potentials to non-military purposes. In conclusion, the chapter considers the future relevance of nuclear weapons to African security.

Abiodun Alao and Funmi Olonisakin discuss the role of ethnicity in the post-Cold War order in chapter six. Their primary concern is how ethnic conflicts have changed in manifestation from what they were in the Cold War period. The chapter also looks at early warning signals to simmering ethnic conflicts in the continent. Although the chapter indicates countries and regions that are having profound ethnic problems, the authors contend that the type of crisis that brought Rwanda to the tribunal of international attention can be prevented if the basic social, political, and economic rights of the minorities in respective African countries are respected.

The inception of new conflicts around the world at the end of the Cold War has necessitated an increased interest in conflict resolution. In chapter seven, Adebayo Oyebade considers this crucial issue of conflict management in post-Cold War Africa. Oyebade focuses attention on the various conflict resolution strategies that have come to the fore of African reality in the aftermath of the end of the Cold War. The chapter examines the potentials of African initiatives in conflict resolution following the obvious wish of the West to stay away as much as possible from African crises.

Ayele Bekerie, in the next chapter, argues that the end of the Cold War has become a major catalyst in the consolidation and expansion of Pan-European Unity. Further entrenched in neo-colonial dependency and exploitation, Africa's unity and security, he contends, could be in greater jeopardy especially when no movements are initiated anywhere in Africa in earnest to match the challenge of pan-Europeanism. Ayele calls for the rethinking of the African position in the new world order. He considers the actualization of a united Europe a lesson for Africa and a call to pursue more vigorously pan-African unity. This, he sees as the only option for Africa to safeguard its security in the twenty-first century.

In the concluding chapter, the editors attempt an overview of the issues discussed in the book and consider possible factors that may affect African security in the future.

NOTES

1. Some of the works on security pertaining to the third world
    include: Mohammed Ayoob, *Regional Security in the Third
    World: Case Studies from Southeast Asia and the Middle East*,
    (London: Croom Helm, 1986); Caroline Thomas, *In Search of
    Security: The Third World in International Relations*, (Boul-
    der: Rienner Publishers, 1987); Muthiah Alagappa, *The Na-
    tional Security of Developing States: Lessons from Thailand*,
    (Dover: Auburn House Publishing Company, 1987); Christo-
    pher Coker, *South Africa's Security Dilemmas*, (New York:
    Praeger, 1987); Edward E. Azar and Chung-in Moon, *Na-
    tional Security in the Third World: The Management of In
    ternal and External Threats*, (Aldershot: Edward Elger Pub-
    lishing Ltd., 1988); and Brian L. Job, (ed.), *The Insecurity Di-
    lemma: National Security of Third World States*, (Boulder:
    Lynne Rienner Publishers, 1992).
2. Barry Buzan, *People, State, and Fear: The National Security Prob-
    lem in International Relations*, (Chapel Hill: University of North
    Carolina Press, 1983), 6. For useful thoughts on the defini-
    tion of *security*, see Brian L. Job, "The Insecurity Dilemma:
    National, Regime, and State Securities in the Third World,"
    in Job, (ed.), *The Insecurity Dilemma*, 14-17.
3. Barry Buzan, "The Concept of National Security for Devel-
    oping Countries" in Mohammed Ayoob and Chai Anan
    Samudavanja, *Leadership Perception and National Security: The
    Southeast Asian Experience*, (Pasip Panjang: Institute of South
    east Asia Studies, 1989), 2.
4. *ibid.*
5. As quoted from Clement Eme Adibe, "Weak States and the
    Emerging Taxonomy of Security in World's Politics," *Fu-
    tures*, 26 (5), June 1994, 491.
6. As quoted from *ibid.*
7. The literature on the United States national security policies
    during the Cold War is quite enormous. For a good synthesis,
    see John Lewis Gaddis, *Strategies of Containment: A Critical*

Appraisal of Postwar American National Security Policy, (Oxford: University Press, 1982). Also useful are "X" (George F. Kennan), "The Sources of Soviet Conduct," *Foreign Affairs*, XXV, July 1947, 566-82; "NSC-68: A Report to the National Security Council by the Executive Secretary on the United States Objectives and Program for National Security, April 14, 1950," *Naval War College Review*, XXVII, May-June, 1975, 51-108.

8. See Maria Helena Alves, *State and Opposition in Military Brazil*, (Austin: University of Texas Press, 1985).

9. Norman Myers, *Ultimate Security: The Environmental Basis of Political Stability*, (New York: W. W. Norton, 1993).

10. Alagappa, *The National Security of Developing States*, 3.

11. *ibid.* For similar submission, see Stephen D. Frasner, "National Security and Economics," in Thomas Trout and James E. Harf, *National Security Affairs*, (New Brunswick: Transaction Books, 1983), 320-321; Harold Brown, *Thinking about National Security*, (Boulder: Westview Press, 1983), 14.

12. *ibid*

13. From the Chapter of the OAU; quoted in Zdenek Cerneka, *The Organizatio of African Unity and its Charter*, (Academica; Praha 1968), 86.

14. Article II, section C.

15. Article III, section 6.

16. Cervenka, *The Organization of African Unity*, 15. See 15-17 for detailed analysis of the resolution on decolonization.

17. Kwame Nkrumah, *Africa Must Unite*, (New York: Praeger, 1963), 174.

18. See the following for insight into external influence in the Congo crisis: Edwin S. Munger, "Conflict in the Congo: External Pressures," *Report Service: Central and Southern Africa Series, 3(4), 1960;* Inda Jit Rikhye, *Military Adviser to the Secretary-General: U.N. peacekeeping and the Congo Crisis*, (New York: St. Martin's Press, 1993); and Alan James, *Britain and the Congo Crisis, 1960-63*, (New York: St. Martin's Press, 1996).

19. Nosakhare Obaseki, *Managing African Conflict*, (New York: International Peace Academy, 1982), 10.

20. *West Africa*, May 1980.

21. *African Research Bulletin*, (Political Series), 1-31, July 1978, 4839.

Chapter 2

ECONOMIC DEVELOPMENT AND THE PROSPECT FOR ECONOMIC SECURITY IN AFRICA

Victor Oguejiofor Okafor and Sheriffdeen Tella

INTRODUCTION

Clearly, Africa has suffered most from the current global economic recession. With an outstanding external debt of $147 billion culminating in net official transfer of about $5,468.4 million in 1990 alone, and a prediction that the population below poverty line will rise from 47.8 percent in 1990 to 49.7 percent in the year 2000,[1] it is fair to say that the continent is, and will probably remain the poor house of the world in the year 2000 and beyond.

The above dismal picture not only has economic, political, and social implications for the continent, it has also fundamental security repercussions. Indeed, for African security to be fully guaranteed, a viable economy is a *sine qua non*. This is particularly imperative in the emerging global order where post-Cold War changes have a necessary correlation with economy. For instance, now that the Cold War is over, African countries which used to benefit from that rivalry have lost a major avenue of material assistance. The

Commonwealth of Independent States and the other former nations of the Soviet Union, are now themselves at the feet of the West with pleas for economic assistance. Another post-Cold War implication for Africa's economic security is the unification drive in Western Europe. If, as separate powers, the European countries could exploit African natural and mineral resources as they have historically done, what happens when those forces come together as one economic unit? As Western Europe gravitates toward economic unity, African countries, despite wobbly regional attempts at economic cooperation, are politically divided and would continue, at least in the foreseeable future, to deal individually with a unified and much more powerful Europe. Obviously, the odds of the bargaining process will be against a divided Africa. The manifestation of change currently being experienced in Africa, therefore, has a direct bearing on the economy. The end of the Cold War has consequently led to the expansion of the scope of security such that economic development occupies a core value. It is impossible to discuss here all the ramifications of economy and security; thus, all that this chapter attempts is a selection of some of the key economic issues that are relevant to security in the post-Cold War era. The chapter opens with an overview of the current economic crisis in Africa and how this has impinged on continental security. It then proceeds to give a panoramic survey of the causes of Africa's economic problems. The thrust of the chapter is a consideration of some of the key economic issues that could underline security in the post-Cold War order. Some of the issues identified include the implications of the debt burden on national security, the economic implications of post-war reconstruction in some of the African countries recovering from wars, and the issue of defense spending in the post-Cold War order. The chapter also attempts to prescribe ways of dealing with the problem of economic development.

AFRICA'S ECONOMIC SITUATION: AN OVERVIEW

To say that Africa's economic situation is in a lamentable state is to acknowledge the obvious. According to the World Bank categorization, three-quarters of sub-Saharan African countries belong to the lowest income group in the world.

In 1992, about 30 million people on the continent (mainly in the Horn) were said to be facing starvation.[2] The ominous nature of the state of Africa's economy is best captured in a document, the *African Charter for Popular Participation in Development and Transformation*, adopted in Arusha, Tanzania, in 1990. This document states:

It is a crisis of unprecedented and unacceptable proportions manifested not only in abysmal declines in economic indicators and trends, but more tragically and glaringly in the suffering, hardship, and impoverishment of the vast majority of African people.[3]

Economic issues such as low income, population growth, level of industrialization, and debt burden are relevant indices of security in developing nations and, therefore, a prism through which to examine the question of Africa's economic crisis.

Low Income

Africa has the lowest per capita income in the world, along with the lowest life expectancy. This implies that majority of Africans would not be able to afford basic necessities like clothing, shelter, nutritious food, and medicare—all of which contribute to good health and long life.

Population Growth

Africa's population growth in relation to the continent's economic growth is also problematic. The continent ranks a distant third in terms of the total population of the world; yet it has the highest population growth rate.[4] The implications of this are two-fold. First, the continent constitutes a small market for viable expanding production. In other words, where population is an important consideration for investments, particularly by multinationals, Africa could not be seen as an important market. Secondly, the high growth rate in population implies that unless there is a rapid increase in exploitation of its resources and output in general, the level of poverty will increase since the ratio of output per person would fall continuously.

Low Level of Industrialization

African economies have largely depended on primary goods, agricultural and mineral. Industrialization, which has generally been seen as the pathway to development, has so far played minimal role in Africa's economic development. Although between the mid 1960s and early 1970s, industrial production grew at 14 percent a year, this slowed down to an annual 5 percent after the first oil shock of 1973/74 when costs of operation suddenly shot up. In 1980, the industrial sector in Africa produced 35 percent of income and employed about 8 percent of the labor force. This declined to 6 percent of the labor force in 1985, and since then there has been a further decline.[5]

Lacking industrialization, the consequent dependence of most African countries on primary goods and their inability to control the prices of these goods, combine to subject the continent's economic prospects to the whims and caprices of the developed world. Deliberate manipulation of prices of primary products by the industrialized world has often compelled African governments to engage in borrowing from the international capital market.

External Debt Burden

Africa's external debt as a percentage of the Gross National Product (GNP) in 1970 was moderate at 13.1 percent, which compared favorably to that of other regions. However, by 1980, it had doubled at 26.8 percent. By 1989 the percentage had quadrupled and overshot the debt/GNP ratio of other regions by as much as 30 percent.[6] Furthermore, whereas Africa's debt/export ratio was one of the lowest—96.8 percent in the developing countries in 1980—it became the highest, at 362 percent, in 1989.[7] This means that the debt value is three times more than exports value. Servicing the debt alone rose from 5.3 and 10.9 percent of total exports in 1970 and 1980 respectively, to 22.1 percent in 1989.[8] The rising trend in Africa's debt service payment has continued in the 1990s.

Also, the progressive net transfer of funds from Africa became alarming. In 1985, it stood at $1,149.3 million, but grew to $9,018.9 million and $19,373.2 million in 1988 and

1990 respectively. The transfer to official creditors in 1990 was $5,468.4 million and the total debt service was $12,665 million.[9] Between 1984 and 1990, Africa's net flow of fund to the World Bank and the IMF had amounted to $4,868 million.[10] This capital outflow, still in progress has had great economic, social, and security implications for a region that is in dire need of both domestic and external capital for development.

The picture of Africa painted above indicates that the continent has serious economic problems. Before discussing the implications of this for Africa's security, it is pertinent to briefly examine the salient factors responsible for the continent's economic woes.

CAUSES OF AFRICA'S ECONOMIC PREDICAMENT

A myriad of complex economic, political, social, and historical factors are responsible for the present economic predicament in which Africa finds itself. These have been adequately discussed in the literature, and the fore-going analysis is by no means an exhaustive discussion.

Economic Mismanagement

The mismanagement of the economy is one of the most important causes of Africa's economic predicament. Economic mismanagement on a massive scale has become so endemic that corruption and misappropriation of public funds and resources by state officials are no longer news. Nigeria provides a good example of a mismanaged economy. With a great potential for a viable economy and a sound industrial base, Nigeria, soon after independence, launched itself on the path of economic mismanagement and large scale corruption. The Second Republic especially epitomized the height to which corruption could climb in an African country. In 1979, when the military left the political stage, Nigeria's external reserve was $5.1 billion. The country, in addition, earned some $51.6 billion from petroleum and non-oil exports between 1979 and 1983. But by the time the civilian administration was terminated by a military coup in December 1993, the country was indebted externally and internally to the tune of $26 billion. This means that in four years, the government of the Second Republic had access to over $82 billion out of which $17.1 billion could not be accounted for.[11] Zaire is another great potential of economic success which Mobutu's graft and outright mismanagement have aborted. There are a host of other African states whose economies have been crippled by corruption and mismanagement.[12]

One of the results of economic mismanagement and corruption is that African states have been forced into external debts which most have found difficult to repay. Significant portions of their fluctuating foreign exchange earnings have thus gone into debt servicing, leaving little for necessary imports like infrastructural equipments and raw materials for local industries.

Political Instability

Africa is bedeviled by political instability, with a result that the continent is lacking in political culture necessary for economic development. Internal factors like incessant military coups, corruption in government, abuse of power, poor accountability and mismanagement, ethnic politics, and religious intolerance have largely contributed to political instability. The lack of a stable political system has given rise to uncoordinated and unsustained economic policies. The frequency of coups ensures that each government's economic policies become truncated before they are fully implemented, or that the normal conduct of economic activities are paralyzed for awhile. Economic policies are thus short term and skewed towards immediate personal gains rather than long term national benefits. Commitment to policy formulation and implementation is also low, promoting opportunism and minimal reward for hard work. The resultant effect is a fall in productivity and general living conditions. As Adebayo Adedeji, former Executive Secretary of the Economic Commission for Africa (ECA) contends, the lack of what he describes as "a democratic culture" in Africa has impeded popular mobilization and effective accountability.[13]

ECONOMIC DEVELOPMENT

Defense Expenditure

Incessant conflicts in Africa have resulted in commitments
of large proportions of African government's expenditures
to the defense sector. The World Bank shows that in the late
1980s, Africa's military expenditures amounted to $860 bil-
lion a year in high income countries, and $170 billion a year
in the low income ones. About $38 billion of the money spent
by the developing countries was for the importation of arms
from industrial countries.

The excessive and ever increasing African defense budget has had adverse effects on essential social services. Many
countries in Africa spend twice as much on the military as
they spend on social services. In the last three decades, military and civilian regimes spent roughly the same share of
their Gross Domestic Product (GDP) on their armed forces.[14]
Thus, money better spent on the social sector is diverted to
defense so that important programs like educational and
health services suffer. Altaf Gauhar captures the mood of
African governments when he said:

> Indeed, it is unpatriotic to question how much
> is being spent on defence...it is recognized that
> the process of development could be acceler-
> ated if some of the military expenditures were
> diverted to social sector, but it is considered
> highly injudicious, if not treasonable, to weaken
> the defence services (by reducing defence bud-
> get).[15]

While the trend in other parts of the developing world is a
reduction in defense expenditure and shift towards increased
finances for education, health, and other social and welfare
services, the reverse is the case in most African countries.
Africa has continually experienced increase in the defense
share of the budget which has led to a reduction in expenditures on the social and welfare sectors. Also, whereas expenditures for the armed forces in developed countries generate income through sales of military hardware to developing countries, in Africa, military expenditure for arms clearly
means importation since, barring South Africa, there is no
known arms producing country in the continent. Arms im-

portation in Africa has thus been a drain on national resources. The disproportionate expenditure on defense could, therefore, undermine internal security through diversion of scarce resources. Indeed, the increased commitment of funds to defense at the expense of social and welfare sector is responsible for the growing poverty and public unrest in many parts of Africa.

Historical Factors

Africa's economic malaise definitely cannot be viewed in isolation from the continent's history of exploitation starting from the great enslavement, through colonialism, to neo-colonialism. As some analysts have argued, the trade in African captives, which dominated European international commerce from the fifteenth to the middle of the nineteenth century, is the real beginning of Africa's economic woes. It is estimated that more than 100 million African lives, including skilled labor, were lost.[16] It has been argued that by uprooting from the continent so many able-bodied men and women to become tools in the development of Western industrial revolution, Africa had been robbed of hands that could have contributed to the development of the continent.[17]

The Western European exploitation of Africa's material and human resources to the detriment of the continent's development continued apace during colonial rule. The colonial economic system delayed Africa's economic progress by producing for the needs of the metropolitan state and not for the needs of Africans. The exclusive production by Africans of raw materials for European consumption effectively discouraged African indigenous industry.[18]

The post independence integration of the African economies into the Western controlled global economy has proved to be devastating to the continent's development efforts. When African countries were freed from colonialism in the 1960s, Western capitalist powers struggled hard to ensure their economic dependence on the West. This was largely achieved through established institutions like the International Monetary Fund (IMF). These institutions proposed the western economic mode as model for the underdeveloped world. Solution to underdevelopment was thus found in indiscriminate application of classic economic principles such as the adoption of 'free markets,' 'free enterprise,' 'modern tax systems,' 'rationalization of the state,' and so on.[19] It is pertinent to note that even the leading centers of "free markets" such as the United States, are known to blend free market ideas with large scale public interventions in the economy.

African states slid into greater economic problems as they began to adopt externally generated economic policies that bear little or no relevance to their situation. The implementation of IMF-type development strategies has not produced any significant solution to Africa's economic problems. In fact, structural adjustment reforms proposed by these bodies have compounded the situation. About two-thirds of African countries that are engaged in economic reforms have had to adopt flexible exchange rate though they have no key currency, and the prices of their exports are determined by the developed countries. Such countries have had to allow market forces, in the spirit of western type economics, to determine their domestic prices as if they have no market mechanism of their own. Further, they have had to implement free trade in economies that are already weighed down by external shocks from the present level of openness and unfair relations with the world capitalist countries.

The Structural Adjustment Program (SAP) formulated by the World Bank and the IMF, to say the least, has not led to improvement in the living standard of the people. The conditionalities of the program, like currency devaluation, for example, have had a crippling effect on a large population of those African states implementing the program. Moshin Khan found that the program negatively affects growth rate immediately after it is adopted.[20] Carol Lancaster has correctly suggested that "the future of structural adjustment in Africa is uncertain."[21]

POST-COLD WAR AFRICAN SECURITY: THE ECONOMIC FACTOR

The end of the Cold War has brought the correlation between the economy and security into sharper focus. It is probably true to infer that in no other place is the level of economic well being an important variable of national security than in Africa. The drastic downgrading of the standard of living of the majority of Africans, more evident in the last few years, undoubtedly has a profound bearing on security. A nation puts its security in jeopardy when the basic needs of its citizens are largely left unmet.

The poor economic situation in many African countries has found expression in anti-social behavior, some of which could be serious enough to threaten national security. Large population of jobless and discontented masses who are unable to make a meaningful living out of the depressed economy have found solace in activities such as armed robbery. The current nose-diving trend of Nigeria's economy has greatly multiplied the number of marauding armed bandits whose operations have defied any solution from the authorities. In the face of a practically helpless police force, life and property of law abiding citizens remain unsafe. The nation is practically held hostage perpetually.

Economic problems have also pushed anti-social behavior within the state to such an extreme that discontented elements engage in crimes against the survival of the nation. Many people dissatisfied with a meager living forced on them by economic stagnation have sought greener pastures within the rank and file of anti-state organized armed groups which are able to provide them some sort of livelihood. Where protracted wars are going on, many people have opted for one armed group or the other, not on account of political or ideological conviction, but because of economic survival. The armed group in Mozambique, the Resistance de Nacionale de Mocambique (RENAMO), swelled its ranks through economically dissatisfied people motivated by the opportunity to exploit a state of perpetual warfare through armed banditry.

What perhaps has created the greatest link between security and economy in the post-Cold War order is the issue of debt repayment. When African countries began to experience economic recession, most of them immediately turned to financial institutions like the IMF and World Bank for short term loans to balance their budget deficit. This action has turned out to have a most damaging economic impact with enormous security implications. Regardless of the situation that brought about their economic problems, African countries receive similar recommendations from the IMF. These include currency devaluation, draconian cuts in government's public expenditure, reduction of food and other consumption subsidies, reduction in wages and restrictions in the availability of credits and privatization of public institutions.[22] The application of this short-sighted therapy has created more problems for African countries.

First, the implementation of IMF recommendations has produced adverse consequences for the living condition of the people. Implementing such programs necessarily led to more restrictive measures like budget tightening and removal of subsidies on certain products and services. The resultant deterioration of the standard of living is a cause of civil strifes capable of threatening national stability and security. Indeed, serious civil unrest arising from unsatisfactory economic well-being of people has occurred in many states. For instance, the removal of oil subsidies in Nigeria in 1992 greatly affected the people and caused tensions that found resounding expression in civil disorder during the abortive 1993 political transition program. In the Sudan, "food" riots led to the overthrow of the government of Jaafar el Nimeiri. The government of former President Kenneth Kaunda of Zambia also nearly fell in 1990 as a result of unrest over the removal of a subsidy for staple food. Public demonstrations in Somalia and Sierra Leone arising from a sudden rise in the cost of living have also led to the overthrow and destabilization of the governments of those countries.

Another dimension of the poor state of Africa's economic situation is that it does not augur well for a stable political system. Those who have hoped that the current wave of demands for political reforms in the continent would usher in a new era of stable democratic governments may be disappointed. This is because the present underdeveloped economy with its attendant problems may prove incapable of sustaining democratic forms of government. Already, most African states are debt ridden, many of them spending a greater proportion of their earnings on debt servicing. This and other economic problems like corruption and mismanagement of resources have considerably lowered the living standard for millions of Africans. The likely inability of an incoming civilian administration to solve the debt problem and cater for the welfare of the citizen could lead to discontentment and social unrest. This is the kind of situation often exploited by the military to intervene in national politics.

ECONOMIC COSTS OF POST-WAR RECONSTRUCTION

Of particular relevance to the discussion of the linkage between economy and security in post-Cold War Africa is the prospect of economic recovery for countries that are currently in, or are just coming out of devastating wars. In all cases, the countries concerned are already in serious debt due to the financial cost of prosecuting such wars. Also, the infrastructure that could put their economies back on course had been destroyed. Apart from these, the economic cost of reconstruction and the cost of maintaining a minimum level of economic prosperity that could prevent a return to crisis are often too much for the country to bear. For example, Liberia's protracted civil war seriously destroyed the economic base of the country. Before the war, the country had depended on the exports of its rubber and diamond for its foreign exchange. Also, the country's fertile lands made it possible for it to feed itself without having to import food. The civil war completely destroyed all these. The country's rubber plantation at Firestone was destroyed and diamond was looted to finance the war. Above all, the general atmosphere of killings and destruction during the war prevented many Liberians from going back to the farm to grow food. The implication of all these for post-war Liberia is that the economic base for rapid reconstruction and sustainable development had almost been wiped out.

Even after peace has been achieved in such a situation of prolonged warfare, there is the other serious problem of getting resources to sustain capital intensive projects such as demobilization, post-war physical reconstruction, recreation of the national army, and so on. Following a study of disarmament and demobilization in six African countries, namely: Angola, Chad, Mozambique, Namibia, Uganda, and Zimbabwe; World Bank consultants came up with three major conclusions: demobilization cannot be cheaply achieved, buying guns back from former combatants only work as part of a broader peace settlement, and ex-fighters need long term job training and help to integrate.[23] Clearly many of the countries in this situation cannot afford these programs. For example, with a completely disarticulated infrastructure and a substantial external debt, it is almost certain that post-war Liberia can only thrive with a massive injection of foreign assistance which, at present, can hardly be guaranteed. The almost certain consequence of this is a return to anarchy, as the basic economic structures that could prevent this cannot be put in place.

Angola is another example in this regard. With the establishment of a crude semblance of order in the country, the only thing that could guarantee a sustained peace is the creation of an economic base for reconstruction. Because of the duration and the extent of the war, the Angolan economy has suffered enormous disruption. External debt as at October 1994 stood at $11 billion, repayment of which would take up to 350-400 percent of annual earnings.[24] By the end of 1994, the annual inflation was at around 800 percent, while the local currency, the Kwanza, had been drastically devalued. All these show that the chances of recovering are considerably slim for Angola. Also, the possible inability of Angola to achieve economic recovery could bring about another conflict. Other countries like Rwanda, Mozambique, Sudan, Burundi and Sierra-Leone are also confronted with this kind of problem.

As earlier indicated, Africa's defense expenditure constitutes an important issue in the continent's security consideration. In the aftermath of the Cold War, three factors continue to affect defense spending in Africa. The first is the attainment of peace in a number of hitherto conflict-ridden states. The second is the democratic movement that necessitates the involvement of a greater section of the society in defense spending policies. The third is the economic strain that has come to affect all aspects of life in most countries on the continent.

Indeed, the attainment of peace in some countries has resulted in the reduction of defense spending, although as it would be shown later, this has also created a number of security problems arising from financial costs of rehabilitating demobilized soldiers. An example in this regard is Ethiopia. The attainment of relative stability in the country has reduced defense spending. According to the figures, Ethiopia's military spending as a percentage of its GNP dropped from 13.5 percent in 1989, to 3.4 percent in 1994.[25] In a letter to the UN, the Ethiopian government further claimed that the country's military spending had been reduced from 50 percent to 10 percent of its national budget, and since the fall of President Haile Mariam Mengistu, no arms had been imported.[26]

South Africa's defense spending since the attainment of majority rule has presented a somewhat contradictory intermix of tendencies. There has been a significant decrease in the expenditure on the type of suppressive weapons that characterized the apartheid regime. However, immediately after the attainment of majority rule, allocations to defense increased, and as at August 1994, they stood at four times the amount earmarked for reconstruction and development programs.[27] There are three possible reasons for this. The first is to prevent the military from derailing the new democratic order. The second is to put the military in the position that it could guarantee domestic and regional peace necessary for foreign investments. The third is the desire to maximize foreign exchange earning from its arms industries.[28] Although there is a temporary concentration of resources on defense expenditure, it is believed that the government is interested in long term reduction in defense expenditure.

It is indeed ironical that, while South Africa is thinking of long term reduction in its defense spending, the country is determined to maximize its earnings from exports of weapons. Even President Nelson Mandela has abandoned his agelong objection to arms trade. He noted:

> I don't think it would be fair to say that a particular country should not engage in trade in arms. Arms are for the purpose of defending sovereignty and the integrity of a country. From that angle, there is nothing wrong in having trade in arms.[29]

Of all the defense legacies of apartheid, one of the few the new government insists on keeping intact, or minimally interfering with is the Armament Corporation of South Africa (ARMSCOR). President Mandela has in fact made it clear that the corporation would be allowed to maintain its business policies, interfering only when there are policies that embarrass the government.

ARMSCOR has since been bringing in new businesses. Towards the end of 1994, it signed seven new counter-trade and offset agreements. The government has since given its endorsement to ARMSCOR's massive drive to increase South Africa's share of the global arms market, and to its plan to expand its arms exports by 300 percent in the next five years.[30] As Sue Willet has noted, the economic rational for this is based on its potential for positive macro-economic effects such as job creation, wealth creation, and balance of trade.[31] She further noted that 1993 arms exports earned South Africa $244 million in foreign exchange and supported 15,000 jobs.

The financial dealings of ARMSCOR have, however, created some diplomatic problems for the government. In 1994, there was the case of the abortive arms shipment to Yemen, while in March 1993, the Angolan government complained of ARMSCOR shipment of arms to UNITA. Again, in May 1994, the Executive General manager of the corporation stated that ARMSCOR had supplied arms worth approximately $30 million to Rwanda over the past five years.[32]

The attainment of peace has, however, caused countries like Mozambique and Angola to reduce their spending. Although it is expected that in the next few years defense issues like disarmament and integration of armed forces could result in increases in defense spending, it is believed that they would not necessarily become a consistent budgetary phenomenon.

A number of other countries have taken some fundamental defense decisions in view of the dwindling economic resources. For example, in September 1994, the Zimbabwean President, Robert Mugabe, announced that the country's armed forces and police/paramilitary forces, which, as of then stood at 70,000, would be halved to 35,000 due to economic difficulties.[33] Also, in 1993, the cash strapped Ugandan government started a demobilization exercise to halve the country's 80,000 strong army by the end of 1994. Although this was not achieved, the Museveni government has continued to pursue this policy under pressure from Western donors who underwrite annual aid of up to $800 million.[34] Tanzania is also expected to cut defense spending and is, in fact, presently considering closing down bases, and the voluntary retirement of some serving members of the armed forces.[35] There are, however, some countries that have refused to carry out specific defense instructions from international aid donors. For example, Zambia refused demands from international aid donors to streamline its 18,000 strong army.[36]

For some of the countries the attainment of democracy has reduced defense spending. There was no longer the need to keep up with heavy defense spending that the previous regimes put in place to suppress democratic values and maintain its hold on power.

POST COLD WAR ORDER:PROSPECTS FOR ECONOMIC RECOVERY AND SECURITY

There is evident need for an African economic recovery in the emerging global order if the continent's security is to be guaranteed. What then are the options for the much needed economic progress? What steps should African states take individually and collectively to build a viable economy capable of sustaining continental security?

In the search for a solution to their economic predicament, African countries have virtually limited themselves to Western induced policies and strategies. The Structural Adjustment Program has been the main economic program pursued by African states with deep sense of responsibility. This is in spite of the shortcomings of the program.[37] Since the beginning of the 1980s when SAP was introduced and adopted by more than half of the African countries, the poverty level and general economic doldrums seemed to have deepened. The number of least developed countries in Africa increased from 21 in 1981 to 29 in 1990. The GDP has continued to fall while debt and debt servicing have continued to rise.[38] Indeed, the World Bank predicts that while the poverty level will decrease progressively through the 1990s to the year 2000 in all other developing countries, in Africa, it will increase from 47.6 percent in 1985 to 49.7 percent in the year 2000.[39]

It cannot be overemphasized that solutions proposed by Western controlled bodies have not been very effective in turning around the downward economic trend in Africa. World Bank reports have argued that those states pursuing religiously structural adjustment programs are doing better economically than those that have abandoned the pro gram.[40] The purported economic "progress" has, however, not been seen translated to better life for the people.

World Bank or IMF strategies remain an inadequate means of meeting the desperate needs of millions of suffering Africans. The reality that the "benefits" of "economic development" have made little difference to the lives of the broad masses of Africans is a major concern of the African Charter for Popular Participation in Development and Transformation. It correctly observes that the nature of socio-economic development in Africa has been such that it alienates the people and impedes their effective participation in the developmental process. One of the consequences of this trajectory of development in Africa is that the "collective and individual creativity of the people have been under-valued and under-utilized."[41] There is thus the need to begin to explore seriously internally generated solutions and development strategies. Consequently, the African Charter for Popular Participation in Development and Transformation has advocated an overhaul of the structures, pattern, and political context of the process of socio-economic development in Africa to allow for popular participation.

It would be incorrect to argue that no attempts have been made to find indigenous solutions to Africa's economic problems. Indeed, there have been some African initiatives. For example, there was the Lagos Plan of Action (LPA) adopted by the OAU in 1980 which emphasized inward-looking strategies and regional integration for Africa. There was the Lome Convention designed to take care of trade areas. There also exists the African Alternative Framework to Structural Adjustment Program (AAF-SAP) developed by the Economic Commission for Africa (ECA) as a more appropriate program for Africa's development.

One of the areas that African states need to explore in order to improve their economic well-being is intra-African trade. At present there is not much horizontal trade among African nations. In 1993, intra-African trade accounted for less than 5 percent of regional trade.[42] Ironically, the lack of intra-state trade is in spite of the fact that Africans had always traded among themselves before the advent of colonialism. During antiquity, Ancient Egypt traded extensively with Nubia in the West and Axum in the Southeast. Between 600 A.D. and 1600 A.D., medieval West African empires like Ghana, Mali, and Songhai prospered mainly on the basis of intra-Africa trade—the trans-Saharan trade between Northern Africa and those empires.[43] The Swahili civilizations of East Africa and their major centers such as Kilwa, Malinda, Mombasa, Sofola, and Zanzibar, which date back to the first millennium A.D., were products of a sub-continental trade between East Africa and Southern Africa. The Swahili merchants served as brokers of gold mined by Africans in Southern Zimbabwe and Mozambique.[44] In other words, long before the Europeans got to the Cape of Good Hope in the 17th century, Africans had been mining the gold of Southern Africa and using the accruing wealth to build civilizations, including the Great Zimbabwe.

In recognition of the abysmal level of intra-African trade, a group of African nations agreed to set up an African Export/Import Bank (Afreximbank) to promote Africa's exports and intra-African commerce.[45] In addition, other organizations have geared up efforts toward forging regional economic cooperation. These organizations include the OAU, the African Development Bank (ADB), Economic Community of West African States, (ECOWAS), the Southern African Development Coordination Conference (SADCC), the Arab Maghrib Union, the Economic Community of Central African States (CEEAC), and the Organization for the Development of the Kagera Basin. They are designed to promote political and economic cooperation, to coordinate economic policies, and to foster collective self-reliance for joint regional development.[46] Although these organizations are bedeviled with financial hardships,[47] their work represents an important stepping stone toward the important goal of economic integration in Africa.

Related to the above is the need for interaction and cooperation between Africa and its diaspora. Common historical and cultural heritage between Africa and the diaspora has not served the cause of African economic development mainly because of lack of a universal African consciousness. Just as European-Americans work cooperatively with European nations in the field of politics, economics, science, and technology, African Americans can forge similar linkages with African nations. The possibility of this has been demonstrated by history which shows that Pan-African cooperation can serve both sides of the Atlantic. For instance,

W.E.B. Dubois' Pan-African Congresses and literary campaigns inspired a generation of African nationalist leaders. In turn, decolonization in Africa served as a psychological prop to the Civil Rights Movement of the 1960s. The Congressional Black Caucus, Trans Africa, and the National Association for the Advancement of Colored People (NAACP), played an effective part in persuading the Congress and the American public and private institutions to adopt and implement economic sanctions against the apartheid regime in South Africa. The role of these African American organizations in the achievement of Namibian independence, and the cessation of the internecine war in Angola are eloquent indications of what Pan-African co-operation could achieve in Africa's economic development. The ongoing realignment of forces throughout the world makes Pan-African linkages all the more important.

Africa also needs to begin to utilize fully its high potentials in mineral wealth, including strategic minerals. Not only has this vast mineral potential not been adequately tapped, Africa's mineral industry is in decline for several reasons, including insufficient exploration and poor management.[48] It is true that Africa has not been able to tap into the boom area of the mineral industry, the profitable precious and strategic metals' market, even though it has rich prospects for such minerals. Instead, the continent concentrated on traditional base mineral mining operations such as copper, iron ore, tin, phosphates, chromite, manganese, zinc, and uranium. A United Nations study has noted that Africa will have to invest some $400 million a year, which represents about four times the current level of investment, in order to reverse the decline of the mineral industry and enable it to compete with low-cost producers in Latin America, Asia, the Pacific Rim and industrialized countries such as Australia and Canada.[49]

Improvement in the industrial sector is also important for economic growth. Instead of spending scarce resources on accumulation of military weaponry, African states must invest more in manufacturing industry. Leonard Gonchanov has suggested that without national industries, any attempt to attain a self supporting growth of the economy and bridge the gap with major capitalist countries in the development levels is impracticable.[50] Industrialization should be geared toward manufacturing goods that satisfy basic needs with the use of indigenous technology that Africans are capable of operating and maintaining. Efforts at industrialization should not be dampened by the experience of the import substitution industrialization scheme of the 1970s. Rather, that experience should guide African countries in new industrialization programs.

The road to economic recovery in Africa also demands revolutionary ideas such as the re-configuration of the geopolitical map of Africa. Any package for solving the perennial economic stress of Africa which does not address this fundamental factor can at best only succeed in addressing the symptoms of the problem. The re-structuring of the geopolitical configuration of Africa is so central to the economic well-being of the continent that it remains a surprise that it has not taken center stage in African political thinking. It is self-evident that Africa cannot sustain itself economically, politically, and militarily on the basis of its fragmentation into a 52-state structure with artificial boundaries. This has served more to hinder the mobility of economic resources than to foster regional economic cooperation and progress. Admittedly, Nigeria, Zimbabwe, South Africa, Zaire, Libya, Egypt, Sudan, and Algeria are relatively speaking endowed with natural and mineral resources which could serve as pillars for self-sustaining economies. But what is the prospect for the survival as independent, sovereign states, of landlocked and economically strapped countries like Burkina Faso, Chad, Mali, Ethiopia, Somalia, Niger, and Mauritania?

It is unfortunate that the OAU has been very conservative on the question of "national geographic boundaries." At the inception of the OAU, the organization affirmed the principle of inviolability of national boundaries bequeathed by former colonial masters.[51] The tendency to continue to uphold this status quo can be discerned in the African Charter for Popular Participation in Development and Transformation. The farthest it could move away from the question of inviolability of national frontiers is to suggest that "people and their popular organizations should develop links across national borders to promote co-operation and interrelationships on sub-regional, regional, South-South and South-North basis."[52] Desirable as it is, the charter's call on Africans to build linkages across national boundaries still indirectly lends approval to the boundaries of the Berlin treaty which have been pin-pointed as an impediment to Africa's economic development. A country's capacity for economic survival and progress depends on its natural and human resources. Africa, in its present fragmented form, cannot withstand the pressures of an economically united (and thus politically stronger) Europe.[53]

Finally, the contemporary trend in African socio-political and economic reality favors an integrative approach to development. African governments must adopt a new strategy for development management. Such a strategy should aim at the revitalization of the public sector, stimulation of the private sector, and encouragement of public participation in the overall development effort. Revitalization of the public sector requires two important steps. The first is the improvement of the policy-making process through the strengthening of skills in policy analysis formulation, implementation and review. The second is the enhancement of the efficiency and quality of African civil services through knowledge improvement, deregulation, and decentralization, among others.[54] As the ECA notes, the development of the private sector depends on entrepreneurs, markets, and a governmental supportive policy framework. Public policies that could enhance entrepreneurial capacity include the encouragement of the informal sector enterprises, efficient infrastructure, foreign investment and joint ventures. It also includes improvement of financial and capital markets, reassessment of training and management education strategies, and delivery systems to support enterprise development.[55] Also, as acknowledged by the ECA, governments alone cannot effect those changes. Business and non-governmental organizations as well as external actors have important roles to play in order to bring them about.

CONCLUSION

Of significant importance to the safeguard of African security, as the foregoing analysis has shown, is the question of economic development. The African continent could not hope to guarantee its security in the new world order as long as its economy remains underdeveloped. More than anything else, serious economic problems such as high costs of living, run-away inflation, mass poverty, massive unemployment or under-employment, and shortages of food and other necessities would continue to pose a serious threat to African security unless the continent urgently addresses the question of economic development.

The chapter has attempted to suggest some solutions to Africa's economic predicament. Suffice it to summarize that for the achievement of long term peace and stability in the continent, it is high time African leaders served their people rather than their selfish interests, allow democracy to develop and flourish, shift emphasis from military accumulation to social and economic development, and show confidence in the ability of their own academic community to provide solutions to African problems rather than relying on foreign personnel. It would not be out of place to conclude that the task of Africa's economic revival rests entirely on the shoulders of Africans. It should be clear to African leaders now that direct foreign investment, or massive foreign aid are no longer easy to come by anymore. The attention of the West has shifted to Eastern Europe where they would want to help democracy and capitalism flourish.

NOTES

1. For details on the figures, see Gerald E. Scott, "Transfer, Economic Structure, and Vulnerability of the African Economy," *Journal of Developing Areas*, 26, 1992, 213-238; Bade Onimode, "The Bretton Woods Institutions and Africa's Development," *Development: Journal of Society for International Development*, 1, 1992, 62-67; and Frankel Jacob and Morris Goldstein, "The Macroeconomic Policy Implications of Trade and Currency Zones," *Policy Implications of Trade and Currency Zones*, (Proceedings of Symposium, Federal Reserve Bank of Kansas City, Jackson Hole, Wyoming), 1991, 157-211.

2. *The Africa Review*, 1992, 11.

3. Quoted in Marion E. Doro, (ed.), *African Contemporary Record: Annual Survey and Documents*, (New York: Africana Publishing Company, 1990), 21, 1988-89, c65.

4. *ibid.* 205.

5. *Prospects for Africa: A Special Report by Save the Children Fund and Overseas Development Institute,* (London: Hodder and Stroughton, 1988).

6. *World Development Report,* 1991, 251. In absolute terms, the debt rose from US$6 billion in 1970 to US$147 billion in 1989, and to US$178 billion in 1991. See World Debt tables for 1989/90 and 1990/91.

7. *ibid.*

8. *ibid.*

9. Dieter Strack and Siegfried Schonherr, (eds), *Debt Survey of Developing Countries,* (Boulder: Westview Press, 1990).

10. Sheriffdeen Tella, "Africa's Economic Prospect After Cold War Era: A Prognosis," paper presented at the 10th Annual Meeting of the Association of Third World Studies, University of Florida, Gainesville, October 1992.

11. See Alaba Ogunsanwo, *The Transformation of Nigeria: Scenarios and Metaphors,* (Lagos: University of Lagos Press, 1991), 19.

12. See Sahr John Kpundeh's, *Politics and Corruption in Africa: A Case Study of Sierra Leone,* (Lanham: University Press of America, 1994), for a discussion of the magnitude of corruption in one of the poorest nations of the world.

13. Adebayo Adedeji, *West Africa,* 11-17, November, 1991, 1878.

14. *World Development Report,* 1991, 141-142.

15. Altaf Gauher, "The Hidden Cost of the Arms Race, *South,* July 1982, 7.

16. John G. Jackson, Introduction to African Civilization. (New York: University Books, 1970), 310.

17. *ibid.*

18. For examples of studies that vividly discuss the effects of European colonial economic system on Africa's development, see Toyin Falola, (ed), *Nigeria and Britain: Exploitation or Development?* (London: Zed Books, Ltd, 1989), and Walter Rodney, *How Europe Underdeveloped Africa,* (Washington DC: Howard Univeristy Press, 1992).

19. See Berberogly Berch, *The Political Economy of Development,* (Albany: State University of New York Press, 1992).

20. Moshin Khan, "The Macroeconomic Effects of Fund Supported Adjustment Program, "*IMF staff papers,* 37, (2), 1990, 195-231.

21. Lancaster, "Economic Reforms in Africa: Is it Working," in Olusegun Obasanjo and Hans d'Orville, (eds.), *The Leadership*

Challenge of Economic Reforms in Africa, (New York: Crane Russac, 1991), 102

22. Irungu Houghton, "The AID industry in East Africa", SAPEM, November 1994, 8.
23. See *The Economist,* 19 March, 1994.
24. *Monthly Regional Bulletin,* Jan., 1995.
25. *International Security Digest,* 1,(9), Ausgust
26. *Jane's Defence Weekly,* 27 August, 1994.
27. *African Confindential,* 26 August, 1994.
28. *ibid.*
29. Quoted from Sue Willet, "South Africa: Arms Trade Dilemma", *International Security Digest,* 2, (2), 1994.
30. *ibid.*
31. *ibid.*
32. *ibid.*
33. *Military Technology,* 9, 1994
34. *Financial Times,* 8 February, 1994,4.
35. *Jane's Defence Weekly,* 16 July 1994, 4.
36. *ibid.,* 19 November, 1994, 11.
37. See the following: *Economic Commission for Africa* Report, 1989; Jan Black, *Development in Theory and Practice,* (Boulder: Westview Press, 1991); and Bade Ominode, The Bretton Woods Institution."
38. *World Development Report, 1991, 186.*
39. *ibid.*
40. See for instance, *The World Bank Annual Report,* 1994.
41. Doro, (ed), *African Contemporary Record,* c65.
42. *Africa Research Bulletin,* 30, (1), Jan. 16-Feb. 15, 1993, 11119.
43. Jackson, *Introduction to African Civilizations,* 202.
44. *ibid.,* 280
45. *Africa Research Bulletin,* 11119.
46. Festus Ugboaja Ohaegbulam, *Towards an Understanding of the African Experience: From Historical and Contemporary Perspectives,* (Lanham: University Press of America, 1990), 250.
47. For instance, in 1992 the staff of CEEAC, which had been hampered by non-payment of membership dues, protested against staff reductions and non-payment of certain allowances. See *Africa Research Bulletin,* 30 (4), March 16-April 15, 1993, 11192. Also at the 57th session of OAU's Council of Ministers in Addis Ababa, Ethiopia, the Secretary-General, Salim Salim complained that member countries owed the or-

ganization $70 million. See *Africa Research Bulletin*, 30, (2), Feb. 16-March 15, 1993, 11155.

48. Howard Schissel, "Mining In the 1990s: An Uphill Struggle," *Africa Review*, 1992, 16.

49. *ibid.*

50. Leonard Gonchanov, "The Critical State of the African Economy: Its Causes, Characters, and Ways to Overcome it," in Obasanjo and d'Orville, (eds.), *The Leadership Challenge*, 27-36.

51. See Article 3 (3) of OAU Charter and the General Resolution on Border Disputes adopted by the Conference of Heads of States in Cairo, July 1964.

52. Doro, (ed.), *African Contemporary Record*, c66.

53. On the question of redrawing the political map of Africa, Molefi Kete Asante has suggested a six-state structure. See Asante, "A Six-State Structure for Africa," *African Concord*, 17 Sept. 1978, 54. *Africa Research Bulletin*, 30.(4). April 16-May 15, 1993, 11228.

Chapter 3

DEMOCRACY AND SECURITY IN AFRICA:
THE CHANGING NATURE OF A LINKAGE

Amadu Sesay and Abiodun Alao

INTRODUCTION

It is perhaps appropriate to begin this chapter by adopting
a working definition of *democracy* and *security* in order to
provide an analytical framework for our discussion. Democracy is a concept that has evoked many emotions. Not unex-
pectedly, there are, thus, several meanings attached to the
concept. For our purpose, we will adopt the basic tenets of
democracy as described by Catharine Newbury. Newbury
sees the characteristics of *liberal democracy* as including

> the presence of institutionalized mechanisms
> by which citizens may change the personnel
> holding power (usually through regular, com-
> petitive elections), respect for the rule of law,
> accountable governance and protection of hu-
> man and civil rights.[1]

Security is also a term of varied definitions. Most often, as
Mohammed Ayoob points out, there are two major assumptions about a threat to national security—that it is externally based; and that it is military in character, requiring an

equally military response.[2] However, as Ayoob also eloquently argues, these notions of security are flawed when considering security in the Third World; this is because security is portrayed almost exclusively as an external phenomenon.[3]

This external orientation of security found full expression in the military alliance system that came into being after 1945; i.e., the North Atlantic Treaty Organization (NATO), and its counterpart, the Warsaw Pact Treaty. Both were geared towards deterring external military attacks from identifiable enemy sources. To be sure, like other states in the international system, Third World countries, in general, and African states, in particular, are also concerned with external threats but that is just a minor aspect of their security dilemma. The major threats to their security come largely from internal or domestic sources, and these are all linked to the complex problems associated with nation building. The linkage between democracy and security is perhaps much more obvious in Africa for these reasons. In this chapter we shall examine critically the link between *democracy* and *security* with special reference to Africa.

Democracy, development, and security have always been interlinked. There is, in fact, a way that they are mutually reinforcing. A stable democratic polity promotes development, ensures freedom of speech, encourages political pluralism, brings about political tolerance, and in the economic realm, creates healthy competition. These "virtues" of democracy constituted the themes exploited by the West in their rivalry against the communist world, especially during the period of the Cold War. Throughout the period, the West argued that its strength, founded on its democratic institutions, not only promoted good life and higher living standards, but that it also guaranteed its security. In the same vein, Western leaders and some liberal scholars believe that the victory of the West over the former Eastern Bloc is, in fact, a victory of democracy over "totalitarianism" and centrally planned economic systems. Whatever the merits or demerits of this position, one thing that is clear is that the post-Cold War international system seems to be moving not only toward a condominium of power, but also ideological uniformity. This is one of the reasons why the period since 1989 has been described as the post-ideological world.

The unexpected collapse of state communism in eastern Europe including the Soviet Union is, perhaps, one of the most important developments that has vindicated the argument presented above. It certainly reinforces the point that democratic polities are much more resilient and secure. Of course, the collapse itself created security dilemmas for some of these countries with which many are still grappling today. For example, Russia, which came out of the dismemberment of the former Soviet Union, is still faced with enormous security problems, including the on-going problem in Chechenya. However, much more significant is the fact that most of these countries have now opted for democracy and free-market economy.

For many decades before the collapse of communism in eastern Europe, western countries had tried to persuade African nations and their leaders that the safest route to development and security was through adoption of democratic systems. The behavior of many western countries during the Cold War, however, contradicted their much advertised preference for democratic values. It was not uncommon for many of them to cultivate close alliances with some of the most autocratic regimes in Africa because of the Cold War expediences. Perhaps the best manifestation of this tendency was western support for the apartheid government in South Africa. The country was seen by the West as a bulwark against perceived Soviet expansion in the Indian Ocean which could pose a threat to western oil supplies from the Middle-east. Also, the geo-political and strategic location of Zaire in the heart of Africa made its government a candidate for western support, in spite of the corrupt and autocratic nature of Mobutu Sese Seko's regime.

The Cold War also provided an opportunity for many African states to resist political reforms. For instance, many of them saw the socialist alternative to development as the answer to both their economic and security needs. African leaders used state communism in Eastern Europe and the Soviet Union to justify the curtailment of the political freedom of their people. Many, in fact, argued that political pluralism which western democracy advocated was unsuitable for their countries because of their ethnic heterogeneity. Indeed, people like former President Siaka Stevens of Sierra Leone argued fervently that multipartism was inappropriate to the African situation because it would only heighten ethnic squablings, promote instability, and hold back progress towards much needed economic development. Multipartism, accordingly, was a luxury on which Africa could not afford to "squander" valuable time and scarce human and economic resources.

AUTOCRACY AND (IN)SECURITY IN THE "OLD ORDER"

One of the most important features of African politics is the ease with which virtually all the post-colonial states, soon after their independence, ended inherited political traditions. Perhaps the most important reason for this was that the political elites that took over after these states' independence were not sincere about the democratic traditions the former colonial powers left behind. Also, most of the new leaders had their own hidden agendas to perpetuate themselves in power. The problems were further compounded by the inability of the inherited institutions, which were hurriedly put into place, to withstand post-independence pressures. Thus, in some cases, the successor political elites merely exploited these loopholes to their advantage. But even the countries that maintained the inherited institutions did not operate them satisfactorily. For instance, in those that maintained a multi party system, it was common to find the same party winning elections all the time, thereby making the country a de-facto one-party state. As will be shown later in this chapter, the long term implication of this became apparent when these countries were eventually forced to adopt multi-party democracy; the political parties that emerged to contest the already established parties suffered enormous disadvantages and failed to compete effectively.

The consequences of the above are just too familiar: political repression, corruption, violation of human rights, and of course, incessant military coup-d'état. In many instances, a handful of individuals or a particular ethnic group holds all political power. This usually leads to tension because those who are denied access to political power resort to non-democratic means of expressing their opposition. As mentioned earlier, some of the most autocratic leaders in Africa did survive for that long because they were beneficiaries of the support and assistance of the Cold War super powers and their allies. Many of these countries were thus able to present a facade of political stability.

The inability of most African states to devise peaceful means of political succession inevitably led to the aberration of the military in government. This later became so rampant that, by the beginning of the 1990s, very few African countries had eluded military intervention in national politics. Although the military claimed to be modernizers and agents of stability, during the early stages of their involvement in politics, following the coups of the 1960s, it became apparent that this claim was false. Indeed, the military became part of the democratic problem in Africa and, in fact, it would appear that it perpetrated much greater political and economic atrocities than its civilian counterparts. Generally, African military governments are guilty of manipulating ethnic cleavages, institutionalizing corruption, nepotism, and indiscipline, and fomenting political instability.[4] In-fighting, rivalry, and petty jealousy within the military have often led to coups and counter-coups, sometimes leading to the overthrow of incumbent regimes, thus promoting political instability.

The history of military involvement in politics has not recorded many examples of democratic transition exercises. More often than not, military regimes in Africa are succeeded by another military administration after a coup. The result of this is a vicious circle in which military regimes change hands. Until the upsurge in democratic pressure after the Cold War, the only example of a successive transition from a military to a democratically elected civilian regime was the one organized by the regime of General Olusegun Obasanjo in Nigeria, which conducted elections and handed over to the civilian administration of President Shehu Shagari in 1979. It was, however, not long before the military came back into politics, as the Shagari administration was overthrown in December 1983 by General Muhammadu Buhari.

Apart from its negative impact on democratic institutions, the involvement of the military in politics also has a major security implication for African countries. In virtually all African countries where the military has played a significant role in politics, most members of the armed forces have become so involved in politics that it has damaged their military professionalism, and that has threatened national security. People typically join the military in order to reach the corridors of power rather than to enhance the security of the country. It is, therefore, little wonder that admission application into the Nigerian Defence Academy (NDA), fell after the Nigerian military got bogged down in the bloody civil war in Liberia.[5] To many Nigerians, the West African peace mission in Liberia (ECOMOG), to which Nigeria contributed the largest contingent, showed the other side of the military, a side that many people had considered unlikely.

THE NEW DEMOCRATIC DAWN AND SECURITY

The end of the Cold War also coincided with what in Africa has been described as the democratic upsurge. The search for democracy in Africa, however, pre-dated the end of the Cold War. Africans had always resisted totalitarian and authoritarian regimes long before the so-called new democratic dawn in the continent. One of the earliest examples of this was the 1967 victory of Sierra Leone's opposition party, the All People's Congress (APC), over the incumbent Sierra Leone People's Party (SLPP), led by Albert Margai, a man whose policies were perceived as leaning towards dictatorship and a one party state. Although Siaka Stevens was prevented from assuming office as prime minister because of the coup in 1967, it is important to note that after a coup a year later, non-commissioned officers in the army summoned him from exile in Guinea and asked him to form a government on the basis of the 1967 election results. Significantly, also, when Stevens himself displayed dictatorial tendencies, several attempts were made to oust him from office. One of the first attempts was made in 1971, ironically by the then Force Commander, Colonel Bangura, who in 1968 had handed over power to Stevens. Bangura opposed the introduction of a Republican status for the country which would have made Stevens an executive president with a lot of powers. Nigeria's long standing political instability has also in part been due to the opposition of Nigerians to military and civilian dictatorships. Again, although it turned out to be negative, the decision of the late Liberian leader, Samuel Doe, to change from a military to a civilian leader, is an acknowledgment that he was aware of the desire of Liberians for democracy, and was willing to strike a balance between his personal ambition and their desire.

In spite of these examples, however, the end of the Cold War added a significant momentum to the process of democratization in Africa. The global denunciation of authoritarianism that followed the end of the Cold War showed many "sit-tight" leaders in Africa that the management of their countries' affairs was no longer an "internal affair," but one which is subject to scrutiny by the international community. One other link between the upsurge in democratic desire and the end of the Cold War is that African autocrats could no longer embrace dictatorial tendencies because the communist ideology on which many relied for inspiration and proof of stability had suddenly collapsed. Since most of the successor regimes in these former communist states started professing their beliefs in liberal democracy and free market economic systems, these African leaders were further alienated.

In the post-Cold War world, both external and internal factors have continued to influence demands for democratic systems across Africa. Apart from the collapse of communism in Eastern Europe and the former Soviet Union, external pressure for change has also come from two other inter-related forces. The first is the "new conditionality" imposed on African states by international financial institutions (IFIs), especially the International Monetary Fund (IMF), and the World Bank. Political conditionalities are not really new. As far back as the 1970s, African countries whose economies were in trouble were expected to carry out some reforms before they were given assistance. However, the prevailing Cold War politics made it difficult to adhere strictly to these conditionalities or requirements. Following the "victory" of the West, it became easier to demand strict adherence as a prerequisite for financial relief, as there was no longer the fear of pushing African countries into the Soviet fold because of tedious conditionalities. Thus, the IMF and the World Bank, have insisted on progress toward multipartism and re-democratization by African countries as a condition for access to new credit lines as well as for debt re-scheduling. Claude Ake summed this up succinctly, when he said "[international institutions] give African leaders the chance to substitute structural adjustment for democratisation."[6]

Another external source of pressure on African countries has come from Western industrialized nations such as Britain, France, the United States, Germany, Canada, and also from Japan. These nations have made African access to Western aid and credit contingent upon clear evidence of their progressive movement towards political accountability, multipartism, and respect for human rights.[7] The limited sanctions that the West imposed on Nigeria since the cancellation of the June 1993 presidential election by Nigeria's former President, General Ibrahim Babangida, is a clear example of this new prerequisite.

In the domestic realm, pressure for democratization has come from varied sources. The first are agitations resulting from the biting economic situation in most of the African countries. In some cases, economic agitation has assumed violent dimensions, especially in those countries where subsidies have been removed from essential items. The ultimate result of all this is the population's desire for an alternative government which will reduce the yoke of economic hardship. Two examples of this are the recurring riots against the Structural Adjustment Policy (SAP) in Nigeria, and the Maize riots in Zambia in 1989.

Internal pressure for multipartism has also come from old politicians who have been left out "of the scheme of things" in their respective countries. These include, for instance, those who have either lost their parliamentary seats in one-party systems, or had fallen out of favor with the government in power. Thus, they call for a wider scope of political participation and dissent in order to effect a change in their political fortunes.

Finally, pressure for change has come from civic organizations and groups such as labor movements, students' organizations, religious organizations, market women associations, and groups which are exclusively dedicated to the restoration of democracy. In Nigeria, these groups, by and large operate under an umbrella organization called the Campaign for Democracy (CD). In Zambia, it was the coalition of opposition elements and labor movements that ousted former President Kenneth Kaunda. A similar coalition was also evident in Kenya, where religious organizations and opposition elements joined forces, although ineffectively, against the Kenyan African National Union (KANU) government of Daniel Arap Moi. Also to be included in this category are the activities of individuals who have come to personify the democratic struggles in their respective countries. Some of these individuals are Gani Fawehinmi and Beko Ransome-Kuti in Nigeria, Ngugi wa Thiong'o in Kenya, and Fru Ndi in Cameroon.

The assumption is that the above factors would lead to a smooth transition to democracy. This has proven to be so in a few African countries such as Niger, Benin Republic, Mali, and Zambia. In these places, the process of democratic change was relatively smooth, thus producing very little immediate security implications. In the majority of African states, however, there has been stiff resistance from incumbent regimes who put up a fight in the form of political repression, closure of media houses, and incarceration of opposition leaders. In some cases, too, incumbent regimes have ordered brutal repression of protest demonstrations by pro-democracy agitators, leading to serious loss of lives. In a number of countries repression preceded the granting of democratic concession. It is not surprising, however, that it was in these countries that security problems were most pronounced. South Africa provides a good case in point, for here suppression of democratic yearnings took a racial dimension. The determination of the white minority to prevent black majority rule was to lead to the most extensive militarization in the continent, and it was to have serious security implications for all the countries in the Southern Africa sub-region.

The degree to which security problems accompanied the manifestation of democratic agitations depends on a number of factors. Of considerable importance is the extent to which the incumbent regime resisted change, the extent of international involvement in the process of democratization, and the degree of cohesion among the parties opposed to the incumbent regime. As mentioned earlier, in countries like Niger, Benin Republic, Mali, and Zambia, the transition was done with relative ease. The incumbent governments conceded to democracy without much hesitation. Even in some of these countries, especially Zambia, there was no serious case of human rights violations before the democratic concession. However, in countries like Zaire, Kenya, Cameroon, and a host of others, the incumbent governments opposed the democratic demands of their people, and it was with considerable international pressure that these governments consented to multi-party democracy. In all these countries, there were security problems of varying dimensions, some of which are still prevalent.

The second determinant of the extent of security problems associated with democratization is the depth of international involvement in the transition exercise. On the whole, deep international involvement manifested in the transition to democracy in three countries: Angola, Mozambique, and South Africa. In all these cases, international organizations, especially the OAU, the UN, and the Commonwealth of Nations took active part in the democratic transition. International involvement had two important effects. First, it ensured massive injection of funds into the conduct of elections. This enabled all sides to be actively involved in electioneering campaigns, ensuring mass participation and "fair" conduct of elections. Second, the participation of external monitors removed the so-called "advantage of incumbency," which is often used by incumbent governments to rig elections and keep themselves in power. The successful democratic transitions in Mozambique and South Africa were thus due to significant international involvement accompanied by the citizens' determination to respect the dictates of democracy. Despite international involvement in Angola, the transition program failed; however, the failure can be blamed on one of the warring sides, which refused to respect the election outcome.[8] As a result, a second civil war began after the UN supervised election in 1993.

The lack of cohesion among opposition parties in some African states also created security problems during the democratic upsurge that followed the end of the Cold War. In countries like Kenya, Zimbabwe, and Zaire, opposition parties could not present their case in any sustained and intelligible manner. This made it easier for the incumbent regimes to remain in power after the election. In some of these countries, efforts to articulate opposition against the incumbent governments created problems because the new political parties were formed along ethnic lines. This again heightened ethnic tension within those countries, with all its attendant security risks.

It would appear that there is superficiality in the democratic changes currently going on in Africa, and more than anything else, this signals greater danger to security in the continent. The nature of the external pressure for democracy, especially from the financial institutions, put more emphasis on free and fair elections, leaving out much more fundamental indices of democracy like tolerance, respect for other people's opinion, etc. All these give many people in Africa the impression that the West may not, after all, be interested in durable democracy in the continent. As experience has shown in many parts of Africa, a free and fair election does not automatically lead to ethnic unity and good government. Although Kenya had a "free and fair" election, the government of Daniel Arap Moi is far from a democratic one in the true sense of the concept. The undemocratic character of the Kenyan government became known to the international community in July 1995, when many human rights commissions accused the government of violating human rights and of repressing political opponents.

In some military regimes, the clamor for democratization put too much emphasis on the formal transfer of power, without realizing that democratic governance implies a post-military administration that has shed the toga of military imperatives. Formal transfer of power, then, is a process of civilianization, not democratization. Democratization implies popular participation, free choice, popular will, etc., and it can only take place in an atmosphere devoid of military pressure. But the handing over of power to civilians by the military rarely takes into cognizance these elements of democracy. Thus, many transitions end up as "stop gaps." Although the 1985-1993 transitional program in Nigeria was propagated by its architects as an example of a well thought-out and well articulated hand-over program, the manner in which it was pursued denied it credibility. The very institutions that were hailed as providing the foundations for a stable Third Republic were themselves counteractive to the democratic process in the long run. The manner of behavior of key managers of the program bothered on irresponsibility. Rules and regulations were changed in a haphazard fashion, and candidates were disqualified without reason. The presidential election held in June 1993 was, at the time, declared free and fair and the most peaceful in the history of the country. But in the final analysis, it never translated into democracy. It was annulled without any cogent justification by the erstwhile military administration of General Babangida.

The Nigerian example is just one of many in Africa where a transitional process, instead of leading to democracy, produced political instability. Even is some places where actual transfer of power has taken place, there is a pervading aura of military presence. The actions of the new political class as it assumes power in the aftermath of "successful" transitions presuppose an illusion of durability of democracy. The new political actors act and talk as if they have a limited spell in power before military re-intrusion. This sense of fatalism inspires conspicuous consumption and predatory habits that sooner or later provoke public disenchantment and the longing for salvation. The country is therefore likely to turn again to the army to come in and "cleanse" the society. This is the vicious circle in which democratization in Africa is caught.

RECALCITRANT STATES AND SECURITY IMPLICATIONS

Many African states have, in various degrees, defied all internal and external pressure to democratize. They could be broadly categorized into four. First, there are those states which have not succumbed to democratic demands and are either under undemocratic civilian administrations or military regimes. In this category are countries like: Togo, Sierra Leone, the Gambia, and Nigeria. Second, there are states where the incumbent regimes won elections amidst allegations of rigging and other electoral malpractice. In the third category are those states where incumbent regimes won elections but still continue to suppress the opposition. The fourth category represents states where there are so far inconclusive elections, and where the incumbent regimes still hold on to power in the face of internal and international opposition.

In all the categories of "recalcitrant" states indicated above, the latent security implications are similar. Perhaps the most important of these is political instability. Outright suppression of democratic pressure continues to remain a major cause of violence and political instability. In recent years many African states have seen violence arising from democratic agitation. A striking example is that of Swaziland, traditionally considered as one of the most stable countries in southern Africa. In this country democratic pressure against the government of King Mswati III has turned violent since the king refused to respond fully to the democratic desire of his people. In February 1995, arsonists caused serious damage to the parliament. Two days before this attack, the home of Prince Phinda, the Minister of Broadcasting, Information, and Tourism was also firebombed. In many African states, similar violent opposition to autocratic rule is being manifested. In some, as in Nigeria, there is marked development of organized opposition.

A number of African states could be classified as recalcitrant because of a peculiar circumstance which has made them ill disposed to democracy. These are states that have either recently ended a civil war or are still enmeshed in one. Examples of such states are Chad, Liberia, Rwanda, Angola, Mozambique, Somalia, Sudan, and Sierra-Leone. What are the prospects for democracy in such states? Any attempt to consider the possibility of a stable democracy in these war-torn states must take adequate cognizance of the importance of achieving lasting peace coupled with durable economy. The following examples demonstrate this fact.

Chad has been at war since independence. The bickering between the sides in the conflict has created a zero-sum game type of politics in the country which undoubtedly hurts the chances of democracy thriving. What appears to be the greatest hindrance to democracy in Chad, however, is its completely collapsed economy. Until there is some form of economic stability in the country, the chances of democracy taking root there are remote. Although a "National Conference" was held between January and April 1993, clashes between factions and between security forces and the civilians still make the situation volatile. As previous experiences have shown, Chad's instability has considerable regional implications and absence of democracy in the country may forebode regional instability in the future.

The Liberian situation has also been a complex one. Although disarmament and demobilization exercises have been successfully completed, and as called for by the Abuja Accord, elections have been held in July 1997, which brought to power Charles Taylor and his National Patriotic Front of Liberia (NPFL), before durable democracy can be established there must first be peace. The task before the new government in order to achieve the necessary peace conducive to development include: revamping the shattered economy, creating new national armed forces, rehabilitating the refugees, and creating a harmonious inter-group relations. The ability of the NPFL government to do this, however, remains to be seen.

By the end of the first quarter of 1996, Angola was still hanging in the delicate balance of peace and conflict, but with a slightly greater tilt towards the former. The bedrock of the current semblance of order in the country is the Lusaka Accord, between the MPLA government and UNITA, signed in Lusaka, Zambia, in October 1994. Cold War politics had turned democracy into a source of conflict in Angola since the country's independence in 1975. UNITA fought the MPLA government because it did not receive the mandate of Angolans in a democratic election. It is, however, something of an irony that UNITA was the group fighting for democracy after it rejected the outcome of the first democratic election in the country on the ground of alleged electoral malpractice.

The prospect of democracy surviving in Angola is a bit more complex. Unlike a country like Liberia where an election has ushered in, hopefully, lasting peace, the election in Angola has not yet brought about the desired peace. Although a valid election, the result has not yet been accepted by all sides in the conflict. Yet, this is necessary for peace to hold. Once this is established, the focus would need to move to post-war reconstruction and the development of the country's economic base. This will create a durable base for democracy to thrive. Angola seems to have acknowledged that the concept of "winner takes all" may hurt the country. Against this background, both sides have agreed to some form of power sharing. In the Lusaka Accord, it was agreed that cabinet, governorship, and deputy governorship positions of some districts should be given to UNITA. In the Angolan situation, this may be a necessary decision, and one which may bring peace and stability to the country.

Another potential obstacle to democracy in Angola is the alleged corruption among the top members of the MPLA.[9] If the charges are true, such widespread corruption may affect the country's economic recovery, which will hinder the chances of its democratic success thereby increasing the drift towards civil war.

Mozambique had its first democratic elections in 1994, after RENAMO and the FRELIMO government signed a peace accord that ended the 17-year-old civil war. The FRELIMO government won the elections, and the RENAMO leader, Alfonso Dhlakama, conceded defeat. The rebel leader later confirmed that his organization would not, because of losing the election, resort back to dissidence.[10]

Although RENAMO has promised to respect democratic principles, bringing democracy to Mozambique still requires overcoming a number of hurdles. The most important of these is the country's precarious economic situation. The civil war has left Mozambique with an empty treasury making the country the most aid-dependent nation in the world. Against this background, the most basic economic infrastructure that could guarantee democracy is not available. Two issues are particularly important here. First, democracy, by its nature is an expensive system. Even if RENAMO has completely renounced violence, the organization still needs some money to have all the infrastructure needed to mount political opposition to the government in power. This, Dhlakama claimed, is presently unavailable to his organization.[11] Inevitably, this could affect the quality of opposition to be presented to democratic debates. Second, without the provision for basic economic resources, peace can not be guaranteed, and the whole democratic gains made at the Rome Peace Accords would be destroyed. In this case anarchy could return to Mozambique.

Sierra Leone seemed to have gone around a complete circle in its quest for democracy. After Brigadier Julius Maada Bio overthrew the government of Captain Valentine Strasser in 1995, Sierra Leoneans were given the option of either having peace before election or a democratic transition before peaceful negotiation with the Revolutionary United Front (RUF) rebels. Although it was clear that the new government would prefer to have a mandate to defeat the rebel forces before holding an election, the rest of the country felt otherwise. After a number of constitutional meetings, the Bio government reluctantly agreed to democratic transition. The argument of those who opted for "election before peace" was that a democratically elected government had greater chances of making peace than the military regime. In the subsequent election held in February 1996, President Ahmad Tejan Kabbah was elected. However, democracy was not to last in Sierra Leone, for in May 1997, the civilian government of Kabbah was overthrown in a military coup led by Major Johnny Koroma. Since the inception of the new administration, Sierra Leone has not known any peace. Although the rebel war seemed to have subsided, Major Koroma's government is faced with international opposition. Pressure to relinquish power and re-install the democratically elected government of Kabbah has particularly been mounted by the states of the West African sub-region. Nigeria has taken the lead in this opposition to military government in Sierra Leone. West African regional forces under Nigeria's leadership have blockaded the impoverished state, creating for it a further economic hardship. Sierra Leone would need a massive injection of foreign assistance to resuscitate its economy. But it is unclear how much international sympathy the country could generate given the international opposition to its military government. However, there is the need for a minimum level of economic well-being for the citizens in order to ensure that ordinary people do not resort to armed robbery and other similar means to survive the hardship. A possible massive proliferation of light weapons in the aftermath of the civil war could be a ready tool of havoc in the hands of poverty stricken population.

Somalia's situation appears slightly more endemic than other countries. The decades of civil war in the country, the entrance and later withdrawal of the United States-led peacekeeping mission have introduced real complications to peace in the country. Again, the dismemberment of the country began with the secession of what is now known as Somaliland. Democracy can only come to Somalia after peace has been restored into the country. This appears to be somewhat distant possibility, as the inter and intra clan conflicts still continue. For example, in June 1995, the main rebel leader who attained popularity by defying the attempts of the United States to capture him, Mohammed Farrar Aideed, was again deposed from the leadership of the faction by senior members of the party. Although the new leadership has asked the United States and other agencies to come back into the country, it is almost certain that this will not happen and the factionalization of Somalia is till likely to continue. It is only after peace has come to the country that the Somalis can start any serious discussion about the prospect of democracy in the country.

Rwanda's scenario is quite similar. Although the genocide that attracted global attention in 1993 has since subsided, the relationship between the Tutsi and the Hutu is still tense. What has made the Rwandan case all the more unique is that, even at the outbreak of the civil war, the country was considered "democratic," but that democracy was defined only to a limited extent. Thus, all that is needed in Rwanda for the restoration of democracy is peace. This expectedly would be followed by mutual trust and economic development and reconstruction.

LABOR MOVEMENTS, STUDENT ORGANIZATIONS AND THE MEDIA IN NATIONAL SECURITY CONSIDERATION

In African states, the most potent forces that have re-emerged in the renewed clamor for democracy are labor movements, student organizations, and the media. Labor movements have used their grip on the economy to force the government to concede to certain democratic reforms. Students, with their numerical strength and being perceived as a source of ideas, sometimes force governments to give way to the wishes of the people. Also, the media have been instrumental in disseminating ideas about democracy to the cross section of the population, raising their political awareness. To African autocratic regimes, therefore, these three sectors of the civil society represent an unholy alliance that should be crushed to ensure their perpetuation in office. This section addresses the role these groups have played and the prospects of their active participation in security decisions in African states.

Labor movements in virtually all African countries have always been at loggerheads with both autocratic and democratic governments. The only difference, however, is that, while democratic governments would seek to resolve the situation through dialogue, autocratic governments would use force and intimidation. In most African states, however, labor movements have not succeeded in forming political parties. Their focus has always been to act as pressure groups. In some cases, in fact, clear and concise clauses precluding them from political activities are entrenched in their constitution.

The important role the unions have played, despite their apolitical tendencies, is demonstrated in the rise of the incumbent Zambian president, Frederick Chiluba, to the limelight of politics as a labor union leader.

Nigeria is a good example of an African state where sections of the labor movement became vocal in the wake of the popular demand for democracy. Labor unions especially became visible in opposition to undemocratic forms of government after General Babangida installed the Interim Government following the nullification of the June 1993 elections. The labor movement, by its relentless opposition to the Interim Government, greatly contributed to its eventual removal. It has also continued its opposition to General Sanni Abacha, leader of the military government that overthrew the Interim Government in 1994. Some of the affiliates of the Nigerian Labour Congress (NLC), especially the oil workers, put up the best organized and sustained strike in the history of the country. Although the government eventually put down the strike, it remained a landmark development that effectively destabilized the government and the country.

Students in tertiary institutions have always played important roles in the democratic struggle. It appears, however, that autocratic regimes have found ways of dealing with their persistent demands, that is, through the closure of their institutions. In virtually all African countries where the call for democracy has gone unheeded, institutions of higher learning have been closed down, both as punishment for their involvement in the call for democracy, and because they are seen as a place where students could articulate a coherent opposition to autocracy. Examples of this situation abound. Many institutions of higher learning in Nigeria were closed down for a whole academic year in order to prevent a sustained opposition to the nullification of the 1993 elections. Other countries like Ghana, Cameroon, Zaire, Togo, Zimbabwe, etc., have, in the last five years closed down tertiary institutions in the face of opposition to government. In some of these countries, the alternative to the closures is to keep open the schools and shoot down students when they engage in open anti-government demonstrations. The outcome of these developments include a number of security related problems like restlessness among the citizens, massive intellectual depletion of the academic community, and general political instability.

The media as a body has played a significant, albeit, occasionally inconsistent role in the clamor for democracy in Africa. As as a vehicle for disseminating information, the media has led the way in educating the population in the practice of democracy. However, contradictions often emerge from the undemocratic activities of some media institutions. Since most media in Africa are government owned, they inevitably end up propagating the ideas of the incumbent government.

CONCLUSION

Although the end of the Cold War has resulted in the upsurge of democratic pressures in Africa, it is certain that it will take more than the legacies of the Cold War to advance the cause of democracy on the continent. A series of other measure must be instituted before democracy can thrive in the continent. The most important of these are economic recovery, reduction of state control over resources, general tolerance from the government in power, provisions for the basic needs of the citizens, and the resolution of the existing ethnic conflicts. Until all these are established, having an enduring democracy on the continent is unlikely.

NOTES

1. Catharine Newbury, "Introduction: Paradoxes of Democratization in Africa," *African Studies Review*, 37 (1), April 1994, 2.
2. See Mohammed Ayoob, *The Third World Security Predicament*, (Boulder: Lynne Rienner and Publishers, 1995), 5.

3. *ibid.*
4. Nigeria is a given African country where the military has played a devastating role in national life. A book that examines the role of the Nigerian military in national develop ment is Toyin Falola, et al., *The Military Factor in Nigeria, 1966-1985*, (Lewiston: Edwin Mellen Press, 1994).
5. Jimi Peters, "From Constabulary to a National Force: The Evolution of the Nigerian National Army," (Unpublished Ph.D. thesis), University of London, 1994.
6. Claude Ake, "End of Honeymoon," in *African Concord*, (Lagos), 24 Feb. 1992, 35.
7. These "new" conditionalities have been the thrust of speeches by several western leaders. See, *West Africa*, (London), 28 Oc tober to 3 November 1991, and 24 February to 1st March, 1992.
8. For more on this, see, Abiodun Alao, "Angola: The Second Civil War", in Robert Hall (eds), *The World in Conflict, 1994/ 95*, (London: Jane's Information Group, 1995), 95-97. See Also John A. Marcum, "Angola: War Again," *Current History*, (92) 572, 1993, 218-223.
9. See "Angola: Rebuilding Confidence," *Southern Africa Political and Economic Monthly*, (8) 5, Feb. 1995, 15-17.
10. This commitment was made during the visit of the RENAMO leader to the Center for Defence Studies, King's College, London, in April 1995.
11. *ibid.*

Chapter 4

THE ENVIRONMENT AND AFRICAN SECURITY:
IMPLICATIONS OF CONTINUED NEGLECT

Abiodun Alao

INTRODUCTION

The environment has two interlocking links with security. First, some military measures taken to ensure security often have consequences for the environment. Second, there are a number of environmental issues whose handling and/or mishandling have created, or have the potential of creating security problems between and within nations. It is, however, ironic that it was only recently when environmental considerations like pollution, the greenhouse effect, acid rain, depletion of the ozone layer, etc., became issues for global concern, that the apparently obvious connections between security and environment came to the fore of global concern. Even in technologically advanced countries, where the inseparable link between the two concepts should be more obvious, the environment was for generations considered the passive victim of man's desire to acquire and use technology in the conduct of conflicts.

The history of neglect of some of the environmental implications of militarization is particularly long. Even before advancements in technology devastated the environment, historical methods of warfare, like the scorched-earth-policy, for example, had caused major, and often lasting damage. The first major realization of the environmental implications of militarization came with the use of the atomic bomb on Hiroshima and Nagasaki in 1945. The detonation of the bomb glaringly illustrated some of the environmental dangers of militarism. The gruesome outcome of the experience of Hiroshima and Nagasaki did not, however, deter the world from acquiring nuclear weapons, as was exemplified by the subsequent Cold War arms race. At one stage, the world community had a brief realization of the implication of their indifference to environmental issues. This led to the initiation of the United Nations Conference on the Human Environment in June 1972. The outcome of this conference, "The Stockholm Declaration," and the establishment of the "United Nations Environment Programme" (UNEP), laid the groundwork for constructive international cooperation. In the end, however, the intricate UN bureaucracy and financial difficulties weakened the initiative. The disregard for the environment thus continued until after the end of the Cold War when the world realized the need to pay greater attention to environmental issues.[1]

In line with the wider global trends, African countries after their independence did not consider the need to look at the environmental implications of security. Understandable naivety seemed to have led them into believing that warfare could only have impact on the environment if it was fought on a nuclear scale. Against the background of this thinking, virtually all African countries at independence chose to be "non-aligned" in the then ideological rivalry between the east and the west. Africa was also declared a nuclear free zone. These provisions aimed to immunize the continent from all environmental, physical, and human destruction that could accompany a nuclear war. It was, however, not long before Africa realized that its insurance against the possible fallout of nuclear war was inadequate, and, more importantly, that other numerous links between the environment and warfare existed, even when such wars are conducted on a non-nuclear scale.

The French nuclear tests in the Sahara in 1964 first removed the illusion that declaring Africa as a nuclear free zone or adhering to non-aligned movement were in themselves sufficient protection from nuclear fallout. After the global condemnation of the tests, Africa's indifference towards the link between security and environment continued. Although African countries contributed to all the numerous United Nations calls for disarmament and arms control, the main reason for their concern was the threat against human life, not the threat against the environment.[2] In fact, African countries considered continental issues like decolonization and the eradication of apartheid in South Africa as more pressing than efforts at global arms control or environmental problems. They considered the later as issues which Africa had no power to influence, or largely as European and American problems.

Environmental issues that have created inter- and intra-state tension have also been addressed half-heartedly or totally neglected. Where states made efforts to sign agreements on how best to manage the environmental issues that could cause conflict, nations unscrupulously breached such agreements if their national interest required it. Again, while nations were ready to go to war over some environmental related issues, they often treated the environmental legacies of such actions as being natural consequences of war. The result was the vicious circle of conflicts that became a dominant feature in Africa especially during the Cold War era.

In this chapter, I attempt to investigate the environmental concerns of security in the post Cold War period. Before embarking on this task, however, I will discuss the environmental issues that are relevant to Africa. This is to provide a background to Africa's perception of environmental issues. The chapter then proceeds to discuss the environmental consequences of militarization, and some environmental issues whose management could create security problems for Africa in the post Cold War era. The conclusion assesses the wider implications of the neglect of the environment, and suggests ways of rectifying some of the problems.

PECULIARITIES OF AFRICA'S ENVIRONMENTAL REALITIES

The United Nations Conference on Environment and Development held in Rio de Janeiro, Brazil, in June 1992, illuminated the differences between the developed and the developing world over environmental issues. Although this chapter does not go deep into the controversy that ensued at the conference over the protection of the environment, some of the differences, especially those bearing on security are identified in this section.[3] The first source of disagreement was over the preservation of the tropical forests, whose depletion had already damaged, directly or indirectly, the economies of many African nations, thereby increasing the propensity for internal conflict. The industrialized nations wanted to tackle this problem by declaring the forests as "global commons," and called for the establishment of a separate institution to regulate their exploitation. These measures, they argued, would not only reduce the present scale of deforestation, but would also ensure the replenishment of exploited resources. The developing countries, however, considered this suggestion hypocritical and unfair. They argued that the developed world raped their forests in its search for modernity. They thus wondered why the developed nations now impose recently achieved standards on the Third World when the latter is on a similar process of industrialization.[4] The Prime Minister of Malaysia put the position of the developing world articulately: "we do not cut down our trees foolishly. We need space for agriculture, we need living space and we need money from our timber".[5]

A second source of disagreement at the conference was on the issue of population. The developed North argued that there should be an immediate step towards population control, especially in the developing world where the population growth is most pronounced. The reason advanced for this was the alarming population increase in the Third World which is approaching a phase where the resources available in these countries will soon be inadequate to meet the needs of the population. While the South agreed that over-population is a major problem, it equally argued that it is a socio-economic issue that should be approached by a slow and continuing process of mass education.

A third divergence centered on who was responsible for the present environmental problems and who should be paying for the clean-up. The industrialized North seems to agree that its policies are largely responsible, but is not ready to pay for the repair. Most countries in the North, too, are confronted with environmental problems that require urgent attention. They thus found it incomprehensible to divert their resources to addressing Third World environmental problems. What the industrialized nations were ready to do was to tie aid provision to the developing countries with their readiness to implement environmental protection programs. The South found this unacceptable, arguing that direct attempts at addressing the environmental hardship in the South must come from the North.

There is the need to consider the dimension of natural hazards in Africa, and their effect on the environment, the economy, and security. Two issues inherent in the continent's biospheric condition are worthy of mention here. They are the problem of arid land prevalent in many of the countries in Africa, and the problem of highlands. In many ways, they have imposed a number of environmental restrictions on African countries. Arid lands are characterized by rainfalls that are low, seasonal, and variable. This invariably leads to drought which in turn results in failure of rain-fed agriculture, shortage of fodder, loss of livestock, and human famine. The result in many African countries is severe drought. Further excessive pressures from human exploitation on the arid-land eco-system has led to desertification, a factor which, in turn, triggers emigration across national borders. As will be shown later in this chapter, the disorganized and desperate migration of environmental refugees has led to instability and political strife in many regions and countries in Africa.

The second biospheric factor, the problem of highlands, is less profound but it is, nevertheless, of considerable importance. The topography of a number of African countries is characterized by mountain ranges. Such countries include Ethiopia, Guinea, Lesotho, Malawi, and Niger. The steep slopes in these countries are especially prone to erosive run-off which can be further aggravated by human activities like road construction, mining, dam-construction, over-grazing, over-cutting of trees, etc. The combination of the inherently fragile ecosystem, economic problems, and excessive pressures from human exploitation can lead to the deterioration of the system beyond its ability to recover naturally. Of the 26 members of the Least Developed Countries with desertification problem, 23 are in Africa.[6] With desertification comes economic hardship, which, in turn, could result in intra and inter-state tension.

From all the above, it becomes obvious that while Africa shares in the concern for the catastrophes that could emanate from global environmental issues, the continent has its own peculiar environmental problems. So profound are these peculiar problems in Africa that it has been suggested that global Green organizations in Europe and America would be unable to help and, therefore, Africa should look for its own indigenous responses to its environmental problems.[7] For example, unlike the case in the developed world, the greatest share of the economy of African states is environmentally based and in form of agricultural production, mining of mineral resources, exploitation of oil etc., Because of this, there is a strong triangular link between environment, economy, and security.

Africa's environmental limitations have also been linked to colonialism's impact on its historical and economic evolution. This school of thought argues that before colonialism, Africans maintained a living balanced between their environment and the resources on which they depended, "developing an intimate, organic relationship with nature, characterized by a high degree of sensitivity and respect for the workings of the natural ecosystems."[8] Colonialism is believed to have upset this harmonious relationship by imposition economic systems which made enormous demands on the environment. The belief that the developed world, having secured development at the expense of the global and local environment, and has again come up with environmental issues that do not address Africa's peculiar needs, has heightened this school of thought.

There are a number of factors which make environmental problems in Africa more serious. First, there is limited technological capability at the continent's disposal to cope with the environmental problems that confront it. In 1971, when the United Nations came up with the concept of "Least Developed Countries", most of the countries that fell into this category were African countries.[9] Even in the 1970s and 1980s, after considerable foreign assistance to these countries, Africa still had 28 of the 41 countries identified by the UN as being under-developed.[10] Second, the adverse economic difficulties that have confronted African countries since the introduction of the Structural Adjustment Program (SAP) in the mid/late 1980s have further weakened the capacity of the continent to withstand environmental hazards. This is in addition to the impact of the IMF and World Bank's sponsored initiatives that have created their own set of environmental hazards by sapping the environment more than is necessary to eke out a living in structurally disarticulated societies.

The political situation in most of these countries is connected to the peculiar position of Africa in the management of its environmental affairs, especially vis-a-vis security. The undemocratic forms of government in many African states have had profound implications for the environment. For instance, it has made the evolution of coherent environmental policies difficult.

WARS, MILITARY ACTIVITIES AND THE ENVIRONMENT IN AFRICA

The environmental damage inflicted by the military in its attempt to provide "security" for the citizen has provided some of the bitter ironies in the link between the environment and security. For African states, this has been particularly enormous, as the numerous intra and inter-state conflicts and the efforts to maintain a level of "preparedness" for the military, have dominated African affairs for several decades. The impact of the military on the environment has been more pronounced in southern Africa, which has seen many conflicts in the preceding decades. Countries that have suffered the most as a result are Angola and Mozambique, whose civil wars were fueled by South Africa's destabilization policies.[11]

Perhaps the most disturbing aspect of the environmental link with security in southern Africa is the allegation that some of the sides in the conflicts in Angola and Mozambique employed chemical weapons. This allegation was made against RENAMO in Mozambique, and against the two sides of the conflict in Angola, the MPLA and UNITA. Although there are no independent confirmations, the allegation, if true, introduces a disturbing dimension to conflict in Africa, and to the long-term environmental safety of the affected region. Closely related to this is the problem of mines scattered in most conflict regions, especially in Angola. The explosion damage land fertility and create long-term adverse impact on the environment.

Another ecological disaster that the wars in southern Africa created is the decimation of the wildlife population in the region. Animals that have fallen victim include elephants, buffaloes, hippos and the large buck. It is impossible to get the exact number, but the extent of the devastation is apparent in the threatened extinction of elephants in southern Angola, and in the recovery in 1987 of 19,700 elephant tusks in Mozambique. Both UNITA and RENAMO were believed to have used the tusks of the slaughtered elephants to pay for some of the arms supplied by South Africa in their wars against the MPLA and FRELIMO governments respectively in Angola and Mozambique.[12] This problem is, however, not peculiar to southern Africa. Examples abound, too, in other parts of the continent. There are recorded cases of attack on the wildlife population in Liberia. More recently, the war in Rwanda threatened the existence of gorillas and their declining population has attracted world attention.[13] Because of the violence, veterinary doctors abandoned the clinic caring for the gorillas, leaving them at the mercy of the poachers ready to make illegal living from killing the animals.[14] Apart from the destruction of wildlife, poaching has also strained relations between states. For example, in October 1994, the Zambian authorities accused UNITA and RENAMO rebels of selling arms to poachers and other criminals in Zambia or exchanging weapons for food.[15]

Intra and inter-state conflicts have also resulted in the destruction of forests. All African countries that have fought major wars have suffered from this problem. Two countries that are recent victims of this environmental disaster are Angola and Liberia. In Angola, the war has resulted in massive deforestation of regions in the south-western part of the country. UNITA, in particular, has especially been accused of destroying the forest to provide make-shift accommodations for its soldiers. In Liberia, all the major sides in the war: the National Patriotic Front for Liberia (NPFL), the Independent National Patriotic Front for Liberia (INPFL), and the United Liberation Movement of Liberia (ULIMO), have done damage to the Liberian forest. There are also allegations that the ECOWAS Monitoring Group (ECOMOG), a peace-keeping force sent to Liberia by the West African regional organization, has also contributed to the destruction of the Liberian forests.[16] What has made the problem more profound is that in all these countries replacing the devastated forests with new plantations is rarely attempted.

A major environmental issue in southern Africa is the destruction of oil pipelines. Between 1980 and 1990, RENAMO destroyed the pipelines linking Mozambique to neighboring countries, in particular, Zimbabwe. UNITA, on the other hand, inflicted enormous damage on the Cabinda oil-field. Again, while South Africa was in the war against Angola, the Cabinda oil installation was often frequently attacked. The pollution that has emanated from this is significant. Thus, apart from loosing resources, the affected countries also have to consider the economic cost of cleaning up the pollution that has resulted from such destruction. Because of their relatively small budgets, such environmental clean-ups are either ignored or are not done properly, resulting in long term damage to the environment.

In peace time, the activities of the military to ensure the security of African countries have proved to be as damaging as they could be in the prosecution of war. Although few African countries are exposed to the radiation that often follows "accidents" during nuclear tests in militarily advanced countries, for a long time, South Africa's efforts to acquire nuclear capability exposed the people in the entire region to nuclear hazards. No statistics are available about those who suffered from South Africa's nuclear program, but it is reasonable to assume that projects like those do have large scale and often long-term environmental implications for the nearby environment.

A source of air pollution in Africa is the air forces of many African states. Although this is more prevalent in countries with relatively well established air force like Nigeria and South Africa, virtually all African states have their own share of this pollution source. Residents living in areas around military air fields often complain about air pollution when members of the air force embark on combat practice. People who live near naval bases also often experience similar problem. In addition, air pollution causes damage to farmlands and fish, straining the meager livelihood of people.

The size of land acquired for military use could also constitute an environmental problem. Jackie Cock has argued this point successfully in the case of South Africa. She shows that the South African Defence Forces (SADF) are the fourth largest land controlling authority in the country, "managing some 60 military facilities which cover approximately 600,000 hectares of land."[17] The preclusion of this land from possible economic development is not the only problem. For example, Cock pointed out that the destruction of several rare or endangered species, including the white rhino and antelope, occur on military land.[18] Although figures are not available for other African countries, the situation is similar.

From the brief discussion above, it is evident that whether in peace time or war, the activities of the military have caused enormous damage to the environment. The impact of the damage is magnified because the activities causing it have been going on continuously for decades. Also, the full extent of the damage will not be realized even after the initial cause has been stopped.

ENVIRONMENTAL ISSUES WITH POTENTIAL SECURITY IMPLICATIONS

There are five major environmental issues that can increase the propensity for conflict in the post Cold War dispensation. These are: the problem of population explosion, the struggle over water resources, the continent's refugee problem, degradation of the environment as a result of excessive exploration for oil and other natural resources, and the politics of toxic waste disposal. In most cases, these environmental issues are not recent phenomena, some having been in existence for decades. What has only happened in recent years is that certain factors have pushed them to a level where they have created security problems that African countries can no longer afford to ignore.

Population, Environment and Security

> It may be that to relate population to environ-
> ment optimally is the greatest technological
> task to the end of the century.
> —Lord Florey.[19]

Africa's population has been on a steady and alarming increase since the flush of independence in the 1960s. Policies
to control the continent's population have been poorly
planned and, therefore, unsuccessful. Thus, it has been estimated that the population of sub-Saharan Africa would rise
from 500 million in 1990 to 1,300 million by the year 2005.[20]
It is not within the scope of this chapter to discuss the reasons for the growth of Africa's population. Instead, the security implications of this uncontrolled increase are identified and analyzed.

The most acknowledged link between Africa's soaring
population and security is the rapid depletion of economic
resources. Already, the population crisis on the continent
has reached a stage where the quality and quantity of food
supplies have become a major security issue. Africa's growing population will require a substantial increase in the quantity of food. The quality of the diet is equally of utmost importance. Africa's staple diet is supplied by four chief crops:
maize, wheat, rice, and cassava, which, as David Hamilton
has pointed out, contain low-quality proteins that "lack the
right balance of essential amino acid for man's use."[21] Lac-
tating mothers and newly weaned children suffer the most
because of the these nutritional deficiencies.

In many African states, lack of sufficient food has directly led to internal opposition to the government. Where
there is no direct internal opposition, the starving population has failed to act as bulwark against external threat. Indeed, often acknowledged is the fact that the first line of
defense of any nation is its citizenry. A population that is
adequately fed, physically fit, and mentally alert is likely to
be more willing and more determined to protect the country against any threat. If, however, when a nation cannot
feed its population, this first line of defense usually collapses.

Apart from food, there is a string of social amenities
and infrastructure which would be overstretched by uncon-

trolled population growth. This necessarily imparts on security. For example, when population increase reaches a stage where the government can no longer provide educational facilities for its people, the country runs the risks of producing a mass of illiterate young people. Those most likely to take part in armed robbery or other security threatening behavior are usually from this uneducated class.

The Potential Problems Over Water Resources

> Sources of water supplies have been among the goals of military expansionism. And inequalities in water use have been the source of regional and international frictions and tension. These conflicts will continue—and in some places grow more in intensity—as growing populations demand more water for agricultural, industrial and economic development.[22]

Water serves many purposes, all of which are related to security. Apart from serving as a basic need for human existence and most other forms of life, it has, in the case of rivers, served as boundaries between political and ethnic groupings and as catchment areas for a vast number of human populations. Conflicts associated with water have centered largely on quality and quantity.

Although Africa has not experienced as much conflict over water as in the Middle East, competition for limited supplies of water and a number of other water related problems have created some conflicts. Peter Gleick has identified four elements that are likely to make water a source of strategic rivalry. These are (I) the degree of scarcity; (ii) the extent to which the water supply is shared by more than one region or state; (iii) the relative power of the basin states and (iv) the ease of access to alternative fresh water resources. In varying degrees, these contributed to some inter-state tension in Africa.[23]

The control of international rivers with security importance has always been paramount in the military calculations of the affected states. In Africa, perhaps the most notable is the River Nile. The river is extremely important to Egypt, prompting the age-long saying of "No Nile, no

Egypt". About 97% of Egypt's water resources come from the Nile River. However, 95% of the river's run-off originate in the other eight nations of the Nile basin. This automatically means that additional water development in other upstream nations could reduce the supply available to Egypt. Realizing its vulnerability, Egypt has threatened to use its military might to prevent any disruption of the Nile supply.[24] However, because of other nations in the Nile basin being arid, some attempt to tap the resources of the Nile may, in future years, prove necessary. For example, the Head of the Ethiopian Development Studies in Addis Ababa, Zawole Abate, has signaled a protest on behalf of his country:

> To date, the level of utilization of the Nile waters by the co-basin states varies with their respective socio-economic advancement. Egypt stands high in this regard, utilising 55.5 billion cu.m. of the Nile water to irrigate 28 million ha. Next to Egypt, Sudan has developed 1.8. million ha of irrigated agriculture consuming 18.3 billion cu.m. of water annually...while Ethiopia, contributing about 86% of the Nile water utilizes a mere 0.6 billion cu.m. annually. This huge gap of water resources development between the downstream and upstream Nile countries would not remain for a long time in light of the various demands made upon the waters of the Nile by all the basin states to meet the various development needs of their fast growing population.[25]

Another region where fresh water could cause tension is the Horn of Africa, mainly between Somalia and Ethiopia. Somalia's access to surface water is limited to only two rivers—Shebelle and Juba. These two rivers originate from Ethiopia. The Shebelle flows only during the rainy season and does not reach the Indian Ocean, disappearing instead in a swamp in Central Somalia. It is the area between these two rivers that form Somalia's agricultural zone.[26] Almost all the water utilized for agriculture in Somalia originates from Ethiopia. On the contrary, Ethiopia has enormous water reserves. Its 14 major river basins carry an estimated 116 billion cubic meters surface run-off. However, over the years, due to political instability in the country, a coherent policy on the country's water resources was never formed. With some form of stability now present, Ethiopia has started taking assertive positions on its water resources. Already, spokesmen for the country have been quoted as saying that Ethiopia's inability in the past to make full use of its water resources has resulted in persistent drought. Thus, an all out conflict over water in the region may be a distinct possibility.

Also worthy of note is the controversy that could occur over multi-national hydro-electric projects. These can promote cooperation and peace, as its management would inevitably require some form of understanding between the states. However, it is also possible they could cause tension. An example of a "multi-national" dam in Africa is the Kariba on the Zambezi river. This dam was completed in 1959, and it is being jointly controlled by Zambia and Zimbabwe. Although these countries usually agree about the distribution of energy from the Kariba, they have experienced some minor difficulties in the coordination of activities. Also, the operation of the Kainji dam built on the lower Niger by Nigeria to generate hydro-electric power depends, at least to some extent, on the goodwill of those countries through which the river passes. Power supply from this river has faced so many considerable difficulties, that it is hardly capable of generating electricity for all parts of Nigeria. This has not deterred the neighboring countries sharing the Niger from demanding a share of energy supply from Nigeria. So far, the dam has caused only minor controversy among these neighboring countries. However, since many Nigerians have demanded that electricity should be supplied to these countries only after their needs have been met, it is possible that an attempt to heed this call would strain relations with the states in question. Already, most of these countries, which are mainly French-speaking, are apprehensive of Nigeria's physical size. It is unlikely, though not impossible, that any of them may attempt to dam the Niger at a point before the Kainji dam. If such happens, it will strain relations between Nigeria and the country in question.

The construction of dams has also resulted in the dislocation of several indigenous populations. The table below shows how this phenomenon has affected Africa.

Table of Displaced Population from Dam Construction

Dam	Countries	No. of People displaced
Aswan	Egypt, Sudan	120,000
Akosombo	Ghana	80,000
Kossou	Ivory Coast	75,000
Kariba	Zambia, Zimbabwe	50-57,000
Kainji	Nigeria	42-50,000
Ruzizi 11	Rwanda, Zaire	12,000
Manantali	Mali	10,000

Source: Extracted from Peter Gleick, (ed). *Water in Crisis: A Guide to the World's Fresh Water Resources,* (New York: Oxford University Press, 1993).

Such massive relocations of people have often caused resentment, and any possible extension of these dams could cause tension. Local populations involved in such an imposed migration would demand payment or compensation from the government. With the precarious state of African economies and the uncoordinated bureaucracy in some of them, such payment or compensation would likely be inadequate or delayed. This could damage the relationship between a central government and the affected local population. Also important to consider is the possibility of conflicts between those forced to migrate and those who might lay claim to the area the displaced people are allocated.

Another issue that could create tension is the inability of the government to provide its citizens with water for domestic use. The rapid increase in African population has further shown that scarcity of water is a distinct possibility in the near future. The table below shows this trend.

Per Capita Water Availability in 1990 and in 2025
(Cubic meters/person/year)

Country	Per Capita Water Availability 1990	Per Capital Water Availability 2025
Algeria	750	380
Burundi	660	280
Cape Verde	500	220
Comoros	2040	790
Djibouti	750	270
Egypt	1070	620
Ethiopia	2360	980
Kenya	590	190
Lesotho	2220	930
Libya	160	60
Morocco	1200	680
Nigeria	2660	1000
Rwanda	880	350
Somalia	1510	610
South Africa	1420	790
Tanzania	2780	900
Tunisia	530	330

Source: Peter Gleick, "Water and Conflict: Fresh Water Resources and International Security," *International Security*, Summer 1993, Vol. 18, No. 1.

These figures indicate clear security problems especially in the health area. Considering the appalling economic condition of most African states, the continent hardly has the required resources to address this problem.

The Refugees' "Dual" Connection

> Of the World's 10 million refugees, about 50%
> are in Africa.[27]
> —Gaim Kibreab

An environmental issue that has dual linkage with security is the refugee problem, which could be as much a result of conflict as be the cause. Large scale refugee populations have always emerged after wars as well as following environmental and natural disasters. As far back as 1983, when there was an estimated 5 million refugees throughout the world, Africa had about 50% of them.[28] This number has increased in recent years, as more conflicts and other economic and environmental hazards have resulted in a massive migration of people. Since the beginning of the 1990s, the refugees in Africa have left countries where war has combined with natural hazards like famine. Foremost in that regard are countries like Mozambique, Angola, Liberia, Somalia, Sudan, Burundi, Rwanda and Ethiopia.

There are several ways through which the refugee issue could create tension, especially between the countries of origin and the host countries. First, hosting large scale refugees inevitably imposes a lot of strain on the environmental situation of the recipient countries. For example, working from the 1989 estimates, the United Nations office of High Commissioner for Refugees (UNHCR) concluded that roughly 11 million trees were cut for shelter needs during the initial period of refugee influx on the continent. This represented the deforestation of over 12 million hectares.[29] In addition, about four million tons of wooded fuel were consumed in Africa by the refugees alone.[30] This is just part of the environmental sacrifice which is rarely considered important, but also one which, depending on the capacity of the host state to accommodate pressure, could create considerable tension.

In recent years, when the economies of many African countries took a downward turn, the somewhat "traditional" hospitality which many Africans extended to refugees began to fade. This would appear to validate Gaim Kibreab's position that the much advertised traditional hospitality of Africans is not so much an enigmatic or inborn attitude, as it is a matter of resource availability.[31] There have been many incidents of conflict and competition between refugees and hosts over issues like food supplies, farmlands, education and medical facilities, jobs, etc. For example, in the 1970s, the Ethiopian refugees at the Qala en Nahal Refugee settlement in Sudan clashed with the local Sudanese over cattle and water shortages. The refugees competed with the Sudanese for watering cattle in the hafirs constructed for the indigenous herdsmen by the local council.[32]

Much the same applies to competition over jobs, especially in the low skilled sector. Many of the refugees after arriving at their new homes quickly find a way to make a living, especially in cases where they are not under the care of the UNHCR or any of the voluntary organizations. In most cases, this attempt at making a living often stirs conflict with the local "professionals". For example, shortly after Ghana's economy took a downward plunge in the mid and late 1970s, many Ghanaians became refugees in Nigeria, then on the last phase of its oil boom wealth. Most of these refugees who were unskilled went into easily available jobs, mainly shoe repair and tailoring for men, and prostitution for women. Since the basic intention of the refugees, at least initially, was to get enough income for daily survival, they operated at rates that were far cheaper than the fixed rates demanded by the local professionals. The fact that many of them were willing to hawk their services obviously meant that they got more customers than their indigenous rivals. This strained relations between the refugees and the local professionals, especially in the shoe-repair and tailoring businesses. In some localities professionals made life particularly difficult for the refugees.[33]

Another example of refugee/host rivalry is that of the Eritrean refugees in Sudan. On their arrival in 1975, they were warmly welcomed, and the local inhabitants of Gedaref, where they stayed, contributed 7,000 Sudanese pounds for their initial settlement. This hospitality later turned into hostility when the local people felt that the refugees were encroaching on their economic resources and social infrastructure. In some Sudanese towns such as Gedaref and Kassale, majority of the hospital beds were occupied by the refugees. They also held many primary school positions. Tension exploded in October 1979, when the local inhabitants of Gedaref destroyed the huts and other belongings of the refugees.

The handling of the refugee problem by the host country could further provoke security problems. Desire to forestall refugee influx may lead a host nation to take steps which might enflame either local opposition, or prompt objections from neighboring states. In 1982, in Nigeria, the administration of President Shehu Shagari attempted to put an end to the conflict in Chad partly to stop the influx of refugees into Nigeria from that country. Consequently, it sent an ill-conceived peace-keeping mission to the country (under the auspices of the OAU). This peace-keeping operation which eventually turned disastrous was the beginning of Nigeria's military involvement in Chad. The involvement, to an extent, aggravated regional instability and led to Libya's more assertive presence in Chad, an intrusion which, even if temporary, created regional tension.

An example of a country where the handling of refugees has resulted in domestic opposition, though not particularly intense, is Zimbabwe, where the Mugabe administration initially had to take some drastic actions to control the influx of Mozambican refugees. Many Zimbabweans living on the border with Mozambique objected to what was considered as high-handedness on the part of the government. Most of the people on the border share ethnic and cultural similarities with the repatriated refugees and this influenced their reaction to the situation.

The main theme that could be deduced from all these examples is that, in cases where the resources of the host countries are in short supply, and the social infrastructure underdeveloped, the likelihood of some form of tension between the refugees and the host countries appears increasingly high. This is likely to be more profound in future years, as refugees keep increasing and the local infrastructure in many of the host countries keeps decreasing. Long term tension could also develop between the refugees and their hosts after the instability or the economic problem that sent the refugee out of their homes had subsided, and the refugees returned home. This is more likely in cases where the refugees believe they were unjustly treated by their erstwhile hosts. For example, this problem manifested shortly after Ghanaian refugees went back home from Nigeria. Although it never became a matter of major conflict between the governments of the two countries, many Ghanaians who were once refugees in Nigeria still harbor hatred for Nigerians for what they considered as the unjust and the allegedly inhuman treatment they suffered while they were in the country.[34]

Excessive Environmental Exploration: Security Consequences

The ecological devastation caused by oil drilling, mining etc., could propel the victims of such degradation either to clamor for self-determination or for a proportional share of national wealth. This is a tendency that could aggravate tensions. A case that best exemplifies this is the story of the Ogoni people in Nigeria. A capsule summary of the experience of this people is worth recording here to show the potential dangers inherent in this particular issue of environmental neglect. Shell Oil, responsible for half of Nigeria's oil production, admitted that there was at least two hundred spillages a year of different sizes.[35] Although the company said it was committed to containing and cleaning up such spills, the watery environment of the delta has made it impossible to take effective measures short of burning off the oil altogether.[36] The ultimate result of this is a total upset of the ecological balance of the region. There are more than 12 million people living in the oil producing areas, but one group that has come to symbolize the suffering of these people is the Ogoni.

The Ogoni are a minority ethnic group of about 500,000 people living in the Rivers State; a state that produced most of Nigeria's oil wealth. For more than three decades, multinational oil corporations, especially Shell and Willbros, have allegedly, with the support of the successive Federal Governments, persistently drained oil to the obvious detriment to the Ogoni people. The environmental implications of the operations for the Ogoni people are well articulated by the Movement for the Survival of the Ogoni People (MOSOP). The "Preface" to *Ogoni Bill of Rights*, presented to the international community in 1992 by MOSOP states:

> The once beautiful Ogoni countryside is no more a source of fresh air and green vegetation ... All one sees and feels around is death. Death is everywhere in Ogoni... Ogoni people, Ogoni animals, Ogoni fishes are dying because of thirty three years (as of 1991) of hazardous environmental pollution and resulting food scarcity. In spite of an alarming density of popu-

> lation, American and British oil companies
> greedily encroach on more and more Ogoni-
> land... Mining rents and royalties for Ogoni oil
> are seized by the Federal Government of Ni-
> geria which offers the Ogoni people nothing in
> return. Ogoni is being killed so that Nigeria
> can live.[37]

For all the hardship they have had to bear because of the oil drilling activities in their area, the Ogoni people, in 1990, started a campaign for self-determination and sought a $10 billion reparation from oil explorers and the Nigerian government. Ken Saro-Wiwa, a popular Nigerian writer and publisher, who came to personify the cause of the Ogoni people, led the campaign.[38] The Nigerian Federal Government (then under Ibrahim Babangida) disregarded the claim of the Ogoni people, and warned of dire consequences if the people made any attempt to prevent the multinational corporations and other agents of the Federal government from carrying out exploration. The situation came to a head in April 1993, when many Ogoni villagers discovered that their farms had been bulldozed for the installation of further oil pipes for Shell Petroleum Company. A spontaneous protest by unarmed women and children was met with a gunfire attack from soldiers of the second Amphibious Brigade in Port Harcourt. Eleven people were seriously wounded, and Saro-Wiwa was immediately detained. In November 1995, in an attempt to silence the environmentalists of Ogoniland, Saro-Wiwa and eight other Ogoni leaders were executed by the government after being convicted of what was widely believed a trumped-up charge of murder. It is too early to know what effect this latest suppression will have on the Ogoni people who have vowed to fight for their right to compensation for the environmental damage caused by the oil multinationals.

The plight of the Ogoni people only symbolizes the problem inherent in the environmental neglect of the regions where resources are drained for national comfort. Similar examples abound in other countries on the continent, and it is likely that, with the increase in democratic political awareness, many of the groups that feel they have received so little for so much sacrifice would cry out for redress. The inability of the respective central governments in these countries to satisfy these needs could result in conflict or attempted secession. Countries that are most vulnerable in this regard are those that depend most on a single natural resource, and have thus over-exploited such resource to the obvious detriment of local inhabitants.

The Politics of Toxic Waste Disposal

Unlike other environmental problems that date back to the years immediately following the independence of some African states, the issue of toxic waste disposal is a relatively recent phenomenon. This problem came to the forefront of world attention in the second half of the 1980s when chemical companies in European countries began to transport their toxic wastes to some west African countries. By the end of 1988, toxic wastes had been deposited in countries like Benin, Guinea, Guinea-Bissau, Nigeria, and Togo.

Two major avenues accounted for waste disposal in Africa. First, waste was transported from western Europe and deposited in some African countries without their knowledge. Second, some African countries did actually sign contracts with European chemical companies to take the toxic wastes for payment. A brief discussion on these two avenues of waste disposal to the continent is in order.

Between August 1987 and May 1988, an Italian chemical company deposited nearly 4,000 tons of toxic waste in a town called Koko in the then Bendel state of Nigeria. A local farmer, ignorant or mis-informed about the content and its implications accepted the waste in his compound for the payment of about $100 per month. The existence of this deposit came to the notice of the Nigerian government after Nigerian citizens living in Italy found out about it and contacted their government. The Nigerian government took a stern view of the situation, and by June 1988, an undisclosed number of Italian and Nigerian citizens had been arrested. The Nigerian ambassador in Italy was recalled and his counterpart in Nigeria was asked to leave the country. The deposit created considerable long-term environmental problems. Many people, including the local farmer who accepted the initial deposit, died of diseases believed to be contracted from the toxic deposit. Many people also suffered chemical burns, partial paralysis, and premature births.[39] It is still early as yet to know whether there will be long-term effects from this deposit.

Other cases of dumping of harmful toxic wastes in several parts of Africa have been reported. For instance, consignments of 275 drums of waste reportedly falsely labeled as cleaning fluids were shipped from the U.S. to Zimbabwe.[40] In a similar situation, toxic deposit labeled as fertilizer by an English broker, was dumped in Liberia. Sierra Leone, on its part, had 625 bags of toxic wastes from the United Kingdom dumped in Bomeh.

Benin Republic is an example of a country that intentionally signed contracts with major chemical companies in Europe to accept toxic deposits for payment. What motivated the Beninois officials to enter into this type of arrangement is not known, but it is likely to center around poverty, greed by officials, and ignorance of the immediate and long-term implications of receiving such dangerous consignments. However, no sooner had the contracted wastes arrived in the country than the government realized that it could not handle it. Some countries have taken stern measures against government officials who attempted to collude with foreign companies to receive their waste products in exchange for money. For example, the attempt by some Congolese officials to receive a $4 million payment for the issuance of a three year waste import license was foiled by the government, and the five officials were arrested. The Guinean police also arrested ten officials in connection with a Norwegian firm's dumping of U.S. toxic wastes on Kassa Island.[41]

There are three levels at which the issue of toxic waste deposits could create security problems. The first is between the country of origin and the country on which they were deposited without government consent. The Koko discovery damaged the relations between Nigeria and Italy. Although this did not go beyond official criticisms by the Nigerian government, such actions could in fact result in a more strained relations between states. The second level is between the state that contracted to accept the wastes and its neighbors, who could suffer because of proximity of the waste to their territories and population. For example, Benin's acceptance of toxic wastes resulted in the deterioration of its relations with Nigeria.[42] Finally, the toxic waste problem can affect the internal stability of the host state and government. Benin's acceptance of the toxic wastes affected the stability of Kerekou's regime, and contributed to its ultimate downfall in 1990.[43]

CONCLUSION

I have tried in this chapter to show both how environmental factors are linked with security and the consequences that could emerge if African countries continue the reckless abandon with which they treat environmental issues. The differences in Africa's environmental conditions vis-a-vis those in the developed world, and the extent to which the environment in both societies has been affected by war, means that Africa has somewhat different problems to handle. For example, while the governments in the developed countries may have to contend with problems like nuclear pollution, African countries have to tackle problems like deforestation, control of refugees, etc.

While Africa obviously needs foreign assistance to handle some of its security related environmental problems, there is the need, too, for countries on the continent to come up with concrete measures to protect the environment. African countries should realize the importance of protecting and managing the continent's environment, especially in areas relating to marine resources, wildlife, parks and forests. Some countries have already started taking steps in this direction. For example, Kenya, Lesotho, Malawi, Mozambique, South Africa, Swaziland, Uganda, Tanzania, and Zambia are reportedly in agreement on the creation of "an anti-smuggling force to fight an international crime syndicate dealing in ivory, rhino horn, diamonds."[44] While this is a significant step, it is also the case that many African countries do not realize the importance of the environment, and do not pursue a policy on it. Again, if Africa intends to enter the industrialized world in the next century, the continent should immediately start putting in place policies and measures to cater to the negative by-products of industrialization, especially the management of industrial waste products and pollution.

Environmental issues that could create tension between states are likely to increase in the future. The prevailing economic situation may force many countries to attempt harnessing all resources at their disposal, while, at the same time, less sympathetic to the political and economic plight of their neighbors. This may multiply security tension in the continent in the years ahead. This implies that the need to address environmental situation inevitably has relevance for the economic situation on the continent. Although on the surface, the economic consequences of the poor handling of Africa's environmental problems might appear insignificant when compared with those in advanced nations of the north, the hapless economic situation in Africa, and the lack of technological expertise to handle most of the environmental problems facing it, make the problem more profound. The economic problems of the continent have yet, another dimension. The attempt to eke out a living inevitably forces the people to make further demands on the environment, thereby increasing, in many cases, the propensity for violence.

NOTES

1. Since the superpower rapport that preceded the end of the Cold War got underway, academic attention has focused on the environmental aspect of security. Two interlocking components, societal security and environmental security, became issues now co-considered in any attempt to discuss security. For example, see H. Westing's "Environmental Component of Comprehensive Security," *Journal of Peace Proposal,* Vol. 20, 1989. Other similar studies include: Peter Gleick's articles, "Environmental Resources, and International Security," in Eric Arnett, (ed.), *Science and International Security: Responding to a Changing World,* (Washington: American Association for the Advancement of Science, 1990); and "Environment and Security: Clear Connection," *The Bulletin of the Atomic Scientists,* Vol. 47, No. 3, April 1991.
2. For more on this, see Aforka Nweke, "African Perception of Global Disarmament and Prospects for Denuclearization of

the Continent," *Nigerian Journal of International Affairs*, Vol. 8, No. 1, 1982, 37-59.

3. For more on the agreement of the conference, see Michael Grubb, et al., *The Earth Summit Agreement*, (London: RIIA with EarthScan, 1993).

4. See Leena Beejadhur, "North vs. South," in Vin Ghatate (ed), *Green Paper*, (London: LSE Greenpeace, 1994), 9.

5. *ibid.*

6. *ibid.*, 17.

7. This, for example, is the position of Mohammed Suliman, the head of the London-based Institute of African Alternatives. See "Africa Must Develop Own Green Identity," *Weekly Mail*, (South Africa), 17 May, 1991.

8. *ibid.*

9. The three criteria used to determined these were: (a) per-capital income; (b) literacy rate; and © industrial development.

10. See *Disarmament, Environment and Development and Their Relevance to the Least Developed Countries*, (A United Nations Publication, 1991), 87.

11. Many authorities on southern African affairs have done detailed documentation of the ecological impacts of the conflict in the region. See, for example, Joseph Hanlon, *Beggar Your Neighbours: Apartheid Power in Southern Africa*, (London: James Currey Publishers, 1986).

12. Jakie Cock, "Militarization and the Ecology of Southern Africa: A GEM Discussion Paper," 7.

13. The mountain gorillas in the country featured in the hit movie "Gorillas in Mist."

14. The US naturalist who brought the plight of the endangered gorillas to world's attention, Dian Fossey, was herself killed by poachers in 1985.

15. *International Security Digest*, Vol. 2, No. 2, Nov. 1994.

16. Discussion with Liberian government officials.

17. Cock, "Militarization and the Ecology of Southern Africa." 8.

18. *ibid.*

19. See Lord Florey's final address as president of the Royal Society, 1967. Quoted from Nigel Calder, *The Environment Game*, (London: Secker & Warburg,1867), 8. Florey was co-discoverer of Penicillin.

20. OECD figures, quoted from *Southern Africa Monthly*, May 1994, 52.

21. David Hamilton, *Technology, Man and Environment*, (New York: Charles Scribner's Sons, 1973), 228.
22. Peter Gleick,"Water and Conflict," *International Security*, Summer 1993,Vol. 18, No.1, 83.
23. *ibid.*
24. *ibid.*
25. Quoted in Naigzy Gebremedhin,"The Environmental Dimension of Security in the Horn of Africa: The Case of Somalia,"*Life and Peace Research*, Vol. 5, No.1, 1991, 13.
26. *ibid.*
27. Gaim Kibreab, *African Refugees: Reflections on the African Refugee Problem: A Critical Analysis of Some Basic Assumptions*, (Uppsala: the Scandinavian Institute of African Studies, 1983), 5.
28. Gaim Kibreab, *Reflections on the African Refugee Problem: A Critical Analysis of Some Basic Assumptions*, (Uppsala: the Scandinavian Institute of African Studies, 1983),1.
29. UNHCR figures quoted from Naigzy Gebremedhin,"The Environment Dimension of Security, 12.
30. *ibid.*
31. Kibreab, Reflections on the African Refugee Problem, 81-97.
32. *ibid.*
33. In Oshongo, a town in the Western part of Nigeria, I personally witnessed the "arrest" and "detention" of a Ghanaian "mobile tailor" by members of an association that called itself, "The Association of Oyo State Tailors" (Oshogbo Branch). "After appeals from some members of the public tha he as later released with a warning that if he was caught doing 'mobile tailoring' again, he would be hadnded ober to the police for deportation to Ghana."
34. A Ghanaian who was refugee in Nigeria told me that a popular saying in Ghana shortly after their return home was 'Thank goodness, God is not like a Nigerian."
35. Alice Martin, "Oil, oil Everywhere," *BBC Focus on Africa*, Jan-Mar. 1995, 10.
36. *ibid.*
37. Quoted in *The News*, 17 May 1993, 18.
38. See Ken Saro-Wiwa, *Genocide in Nigeria: The Ogoni Tragedy*, (Port Harcourt: Saros International Books, 1992). Saro-Wiwa was the President of both the Association of Nigerian Authors (ANA) and the Ethnic Minority Rights Organisation

(EMRO). He was also the founder of the Nigerian Society for the protection of the environment (NSPE).

39. Wordsworth Filo Jones, "The Evolution of the Bamako Convention: An African Perspective," *Colorado Journal of International Environmental Law and Policy*, Vol 4, 1993. 326.
40. *ibid.*, 327.
41. *ibid.*, 327 and 328.
42. See Kojo Boakje Djan & Matthew Kelland, "Political Events in Africa South of the Sahara, 1988-89," *Africa South of the Sahara, 1990*, (London: Europa Publishers Ltd., 1990), 18.
43. *ibid.*,
44. *International Security Digest* (London: Centre for Defence Studies, University of London), Vol. 1, No.5, Mar. 1994. 1.

Chapter 5

AFRICAN SECURITY AND NUCLEAR WEAPONS:
PAST FEARS AND FUTURE RELEVANCE

Adebayo Oyebade

INTRODUCTION

> It is argued that the developing countries are
> too patently irresponsible to be entrusted with
> nuclear weapons. The fact is, today the world
> has become increasingly insecure with the pro-
> liferation of multi-polar nuclear nations. It is
> in this circumstance that Nigeria and other
> Third World countries now find themselves
> coping with the development of peaceful use of
> nuclear weapons in the face of growing racial
> intolerance and arrogance from South Africa
> and those who believe in racial supremacy in
> the world today.[1]
> —Ibrahim Badamasi Babangida.

The history of global security in the last half a century
has been such that Africa can hardly be said to have
exerted any significant influence. For the most part, the
nuclearized world system was no more than a nuclear balance of terror between the Western powers, especially the

United States, and the erstwhile Soviet Union. The international system was such that these powers predominated, dictating to the rest of the world the terms of peace and conflict. They were the ones that opened the flood gate of nuclear arms race and sought to out-pace each other in stocking their arsenals with weapons of mass destruction. The Cold War proved, in the final analysis, to be a power tussle between the United States and the Soviet Union. The rest of the world merely served as tool in that ideological and hegemonic warfare.

Although East-West strategic thinking largely defined the global framework of peace and security, as the nuclear era aged and the Cold War expanded beyond the confines of Europe, world peace and security took a new meaning. For the so-called Third World, superpower covert or overt interference in their internal affairs in order to preserve East-West parity, raised questions about their own security. For instance, the tacit approval of the United States to South Africa's nuclear weapons program brought home to Africans more than ever before the security risk the apartheid enclave posed to the continent. Regional security in the developing world thus became important in the light of the threat to their security by superpower rivalry.

Many developing states saw the acquisition of nuclear weapons as a way of safeguarding their security in the international arena.[2] Consequently, new actors, especially in Asia and Latin America, worked hard to enter the fold of the nuclear club. Brazil, Argentina, India, Pakistan, and lately, North Korea, are states believed to be in possession of nuclear weapons, or at least, on the threshold of acquiring them. For Africans too, the dynamics of security were changing fast. Africa's pledge to ensure a nuclear weapons-free continent quickly became anachronistic in the face of apartheid South Africa's nuclear monopoly. The Organization of African Unity (OAU) had at its inception taken the stand that African states must steer clear of acquiring nuclear weapons. The reason for this attitude is simple. African leaders reasoned that the best way to ensure continental security in the nuclear age was to desist from getting involved in the proliferation of nuclear weapons. Hence, the declaration of the continent as a nuclear weapons-free zone. It was thus not difficult for many African states to endorse the Non-Proliferation Treaty

(NPT) that banned non-nuclear states from acquiring nuclear weapons.[3]

The realities of power relations in a nuclearized age, however, proved to many in Africa that shunning the nuclear path would not necessarily make for security. Indeed, there was widespread belief that in order to truly ensure the security of the continent, Africa had to acquire nuclear weapons. The justification for this was often the perceived threat posed to African security by South Africa when it became common knowledge that it had already possessed the atomic bomb. Indeed, to most Africans, South Africa constituted the most dangerous threat to African security. Thus, it was this perceived threat that largely paved the way for the African search for security via nuclear weapons.

The aim of this chapter is to examine the role apartheid South Africa played in Africa's search for security. It will examine pre-democratic South Africa as a nuclear power and the implication of this on the security of the African continent. The chapter will also discuss the evolution and the collapse of a nuclear weapons-free Africa as a strategy for continental security. Obviously, the end of the apartheid system and the enthronement of democracy in South Africa has profoundly diminished the perception of that state as a threat to the continent. In this light, the chapter will also examine the implication of what a new democratic South Africa might mean for African security.

AFRICA AND THE NUCLEAR AGE

It is not often realized that Africa contributed substantially to the advent of the nuclear age. It was from the Congo that the Western powers obtained the uranium with which the American-led Western nuclear industry developed in the 1940s.[4] When the United States unleashed the awesome atomic bombs on Hiroshima and Nagasaki in August 1945, Africa may thus, unwittingly, have contributed to that devastating proclamation of the coming of the nuclear age. Yet, no African state (barring South Africa) ever possessed nuclear weapons and, in the words of a former Nigerian foreign minister, Professor Ibrahim Gambari, Africans "appear to be mere onlookers in the nuclear debate and irrelevant to the issue of strategic weapons deployment in Europe."[5]

Africa as a Nuclear Weapons-Free Zone

When African states obtained their political independence in the early 1960s, it was fashionable for them to adopt a non-align policy which, in principle, would preclude them from an ideological commitment to any of the power blocs. This policy, it was assumed would prevent Africa from being turned into a pawn on the chessboard of superpower ideological confrontation. The non-align principle, therefore, tended to discourage many African states from entering into military or defense agreements with the North Atlantic Treaty Organization (NATO), or with the Warsaw Pact. Some African states vehemently opposed any attempt by policy makers to commit them into a non-African military arrangement, especially one with former colonial masters. This was true of Nigeria, where protests by students forced the government of Sir Abubakar Tafawa Balewa to abrogate the Anglo-Nigerian Defence Agreement of 1960.[6]

In line with their policy of non-alignment, African states' posture toward the big powers nuclear build-up was that of non-involvement. The Non-Aligned Movement conference in Cairo endorsed the OAU declaration of Africa as a nuclear-free zone. The policy of non-involvement was aptly demonstrated in the outright opposition of African countries to the decision of the French government to test its first atomic bombs in the Sahara in 1960. Most of the African public saw this as an attempt to get Africa involved in the nuclear dilemma and opposed it. Following the test itself, the Nigerian government broke diplomatic relations with France and placed embargo on French shipping and aircraft. It also froze French assets in the country.[7] The Ghanaian government of President Kwame Nkrumah likewise responded with series of actions. It placed restrictions on monetary transactions with the French, recalled its ambassador from Paris, and also froze French assets in Ghana.[8]

African leaders who opposed any military entanglement with the big powers feared this development would lead to external intervention in the affairs of the continent. Such intervention, it was thought, would not only threaten continental sovereignty and integrity, but would also compound the African effort in the management of internal conflicts. When the "founding fathers" of the OAU met at the organization's first summit conference at Addis Ababa, Ethiopia, in May 1963, they recognized the dangers a militarized Africa could pose to peace and security in the continent. They thus adopted a resolution affirming faith in general disarmament.[9]

This resolution was a regional initiative at the safeguard of global security. In the next couple of years the OAU adopted other resolutions aimed at African security through non-militarization of the continent. For example, on August 10, 1963, the OAU Council of Ministers adopted a resolution on Disarmament and Nuclear Test. Moreover, African states endorsed the agreement of the 1963 Moscow Partial Test Ban Treaty which outlawed atmospheric testing of nuclear weapons. The treaty was seen as an initial step toward final and complete disarmament. During the second ordinary session of the Council of Ministers in Lagos, Nigeria, on February 29, 1964, the council upheld the principle of denuclearization of Africa.[10] The Assembly of Heads of State and Government in July 1964 formally adopted a resolution on denuclearization of the continent which had earlier been adopted by the Council of Ministers during their ordinary session meeting in Cairo.[11] The resolution on denuclearization emphatically declared Africa's refusal to manufacture or acquire control of nuclear weapons. This was in agreement with the provisions of the NPT.

The Demise of the Strategy of Nuclear Weapons-Free Zone

In the early 1960s, the first years of African independence, two immediate grave dangers threatened the security of the continent. Nkrumah put it well this combination of threats when he stated:

> There are two threatening swords of Damocles hanging over the continent, and we must remove them. These are nuclear tests in the Sahara by the French Government and the apartheid policy of the Government of the Union of South Africa.[12]

These threats to African security were ominous signs about the future of a nuclear weapons free regime in Africa. The French atomic bomb tests threatened African security by directly challenging African continental sovereignty and integrity. The tests also violated Africa's right to keep the continent out of the nuclear struggle of the big powers. But South Africa, already a threat to African security because of its apartheid system, posed even greater danger to continental security when it acquired nuclear capability. The acquisition of the bomb by the white supremacist state was the death knell to the notion of a nuclear-free Africa. For those who advocated that Africa should go nuclear, therefore, their reason was the threat, real or perceived, posed by a nuclear South Africa to its neighbors in particular, but also to the continent in general. The South African possession of nuclear weapon thus constituted the dominant argument for Africa to eschew non-proliferation as a strategy for continental security. Aforka Nweke contended that

> By acquiring the technical capability to make nuclear weapons and the necessary means to deliver them, South Africa has not only shattered the *raison d'etre* of the 'Declaration on the Denuclearization of Africa,' but has also greatly tilled the balance of power in the continent.[13]

In the same vein, Ali Mazrui argued that "African countries should stop thinking in terms of making Africa alone a nuclear-free-zone."[14] In his opinion, this was something relevant in the 1960s but certainly not in the 1980s and 1990s. Consequently, he contented that it was time for African states to aspire to become nuclear powers.[15] With the call for an African nuclear industry, the doctrine of a nuclear-free Africa was practically dead.[16]

The demand for the overthrow of the non-proliferation regime in Africa did not, however, prevent African countries from continuing to pay lip service through the OAU to the notion of a nuclear weapons-free continent. Though conscious of the threat posed to African security by South Africa's nuclear capability, African leaders in a 1986 resolution on disarmament, denuclearization, and development in Africa still "reaffirmed the political will of the OAU to make Africa a nuclear-free zone."[17] Such a pronouncement can be assumed to be a diplomatic nicety to appease the superpowers, especially the United States, which was determined to prevent the spread of nuclear weapons. Thus while OAU leaders were playing with the rhetoric of 'denuclearized continent,' some African states were well on their way in the development of nuclear capability. Egypt, Libya, and Nigeria began their respective nuclear programs in the mid-seventies. Egypt's intention to go nuclear first became common knowledge in 1974 when the United States proposed selling it two power reactors.[18] Libya's nuclear program, on the other hand, dates back to 1971 when it unsuccessfully attempted to purchase an atomic device from the Chinese.[19] Libya's nuclear program took real shape in 1973, when the country established an Atomic Energy Commission to produce nuclear weapons. Nigeria entered the nuclear race when it established an Atomic Energy Commission in 1976. This commission ostensibly had the task of developing nuclear energy for peaceful purposes.[20] By 1977, Nigeria had established what it called "centres of excellence in nuclear science and technology" at two of its institutions of higher learning, the University of Ife (now Obafemi Awolowo University), and Ahmadu Bello University.[21] Gabon, which many analysts would regard an unlikely candidate to embark on a nuclear weapons project because of the huge financial commitment involved, nevertheless, expressed its interest in 1983.[22] Gabon's rich uranium deposits seemed to have influenced its decision to develop the bomb.

PRE-DEMOCRATIC SOUTH AFRICA:THE BOMB AND AFRICAN SECURITY

The Clarion Call For Nuclear Capability

The demand for Africa to go nuclear in the 1980s was made even though a majority of African states were signatory to the NPT. In the face of apartheid South Africa's sophisticated military arsenal and its possession of nuclear weapons, it was argued that if African security was to be safeguarded, the continent must join the nuclear arms race. This contention was expressed over and over again in some African states by prominent scholars and policymakers alike. Ali

Mazrui, who has been described as "the most provocative Third World advocate of nuclear weapons,"[23] called on African states to consider setting up a "continental nuclear consortium" for the purpose of developing a small nuclear capability.[24] According to Mazrui, Africa needed to join the nuclear race in order to come of age. "Africa," he says, "under its triumvirate of diplomatic leaders, partly endowed with nuclear credentials, will have begun to enter the mainstream of global affairs."[25] Mazrui implied that by acquiring nuclear weapons, Africa would no longer be bullied by imperialist powers holding a monopoly of nuclear capability.

The call for Africa to join the nuclear world was particularly strong in Nigeria, a country in the 70s and 80s widely believed to have the wherewithal to build nuclear weapons. Besides, Nigerian leaders of the period felt particularly uncomfortable at the prospect of South African nuclear capability. Thus, former President Shehu Shagari in an independence anniversary address on October 1, 1980, hinted that Nigeria would acquire nuclear weapons in order to protect itself "if racist South Africa persisted in acquiring the deadly weapons to threaten the continent."[26] On subsequent occasions, the Nigerian President reiterated his country's willingness to match South Africa in arms race if it was necessary to bring down the apartheid regime.[27] His Defense Minister, Professor Iya Abubakar, also expressed the need for Nigeria, "the largest black nation on earth" to become a nuclear power "at any price" since "protagonists of apartheid have access to nuclear capability."[28] By 1981, the interest in the nuclear industry seemed to have advanced so much that Shagari's government allegedly made a decision to start initial research into nuclear development.[29] Before its collapse in December 1983, Shagari's government consistently emphasized the need for Nigeria to develop its nuclear potential.

But Shagari was not the first Nigerian leader to voice his country's belief that nuclear capability was needed to match South Africa's threat. Former Head of State, General Olusegun Obasanjo, during a state visit to the United States in 1977 was reported to have hinted Nigeria's preparedness to go nuclear if South Africa would defend apartheid with nuclear weapons.[30] In a lively debate over the question of acquisition of nuclear capability, several prominent Nigerians argued in favor of the country going nuclear principally because of South Africa.

Perhaps the most significant call among policymakers for Africa to develop nuclear weapons to counter South Africa was one made by Edem Kodjo, the former Secretary-General of the OAU. Reporting to the opening session of the 19th summit conference of the organization in Addis Ababa on June 9, 1983, Kodjo urged member states to acquire nuclear weapons in order to match those of South Africa. He warned that South Africa's aggression on her neighbors risked spreading northward and as such it was the duty of those African states who were capable of building nuclear weapons to go ahead and do so.[31]

Edem Kodjo's call for Africa to embark on the nuclear weapons path is important in the light of his position as the Secretary-General of the OAU. His call was in direct conflict with the official policy of the organization of which he was the scribe. But this only reflected the changed attitude of most African leaders to a security strategy based on non-acquisition of nuclear weapons in an age of increased threat from South Africa.

It should not be assumed that there was a consensus in Africa to go nuclear. There were also counter arguments to the proposition. Although, most opponents of a nuclearized Africa believed that South Africa was, indeed, a threat to African security, they did not see Africa acquiring nuclear capability as the solution. The late Nigerian veteran politician and former presidential aspirant, Chief Obafemi Awolowo, warned during the nuclear debate in Nigeria that the Federal Government should not waste its time in developing nuclear power in order to fight South Africa."[32] Mohammed Babu, a former minister of Economic Affairs and Development Planning in Tanzania, condemned Edem Kodjo's call for an African nuclear capability describing it as a displaced one in terms of the military and political requirements for liberating South Africa. Rather than plunging headlong into the nuclear race because of South Africa, Babu was of the opinion that emphasis should be placed on the strengthening of guerrilla forces, and not even on conventional military capability.[33] Felix Houphouet-Boigny, former president of Cote d'Ivoire, opposed any form of military confrontation with South Africa. To him, the only solution to the South African dilemma was dialogue with Pretoria.

The Apartheid Bomb As Threat

South Africa first admitted it had nuclear weapons on March 24, 1993, during a speech delivered by the country's erstwhile president, F.W. de Klerk, to the joint session of Parliament. The South African president revealed that Pretoria had produced six of the projected seven nuclear bombs. Before the announcement, especially between 1974 and 1990 which was the period of South Africa's active nuclear program, South African officials deliberately maintained an ambiguous position on the country's nuclear status. In these years, South Africa never confirmed or denied having nuclear weapons.

Before South Africa admitted being a nuclear power, political observers around the world had for years suspected that Pretoria was capable of producing nuclear weapons. Most observers in Africa believed that South Africa, indeed, already had the bomb in its arsenal. This was reinforced in 1979 after the alleged South African nuclear test.

The first legitimate information about South Africa's possession of nuclear weapons came in August 1977, when the former Soviet Union and the United States' reconnaissance satellites captured what was believed to be South Africa's preparation for an underground nuclear weapons test in the Kalahari desert. The planned test was reportedly shelved following pressure put on South Africa by the U.S. and Soviet Union.[34] But what appeared to be an actual detonation of a nuclear weapon by South Africa took place two years later, on September 22, in the southern Atlantic. On that day, an action that has been variously described as "double flash," "blast," or "explosion" occurred at night off the South African coast. This unusual phenomenon was reportedly picked up by a United States' surveillance satellite over the Southern Atlantic. A Central Intelligence Agency (CIA) document which provided, for the first time, an insight into the previously classified information about the incident described the explosion as "a yield of less than three kiloton, about a quarter the size of the Hiroshima bomb and equivalent to the yield of a nuclear-tipped artillery shell."[35]

To the world, South Africa appeared to have conducted a nuclear test.[36]

South Africa did deny testing a nuclear weapon[37], but few observers in Africa were persuaded by Pretoria's rhetoric. The explosion was seen as a confirmation of South Africa's nuclear capability and this added a new dimension to the perceived danger posed by the racist state to African security. It became a source of worry to many African states especially the Frontline States (FLS) of: Zimbabwe, Angola, Mozambique, Zambia, Botswana, and Tanzania. African states were justifiably worried by the escalation of South Africa's military capability through its acquisition of nuclear weapons. Already the apartheid system that dehumanized the black population in South Africa was a threat to continental security. Indeed, of the many security problems that plagued Africa, the South African apartheid system was seen as the most dangerous.[38] By subjecting the voteless black majority to white minority rule, the system was a breeding ground for internal violence detrimental to Africa's security. Beyond apartheid at home, the racist state's aggression against the Frontline States, attempting to cripple their economy as well as to destabilize their governments, constituted further threat to continental security. In the early and mid-1980s, desperate to hold on to the apartheid system threatened by the decolonization process in southern Africa, South Africa launched attacks on the neighboring states of Mozambique, Angola, Zambia and Botswana.

The OAU was most concerned about the South African threat to the security of the states bordering the racist state. In 1985, at the height of Pretoria's unprovoked aggression on its neighbors, the acting Secretary General of the OAU, Peter Onu, observed that:

> The apartheid regime in South Africa continues to be not only a threat to peace and security in the region, but also a danger for the entire continent.[39]

South Africa's onslaught on its neighbors also prompted the OAU to pass series of resolutions condemning the attack and calling for concerted international action against the minority regime.[40] In the sub-region, many observers believed that nuclear weapons would give South Africa the upper hand in the struggle against the Frontline States.

The knowledge that South Africa was militarily more powerful with its possession of nuclear weapons was not only of major concern to the black population in the country and to the Frontline States, but also to other African states which viewed themselves as being directly threatened. Many African states believed that South Africa, bent on defending apartheid, would resort to using the bomb to intimidate them. Some observers have even argued that South Africa would not hesitate to use the weapon. Ravi Shastri observed that "the actual use of nuclear weapons by the white minority regime remains a real possibility."[41] It was believed that South Africa had the military wherewithal to deliver the weapons.[42] It was also thought that the capital city of every African country was within the range of South Africa's attack.[43]

Nigeria considered itself a prime target of Pretoria's hostility and possible military attack because of its consistent support for the liberation struggle in Southern Africa and its commitment to black majority rule. This sentiment was expressed by a number of government officials. Ibrahim Gambari, for instance, declared that South Africa identified Nigeria, "the most populous black African state with the greatest potential ability to undermine apartheid, as a prime target for possible retaliation."[44] Nigeria's assistance to the liberation struggle was cited as the principal motivating factor for an alleged South African plan to strike on oil fields in the country including the refineries in Port Harcourt, Warri, and Kaduna.[45] The air force base at Markurdi was also thought to have been another target of South Africa's attack.[46] The stories of the impending attack were corroborated by the then Chief of Army Staff, General Sanni Abacha.[47] South Africa's presence in Malabo in the neighboring Equatorial Guinea from the mid 1980s was also perceived in Nigeria as a direct threat to national security. It was alleged that South Africa had a military base in that Central African country and that Pretoria would use it as an operation ground for an attack on Nigeria.[48] Nigeria was particularly alarmed at Equatorial Guinea's flirtation with South Africa. It had to employ all diplomatic tactics at its disposal to ensure that the Central African state was not used by South Africa.[49]

Nigeria could be said to have done more to end apartheid in South Africa than any other African country except, perhaps, the Frontline States. One of the cardinal principles of the Nigerian foreign policy, especially during the early 1970s, was the end of minority supremacist regimes in Southern Africa. The civil war of 1967 to 1970 radicalized Nigeria's perception of the threat posed by these regimes to its national security. During the war, Rhodesia (now Zimbabwe) and South Africa actively supported the secessionist cause by aiding Biafra militarily. After the war, Nigeria's position was consistently that the continued existence of minority regimes in Southern Africa was detrimental not only to Nigeria's security, but also to the security of the entire continent. Nigeria thus assumed the leadership role in the fight against institutionalized racism in Southern Africa. Its diplomatic, financial, and material assistance to the liberation struggles was enormous. Although Nigeria did not militarily intervene on behalf of the liberation organizations, as called for in many quarters, its support, especially in diplomatic terms, was of considerable importance in the struggle. An indication of this was the leadership role Nigeria played in the recognition of the Angolan nationalist organization, the Popular Movement for the Liberation of Angola (MPLA).

Why did Pretoria acquire nuclear weapons? During the active days of South Africa's nuclear program, it was widely believed that the apartheid state was prepared to defend its racist system with nuclear weapons. But in the dying days of the apartheid regime, and after announcing that it had dismantled its nuclear technology, South Africa claimed that the bombs acquired were never going to be used. In his March 1993 address to the Parliament, de Klerk said that the weapons were planned only for deterrent purposes. According to de Klerk, South Africa wanted a limited deterrent capability which would dissuade a possible attack by forces from Angola and Mozambique, backed by Soviets and Cubans. The decision to acquire the bomb was thus taken, de Klerk said, "against the background of a Soviet expansionist threat in Southern Africa, as well as prevailing uncertainty concerning the designs of the Warsaw Pact."[50] South Africa's nuclear strategy, according to de Klerk, was that:

> If the situation in Southern Africa were to de-
> teriorate seriously, a confidential indication of
> the deterrent capability would be given to one
> or more of the major powers, for example the
> United States, an attempt to persuade them to
> intervene.[51]

This strategy, in other words, was that a South African threat
to explode nuclear bombs would 'blackmail' the United States,
or any of the Western powers, into intervening in Southern
Africa on behalf of Pretoria if a major conflict with Soviet-
backed forces in Southern Africa threatened South Africa.

That the nuclear weapons program was directed at the
states in the sub-region struggling against South Africa's
destablization was enough justification for African states to
feel threatened by the weapons. The nuclear project, indeed,
began in the mid-1970s, a time when the struggle against
racial oppression was intensifying in Southern Africa. By
1975, Angola and Mozambique had obtained their political
independence and the struggle for Namibian independence
was well under way. The rapidity at which black-controlled
governments were springing up in Southern Africa frightened South Africa which may have decided to defend apartheid by seeking refuge in nuclear weapons. This was at least
the perception in Africa.

POST-APARTHEID SOUTH AFRICA: IMPLICATION
FOR AFRICAN SECURITY

South Africa and Change

When South Africa voted to end the apartheid system and
embrace democracy, the threat posed to African security by
that racist state began to disappear. In December 1988, a
tri-partite agreement was signed by Angola, Cuba, and South
Africa on the question of Namibian independence and the
withdrawal of Cuban troops from Angola. With the Cuban
troops out of Angola, the withdrawal of the Soviet Union
from Southern Africa and, consequently the end of "Communist threat" to South Africa, Pretoria was prepared to
embark on far-reaching changes.

The demand for democratic forms of government around the world following the end of the Cold War and the disintegration of the Soviet Union further gave impetus to the need for change in South Africa. In February 1990, incumbent President, de Klerk, announced that the state would end apartheid and begin talks with black political organizations with a view to establishing a future democratic society with a government based on majority rule. To pave way for this major reform in the South African political system, discriminatory laws were repealed, the African National Congress (ANC) was legalized, and its jailed leaders, including Nelson Mandela, were released from prison. The reform program of de Klerk was endorsed in an all-white referendum on March 17, 1992, and the stage was thus set for a rapid movement toward social and political change. Despite increased tension and violence, the nation moved forward to hold the first multiracial election in April 1994 which formally installed democracy.

The emergence of an ANC-led democratic government in South Africa has important implications for African security. In the first place, the former supremacist state no longer constitute a threat to the rest of Africa. In fact, since the early 1990s, South Africa through its reform strategy had begun to pave the way for its reconciliation with African states. By adopting a deliberate policy of wooing African states, de Klerk aimed at removing his country from its pariah status in Africa. This policy involved, in part, diplomatic overtures to notable African countries. By mid-1992, de Klerk had made shuttle visits to about thirty-three African countries including Cote d'Ivoire, Kenya and Nigeria.[52] Though some Africans were still skeptical of South Africa's real intention, there was a general warm response to its overtures. Some African leaders responded by paying reciprocal visit to South Africa. President Daniel Arap Moi of Kenya, for instance, visited the country on June 9, 1992, becoming the first African leader to visit South Africa in over two decades. Political observers viewed the visit as a major step for South Africa in its attempt to improve its relations with African States.[53]

De Klerk's "breakthrough" visit to Nigeria is particularly important because of its special significance for South Africa's rapprochement with African states. The visit, the first in decades by a South African white leader to Africa's most influential state, and certainly one of the staunchest opponents of apartheid, signified South Africa's acceptance into the family of African states. Given Nigeria's impressive track record in the struggle against racist minority regimes in Southern Africa, de Klerk's triumphant landing on Nigeria's soil was, indeed, a symbolic end to South Africa's isolation in Africa. The visit opened the gate to new ties between African states and South Africa. For example, Malawi and Cote d'Ivoire immediately instituted diplomatic relations with Pretoria.[54] Renewed relations were also pronounced in the field of economic cooperation. Djibouti lifted its trade and travel restrictions on South Africa.[55] Zaire, (now the Democratic Republic of Congo), officially sanctioned imports from South Africa.[56] By the end of 1989, about one-third of South Africa's exports of manufactured goods were said to be going northwards to African states.[57] Today, rather than constituting a danger to Africa's security, the new South Africa is poised to assume a constructive role in regional peace and security. Its Defense Minister, Joe Modise, has indicated the preparedness of his country to accept regional defense role particularly in the politically unstable Southern African region, and in the continent as a whole.[58]

Africa as Nuclear Weapons Free-Zone

The new era of democracy in South Africa has also brought back the continent to the nuclear weapons free-zone status quo. When de Klerk embarked on his reform program he had also extended it to the military sector. Soon after his ascension to power, he decided to do away with South Africa's sophisticated weapons system. Early in 1990, the Republic's entire nuclear weapons program was halted, nuclear plants were closed down, and the destruction of the nuclear weapons so far produced began. At the end of the exercise of dismantling South Africa's nuclear technology, the country had become "the first nation to give up its nuclear capability voluntarily."[59] To show that "our hands are clean," de Klerk signed the NPT in July 1991, something South Africa had shunned over the decades of the development of its nuclear program. Moreover, South Africa opened its doors to the International Atomic Energy Agency (IAEA), promising the organization which is responsible for monitoring nuclear programs, "full access" to the dismantled nuclear weapons facilities. With the order to destroy the existing bombs in February 1990, Africa was once again on the way to becoming a nuclear weapons free-zone.

Since the government of Nelson Mandela has not indicated any interest in a nuclear weapons program, it is most probable that Africa will continue to exist as a denuclearized zone. The reasons for this are convincing. First, as already mentioned, a black-government ruled, non-nuclear South Africa no longer poses a threat to Africa's security. Nelson Mandela's government, also as stated earlier, is not interested in rescinding the decision to close South Africa's nuclear plant for good. Mandela reportedly affirmed that "the ANC will abide by the Nuclear Non-Proliferation Treaty," and that "we fully support the declaration by the Organization of African Unity calling for the establishment of the African continent as a nuclear-weapons-free zone."[60] Mandela's government rather has been preoccupied with the reorganization of the new armed forces, the South Africa National Defense Force (SANDF). South Africa's priority presently is to integrate into SANDF, the armed wings of the former nationalist groups such as the ANC, the Pan-Africanist Congress (PAC), and also the armies of the erstwhile independent homelands.

Second, the present worldwide economic crisis to a considerable extent will affect the capacity of African states to meet up the financial obligations of a nuclear weapons industry. It is an understatement to say that African countries are the worse hit by this economic depression. Nigeria, which has often been assumed to sport the greatest urgency to produce nuclear weapons among the African contenders, has not gone far in this bid. Indeed, in spite of its nuclear rhetoric, no Nigerian government has wholeheartedly pursued a nuclear weapons program. The depressed Nigerian economy has not permitted the government to give priority to its obvious wish that the country should become a nuclear power. It is precisely for the fact that nuclear program is very expensive that some of its opponents regard it as a grandiose or white elephant project in the face of limited resources which could be better managed.

Third, the African contenders for nuclear weapons, probably with the exception of Nigeria, have not proven that they
have the necessary technical expertise. Libya's desperate bid
to acquire the weapon has not been successful partly because it lacked the required technology. In the early stages
of Libya's nuclear program, Muammar Gaddafi attempted
to buy atomic devices from the Chinese, and later from the
Indians without any success. The Libyan leader at one time
turned to German scientists for help.[61] President Omar
Bongo's dream of a small but powerful nuclear state is also
not likely to materialize. Though Gabon is rich in uranium,
the central African state lacks nuclear expertise, and Bongo's
request for French assistance was not heeded. It is doubtful
whether any African state still wishing to build nuclear capability will succeed in acquiring the services of nuclear
physicists rendered jobless in the former Soviet Union. Also,
no African state has been reported to be involved in the so-
called "black market" for nuclear weapons essential materials. This is an open market where interested states can buy
weapons-grade plutonium or uranium, other nuclear weapons materials, or even complete warheads allegedly smuggled
out of the Soviet Union after its disintegration.[62]

Fourth, there has been in the post Cold War period a
sustained campaign by the West, particularly the United
States, for nuclear weapons non-proliferation. This is demonstrated in the staunch opposition to the Iraqi nuclear and
chemical weapons programs after the Gulf War. The U.S.
insistence that North Korea should open its nuclear facilities to the IAEA for inspection is another example. As a
matter of fact, President Bill Clinton stated that non-proliferation of nuclear, chemical or biological weapons was "one
of the highest and most urgent priorities," of the United
States. The president hoped to "weave non-proliferation more
deeply into the fabric of [America's] relationships with the
world's nations and institutions."[63] Most definitely, the West
will not tolerate a South Africa whose government is dominated by blacks to have nuclear capability. The politics of
the destruction of South Africa's nuclear capability before
the collapse of apartheid suggests this. Pretoria's declared
reason for discontinuing its nuclear program was the result
of the prevailing global and domestic changes which made
nuclear deterrent, as de Klerk put it, "not only superfluous,

but in fact an obstacle to the development of South Africa's international relations".[64] But as analysts have noted, the decision to destroy the bombs was largely determined by the white minority regime's fear that the control of the weapon would eventually fall in the hands of a black majority government. The *Washington Post* noted that "there was a very real fear by the white community that [the weapons] would be mis-used" by the ANC when it took over the reins of power.[65] The United States also held this view and was particularly fearful of a possible nuclear cooperation between a black-ruled South Africa and Libya. The United States on many occasions expressed misgivings at the ANC links with Gaddafi, believed, not only to be funding the black political movement, but also providing it military support.[66] The U.S. thus reportedly pressurized South Africa to destroy its nuclear weapons and its high grade uranium before a change of government which, as expected, swept into power a black majority.

It is rather too early to state categorically the extent to which the pursuit of an "Islamic bomb" by some North African states namely Libya and Egypt would militate against a nuclear weapons free regime in Africa. Both Libya and Egypt perceived Israel as a threat to North Africa especially with its nuclear capability. Indeed, it was the Israeli acquisition of nuclear weapons that persuaded Egypt and Libya to seek them. In their calculation, their nuclear weapons would provide a counter force to those of Israel. The standard agreement of Egypt and Libya in opting for nuclear capability was the desire to redress the power equation in the Middle East. To Gaddafi, a Libyan bomb would remove strategic inferiority of the Arab world relative to Israel.[67]

It would seem that the signing of the peace accord between the Palestinian Liberation Organization (PLO) and Israel would dissuade Libya, or at least, Egypt from further seeking the bomb. But because the peace process has repeatedly been stalled indicates that the foundation of a lasting peace in the Middle East is not anywhere in the nearest future. The knowledge, therefore, that Israel still has nuclear weapons may continue to cause some apprehensions for the North African Arab states. Indeed, worried about Israel's nuclear capability, Egypt continued to campaign against its nuclear monopoly.[68] In November 1993, it submitted a draft resolution to the U.N. asking for the establishment of a de-nuclearized zone in the Middle East.[69]

So far, however, Africa has remained a nuclear-free con-tinent since the dismantlement of the South African nuclear weapons. This is likely to remain so in the post-Cold War period given the desire of African states to see the continent free of the weapons. In this light, resolutions have been adopted by the OAU and the U.N. For example on Novem-ber 8, 1993, Algeria on behalf of African states sponsored a United Nations draft resolution titled: "Establishment of a Nuclear-Weapons-Free Zone in Africa." The draft resolu-tion was adopted by the General Assembly on December 16.[70] Finally, on April 11, 1996, forty-three member states of the OAU signed the Pelindaba Antinuclear Treaty, by which those states pledged not to build, test, or stockpile nuclear weapons.[71]

CONCLUSION

The early 1960s consensus in Africa that the continent should be a nuclear weapons-free zone had by the 1980s effectively been challenged. As we have seen, internal dynamics were changing fast. Africa of 1964 when OAU members could resolve to make the continent a denuclearized zone was dif-ferent from Africa of the 1980s when South Africa was equipped with nuclear weapons and, therefore, posed a grave threat to the security of African states. The two decades that had elapsed between the 60s and the 80s showed quite glar-ingly the futility of an African security system based on de-nuclearization of the continent. The search for security in-evitably brought many states into the mainstream of the arms race. Those particularly vulnerable to nuclear threats from South Africa were forced to toy with the idea of acquiring a deterrent capability.

However, post Cold War events in the world generally and particularly the momentous changes in South Africa including the institution of democracy and the destruction of the state's nuclear weapons system have restored Africa as a denuclearized region. South Africa has consistently pledged its commitment to the principle of non-nuclear Af-rica as a strategy to guarantee the security of the continent.

Since the dismantlement of the South African nuclear industry, African states have renewed their determination to ensure the establishment of a nuclear weapons-free zone in Africa.

NOTES

1. Quoted in "Address by General Ibrahim Babangida, Commander-in-Chief of the Nigerian Armed Forces, to the All-Nigeria Conference on Foreign Policy at the Nigerian Institute of Policy and Strategic Studies, Kuru, on April 7, 1986." For full text of the address, see Ibrahim Badamasi Babangida, "National Interest is National Security," *Nigerian Journal of Political Science*, 5 (1-2), 1987, 105-110.
2. For a good synthesis of the search for security in the Third World through nuclear weapons, see Caroline Thomas, *In Search of Security: The Third World in International Relations*, (Boulder: Lynne Rienner Publishers, 1978), 121-145.
3. The NPT was instituted in July 1968 but did not come into operation until March 1970. See the provisions of the treaty in J. Goldblat, (ed.), *Non-Proliferation: The Why and the Wherefore*, (London and Philadelphia: SIPRI, 1985), 247-250.
4. See U.S. Department of State, *The United States and Africa*, Africa Series, no. 40, (Washington D.C., 1964), 30.
5. Ibrahim A. Gambari, *Theory and Reality in Foreign Policy Making: Nigeria After the Second Republic*, (New Jersey: Humanities Press International, 1989), 187.
6. For an analysis of the agreement, see Gordon J. Idang, "The Politics of Nigerian Foreign Policy: The Ratification and Renunciation of the Anglo-Nigerian Defence Agreement," *African Studies Review*, 13, (2), Sept. 1970, 227-251.
7. See Gordon J. Idang, *Nigeria: Internal Politics and Foreign Policy, 1960-1966*, (Ibadan: University Press, 1973), 41, 76, and 82.
8. W. Scott Thompson, *Ghana's Foreign Policy, 1957-1966: Diplomacy, Ideology and the New State*, (New Jersey: Princeton University Press, 1969), 99.
9. AHG/RES 12 (II).
10. CM/RES 28 (II).

11. CM/RES 38 (III). Resolutions on denuclearization of Africa were also adopted at the U.N. See, for instance, Resolutions 1652 (XVI) of November 24, 1961 and; 2033 (XX) of December 3, 1965. The OAU also tried to work through the UN to ensure the denuclearization of the continent. In 1976, it submitted a proposal, "Implementation of the Declaration on the Denuclearization of Africa," to the 31st Session of the UN General Assembly. See *Official Records of the General Assembly, Thirty-First Session, First Committee,*(A/C 1/31/PV, 20-25).

12. Kwame Nkrumah, *I Speak of Freedom: A Statement of African Ideology,* (London: Heinemann, 1961), 213.

13. G. Aforka Nweke, "African Perception of Global Disarmament and Prospects for Denuclearization of the Continent," *Nigerian Journal of International Affairs,* 8, (1), 50.

14. Ali A. Mazrui, *Niger-Saki: Does Nigeria Have a Nuclear Option?,* The Nigerian Institute of International Affairs, Lecture Series no. 33, 17.

15. Mazrui was particularly outspoken against the Non-Proliferation Treaty to which many African states are signatories. The noted scholar saw no rationale in embracing this treaty which, he argued, was designed to prevent other states from acquiring nuclear capability while those who already possessed it continued to develop it.

16. For an appraisal of nuclear non-proliferation in Africa, see Oye Ogunbadejo, "Nuclear Non-Proliferation in Africa: The Challenges Ahead," *Arms Control,* 10, (1), 1989, 68-86, and; Nweke, "African Perception of Global Disarmament," 37-59.

17. AGH/Res. 126 (xx).

18. Oye Ogunbadejo, "Africa's Nuclear Capability," *Journal of Modern African Studies,* 22, (1), 1984, 26.

19. *ibid.*

20. See *Financial Times,* (London), 3. Sept. 1976.

21. For an expanded discussion of Nigeria's nuclear power program, see G. Aforka Nweke, "Nuclear Power and Nigeria's Defence policy," in A.E. Ekoko and M.A. Vogt, (eds.); *Nigeria's Defence Policy: Issues and Problems,* (Lagos: Malthouse Press Ltd, 1990), 145-161.

22. Ogunbadejo, "Africa's Nuclear Capability," 39.

23. Thomas, *In Search of Security,* 131.

24. Ali A. Mazrui, "Africa's Nuclear Future," *Survival,* March-April, 1980.

25. Ali A. Mazrui, *The African Condition: A Political Diagnosis*, (London: Cambridge University Press, 1980), 122.

26. President Shehu Shagari, *Address to the Nation on Nigeria's 20th Independence Anniversary, 1st October, 1980*, (Lagos: Government Printer, 1981).

27. See Stephen Wright, "Nigerian Foreign Policy: A Case of Dominance or Dependence?" in Timothy M. Shaw and Olajide Aluko (eds), *Nigerian Foreign Policy: Alternative Perceptions and Projections*, (London: Macmillian Press, 1983), 105.

28. *West Africa*, May 19, 1980, 837.

29. *The Punch* (Lagos), 2 July, 1981.

30. *West Africa*, Oct. 24, 1977. The government's statements on acquisition of nuclear capability, in the final analysis, proved to be mere rhetoric.

31. See "Match Nuclear Threat by South Africa, Kodjo Tells OAU," *The Herald*, (Harare), June 10, 1983. See also *West Africa*, June 20, 1983, 1438 and, *Kessings Contemporary Archives*, Bristol, 1983, 32420.

32. *The Punch*, 17 Nov. 1980.

33. See Abdul Mohammed Babu, "Africa and the nuclear Bomb," *Africa Now*, July 1983, 47-48.

34. Declassified CIA reports were later to confirm this intended test and its cancellation because of international pressure. For summary of the CIA reports, see *The New York Times*, Sept. 27, 1990, A16.

35. Quoted in *ibid.* For details, see Central Intelligence Agency, *The 22 September 1979 Event*, Interagency Intelligence Memo randum, Office of the Director of the Central Intelligence Agency, December 1979. This document was declassified in July 1990 and obtained under the Freedom of Information Act by the Natural Resources Defense Council, Washington, D.C.

36. Other alleged South African nuclear tests over the southern Atlantic were reported in 1980 and 1987. See, for instance, Phyllis Johnson and David Martin, *Frontline Southern Africa*, (Peterborough: Ryan Publishing Co., 1989), 301-302. For more details on the South African nuclear tests, see Ronald Walters, *South Africa and the Bomb: Responsibility and Deterrence*, (Toronto: Lexington Books, 1987).

37. Later, while admitting that South Africa attempted to con duct a nuclear test, de Klerk insisted that his country never did conduct any clandestine nuclear weapons test. See, David

Albright, "South Africa Comes Clean," *The Bulletin of the Atomic Scientists*, 49, (4), May 1993, 4.

38. See, for example, Gambari, *Theory and Reality*," 193.
39. Peter U, Onu's Inaugural Address at the Conference on Security, Disarmament and Development in Africa, Lome, Togo, 11-12 August 1985. See the proceedings of the conference published by the United Nations, 18.
40. For such resolution, see Resolution on the Security of Countries Nearest to the Southern African Battleground, AHG/ RES. 80 (xiii).
41. Ravi Shastri, "South Africa and Nuclear Weapons: Deterrence or First Use," *Strategic Analysis*, (New Delhi), 12, (8), 1988, 879 and 889. There is dissenting view, however. J.E. Spence concludes that "it is difficult to see any military utility for nuclear weapons, either as deterrent or defence." See his, "South Africa: The Nuclear Option," *African Affairs*, 80, (321), Oct. 1981, 445.
42. See, for example, Johnson and Martin, *Frontline Southern Africa*, 283.
43. *ibid.* 193.
44. Gambari, *Theory and Reality*, 116.
45. *The Guardian*, Nov. 23, 1986.
46. *ibid.*
47. See *West Africa*, Dec. 15, 1986, 2623. Reacting to the rumors of the alleged planned South African attack, the Chief of Air Force Operations, Air Vice-Marshal George Osho, said Nigeria was prepared. However, External Affairs Minister, Bolaji Akinyemi described the reports as "mere speculations." See *ibid.*
48. *The Guardian*, Nov. 23, 1986. Equatorial Guinea's Charge D'Affair in Nigeria, Mr Narciso Ncugu Abeso, however, denied any complicity of his country with South Africa in the alleged planned attack on Nigeria. He said Equatorial Guinea would not permit the use of its territories for any military attack on Nigeria by South Africa. See *West Africa*, Dec. 15, 1986, 2623.
49. Some discussions of South Africa's activities in Equatorial Guinea can be found in Olusola Akinrinade, "Threats to Security and Stability in Nigeria: Perception and Reality," *Geneve-Afrique*, 26, (2), 1988, 58-60.
50. Quoted in *Africa Report*, 38, (3), May/June, 1993, 6.
51. Quoted in Albright, "South Africa Comes Clean," 3.

52. *African Concord*, June 22, 1993, 14.
53. For a report on the visit, see *ibid.*
54. See *Africa Research Bulletin*, 29, (4), April 1-30, 1992, 10527.
55. *ibid.*
56. *The New York Times*, Dec. 5, 1989, A-11, provides some insight into Zaire's increased trade with South Africa.
57. See *ibid.*
58. See Helmoed-Romer Heitman, "New South African Defence Force Takes Shape," in Robert Hall, (ed), *The World in Conflict, 1994/95*, (London: Jane's Information Group, 1995), 89-90. See chapter 7 for a discussion of the role South Africa is likely to play in the management and resolution of conflict in Africa.
59. *The Philadelphia Inquirer*, May 16, 1993, C1.
60. See *The Bulletin of the Atomic Scientists*, July/August, 1994. However, "a few isolated individuals" within the ANC are said to have expressed the wish that the government would revive the nuclear weapons program. See *ibid.*
61. See *World Press Review*, Dec. 1991, 11.
62. *Time*, Aug. 29, 1994, 47-51. The territory of the former Soviet Union is said to house about 15,000 tactical nuclear weapons and 12,00 strategic weapons. See Helmut Schmidt, "The Search for Global Order: The Problems of Survival," *Security Dialogue*, 22, (3), 1992, 44. For further discussion of nuclear weapons "black market," see Kirill Belyaninov, "Nuclear Nonsense, Black Market Combs, and Fissile Flim-Flam," *The Bulletin of the Atomic Scientists*, March/April, 1994, 44-50.
63. *United Nations Disarmament Yearbook*, 18, 1993, 2.
64. Quoted in Albright, "South Africa Comes Clean," 3-4.
65. *The Washington Post*, March 18, 1993.
66. *ibid.* See also, *Africa Report*, 38, (3), May/June, 1993, 6.
67. Oye Ogunbadejo has adequately summarized the Libyan leader's concern in this regard: "It is an open secret that Quaddafi has, for a long time, been one of the foremost and most militant Arab apostles of producing an `Islamic bomb' that would be able to face up to the nuclear threat posed by Tel Aviv." See Ogunbadejo, "Africa's Nuclear Capability," 27.
68. See P.R. Kumaraswamy, "Egypt Needles Israel," *The Bulletin of the Atomic Scientists*, March April 1995, 11.
69. See *The United Nations Disarmament Yearbook*, 18, 1993, 159.
70. See U.N. RES/48/86.
71. *Los Angeles Times*, April 12, 1996, A15.

Chapter 6

POST COLD WAR AFRICA:
ETHNICITY, ETHNIC CONFLICT
AND SECURITY

Abiodun Alao and Funmi Olonisakin

INTRODUCTION

The tragedy that started unfolding in Rwanda during the first half of 1994 focused the world's attention on an extreme example of ethnic conflict in Africa. If it wasn't for its extent and timing, the Rwandan crisis would have been dismissed as another example of Africa's perennial ethnic conflicts. However, with a casualty of almost a million, at a time of post-Cold War euphoria, the Rwandan ethnic conflict has come to be a reference point in post-Cold War ethnic conflicts. Perhaps more than anything else, the conflict brings to focus, once again, the need to consider critically the link between ethnicity and conflict in the new global security dispensation.

Although ethnicity is by no means an understudied concept, the ramifications surrounding its usage in any given context should be clearly defined. Because of the multi-dimensional nature of ethnicity, and the depth of emotion and partisanship evoked in most discussions of the term, the

main intention and focus of most analyses are easily mis-
placed. In this chapter, Anthony Smith's definition of an ethnic group will be adopted. Smith defines an ethnic group as:

> a named human population with a myth of com-
> mon ancestry, shared memories and cultural el-
> ements, a link with an historic territory or
> homeland and a measure of solidarity.[1]

Engeen Rosen further elaborates that members of an ethnic
group inevitably "make use of certain cultural traits from
their past to ensure perpetual cohesion."[2]

In considering the appreciable literature that ethnicity
has attracted in recent years, one is often tempted to forget
that the development of the sociological and anthropologi-
cal theory of ethnicity dated back only to the late 1960s and
the early 1970s when the experience of the multi-ethnic state
pointed out the flaws in nation building.[3]

Although this chapter will not explore in detail the diverse links between ethnicity and war, certain basic connections between the two concepts deserve some passing mention.[4] As Winston van Horne and Werner Prange have noted,
the most compelling attribute of war-politics is the molding
and nurturing of undifferentiated mass social psychology
that inclines and impels individuals to perceive common
mortal foes, and feel a strong inner need to destroy them.
The mobilization of this common perception is much easier
under an ethnically underlined conflict. The "we are good,
they are evil" type of perception that often underlines most
conflicts becomes easier to create and sustain under an ethnic situation.

It has been argued that the deep divisions within ethnic
groups in such societies have been created largely by psychological concerns.[5] Amongst several such factors which
normally generate ethnic conflict are: the fear of relinquish-
ing or losing political dominance, the need by a group to
assert its worth,[6] a politically or economically dominant
minority group's belief that it is superior to others,[7] and the
avowed determination of some groups to oppose a ruling
group's attempt to spread its culture and influence. Donald
Rothchild argues that in instances where there is fear of "consequences of a fundamental re-ordering of regime proce-

dures" by the ruling elite, or "where political minorities remain deeply anxious over their subordination or their cultural or physical survival," the resultant ethnic conflicts could be violent, involving loss of lives and property.[8] Compromises are difficult to reach in such situations, as groups perceive their rivals as basic threats to their survival.

How ethnicity is perceived determines to a large extent on its linkage with conflict. Rudolf Stavenhagen has identified three approaches: (a) ethnicity as an inherent, primordial affiliation responding to a deep psychological need for a sense of belonging and security within a community; (b) ethnicity as a framework of social organization through which people relate to members of their immediate communities and those outside; (c) ethnicity as a political and economic resource, a major factor in the distribution of power and wealth.[9]

Robert Cooper and Mats Berdal have identified two important characteristics of ethnic conflicts. The first is that such conflicts seem to last for a long time. This, according to them, is because the parties to the conflict have some unalterable or nearly unalterable characteristics like race, religion, or language. The second is that in most cases, ethnic conflicts are often between governments and ethnic movements, i.e. between "legally recognised authority on the one hand, and a rather ill-defined and possibly illegal movement on the other."[10] What is certain, though, is that ethnic conflict will not disappear quickly. More than anything, it seems the end of the Cold War has evoked more factors that support this prediction. As David Welsh has noted, of the approximately 180 states presently in existence, fewer than 20 are ethnically homogenous (where the minority is less than 5% of the population).[11] Against the background of the certainty of ethnic conflict occurrence in such states, methods of management of these conflicts should be sought and put in place in anticipation.

Ted Gurr and Barbara Harf have identified four important types of politically active ethnic groups within the modern state system. These are ethnonationalists, indigenous peoples, communal contenders, and ethnoclasses.[12] These types of politically active groups could be grouped into two. The first two, ethnonationalists and indigenous peoples want separation or autonomy from states that rule them. The latter two, communal contenders and ethnoclasses seek greater access or participation within the existing state structure. Gurr and Harf have enumerated the differences between the two groups. According to them, ethnonationalists are usually independent, aspiring always to establish or re-establish their own states, and the indigenous people are concerned with protecting their traditional lands, resources and culture. On the other hand, communal contenders are after sharing of political power, while ethnoclasses "want equal rights and opportunities to overcome the effects of discrimination resulting from their immigrant or minority status."[13]

The historical experience of the emergence of African states makes ethnicity a most significant denominator of internal affairs. Key issues like politics, economics, education, revenue allocation and resources distribution are, to a large extent, determined by, or perceived to be determined by ethnic cleavages and considerations. However, the area where ethnicity has attracted most attention is its association with conflicts in post-independence Africa. Where it has not caused or inflamed tension between different groups, it has been employed to explain security actions and/or indecision.

This chapter looks at the relationship between ethnicity and conflict in post-Cold War Africa. With Yugoslavia bringing to European and American attention the extreme manifestation of ethnic conflict in Europe, this chapter takes a deep look at ethnic related conflicts in Africa, and investigates how their character has changed, and could yet change again in the post-Cold War order. In doing this, the chapter first analyzes the root causes of ethnicity in Africa. It then proceeds to discuss how ethnicity has graduated through the Cold War to the post-Cold War era. The legacies the end of the Cold War bequeathed in this regard and the future of ethnic conflicts are also analyzed. The chapter further discusses the crucial issue of foreign involvement in Africa's post-Cold War ethnic conflicts with regard to the regions of the continent currently undergoing simmering ethnic strife.

TRACING THE ROOT CAUSES OF ETHNICITY: VICISSITUDES OF COLONIAL DIVISIONS AND THE ACTIVITIES OF THE "INHERITANCE" ELITE

Tracing some of the roots of post-independence ethnic conflicts in Africa to colonialism is almost effortless. First, the creation of artificial national boundaries which, for administrative convenience, brought together people of different ethnic, social and religious identities sowed most of the seeds of the problem. Second, it was also often the case that most of the colonial powers deliberately and/or inadvertently, showed favoritism towards certain groups to the detriment or annoyance of the others. Thus, during the colonial rule, the structures that would create ethnic tension had been well laid. However, once colonialism had sown the seed, the development of ethnic phenomenon in post-independence years, was left to the core of elites that inherited the mantle of leadership. This started with the creation of ethnically based nationalist movements which paved the way, after independence, for weak political parties, badly compromised constitutions, fragile democratic arrangements, unstable socio-economic policies, and essentially weak structures incapable of withstanding the pressure independence was to bring. All these provided fertile grounds on which post-independence ethnicity and ethnic related tensions were to thrive in later years in Africa.

Although the link between colonialism and the activities of the earliest crop of elites in post-independence Africa to the development of ethnicity in the continent has been well established, some of the features of the argument relevant to our discussion in this chapter will be briefly identified. With the possible exception of Somalia, where another variant of primordial divisions was to bedevil the nation state, all African countries are ethnically heterogenous. What perhaps compounded the difficulties of unity in the newly independent nation states was that, most of the groups brought together within the same national borders, were neighbors that had fairly long histories of rivalry in the pre-colonial period. In short, right from the time they were forced to co-exist, rivalry, tension, and mutual suspicion had been at the background of their relationship. Although the might of colonial authority often suppressed these rivalries, they later surfaced in the post-independence era.

Some scholars have argued that colonial masters did make attempts to set the various ethnic groups in their respective territories against each other, as a way of destabilizing the territories after independence. The controversial nature of this position means that more research would be needed before conclusive deductions are made. However, it has been established beyond reasonable doubts, that, in some of the former colonies, the colonial masters did show favoritism towards certain groups against others. Whether this was to curry favor from those groups, or to reward them for being loyal, would remain some of the tantalizing questions of colonial history. Again, whether this policy was only to serve short-term gains, or had hidden desires to frustrate the post-independence policies of the new states, awaits its own historians. However, it is a matter of fact that colonial masters showed preferential treatment for certain ethnic groups in the creation of sensitive post-independence structures, especially the armed forces, the profession that was to play a most redoubtable role in the post-independence power structure and power struggle in Africa.

The activities of the "inheritance elites" (the core of the elites who took over the administration of African countries at independence) in perpetrating ethnic divisions has been established. At independence, ethnicity was the easiest and most available tool at the disposal of the new elite to establish their grip on power. Since the independence political movements were formed along ethnic lines, stirring ethnic emotions against real and imagined rivals became a way of maintaining their positions in power.

What then are the implications of all these? The first is that at independence ethnicity was already well established and would underline virtually all areas of national life. Second, the crop of political elite that took over the administration of the new states showed readiness to exploit ethnicity to perpetrate its hold on power. Third, ensuing socio-political structure at independence was conducive to ethnic conflicts. Finally, Cold War politics which underlined most global conflicts during the period were set to play a primary role in influencing Africa's ethnically tainted conflicts.

THE PAST AS LEGACY FOR THE PRESENT: ETHNIC CONFLICTS IN THE OLD ORDER

It is impossible here to make a detailed discussion of Africa's ethnic conflicts during the Cold War era. Instead, what is attempted is a brief discussion of some fairly consistent trends of the phenomenon. The intention in this regard is to investigate the extent to which manifestations of ethnic conflicts have changed between these two phases, and to assess whether old prescriptions for preventing ethnic conflicts during the Cold War era are still valid in the post-Cold War dispensation.

Perhaps the first characteristic of the Cold War ethnic conflict is that in most cases, it is expressed along the desire for self-determination, which again is manifested in explicit territorial terms. Groups of people experiencing real or perceived persecution within the existing state framework often clamor for self-determination. In some cases, however, self determination, may be unrelated to real or perceived victimization. Alleged victimization could be a front for other hidden considerations. For example, people in a given geographical region with considerable mineral resources may anticipate a better future if they can find a way of seceding from an existing constitutional arrangement. The desire of the Cabinda to secede from Angola is a manifestation of this sort of self-determination.

Secondly, most of these conflicts often attracted external intervention soon after their commencement. More often than not, external involvement in African internal conflicts was exploited by Cold War adversaries who took opposing sides. There are many examples of the paramountcy of the Cold War politics in African conflicts. Perhaps this was best manifested in Angola, where the ethnic war was intermixed with other complications like sub-regional politics, internal political differences and an un-coordinated decolonization process. However, external involvement in Africa's ethnic conflict could also cut across the Cold War divide. For example, during the Nigerian civil war, both the former Soviet Union and Britain (admittedly in varying degrees) supported the cause of the Federal government while France sided with secessionist Biafra.

The only country that appeared to have handled its ethnic conflict with the least possible external intervention was Zimbabwe. During the short-lived ethnic differences between the Ndebeles and the Shonas, the only form of external involvement came from South Africa, and this involvement was minimal, when compared with the apartheid state's involvement in other regional ethnic conflicts. Several factors accounted for this somewhat unusual situation in Zimbabwe. First, the ethnic conflict emerged at a time when all countries around the world were interested in having normal relations with the newly independent country. Because of this, no country was willing to assist the anti-government forces. Second, the rebel forces did not have any organized structure or political leadership that could attract such sympathy. Third, the duration of the conflict was relatively short, between 1983 and 1987.

Another characteristic of some ethnic conflicts during the Cold War was the influence of political and/or religious factors. In Angola, for instance, the ethnic conflict was influenced by the MPLA/UNITA political antagonism. In Sudan, the North/South ethnic division became intermixed with Christian/Muslim antagonism. The intermixture of ethnicity with other considerations served to make the conflicts more endemic, and the issue of external support more complex. For example, one of the declared reasons why France supported the Biafran cause was that the country saw the Ibos as fellow Christians facing persecution from the Muslim north. In the Sudan, the Saudis supported movements fighting for the preservation of Muslim interests.

Having identified some of the trends that cut across Africa's ethnic conflicts during the Cold War era, it might be necessary to consider the conflicts that overlapped the Cold War and the post-Cold War phases. These conflicts have one major characteristic: they had existed for at least a decade and had become considerably entrenched. Some of these major conflicts include the clan conflict in Somalia, the debacle in Angola, and the civil war in the Sudan. The extent to which these conflicts were influenced by Cold War politics varied—ranging from the deep external and great power involvement as was the case in the Angolan conflict, to the relatively low external involvement in the case of Sudan. The success that has attended the post-Cold War efforts to resolve these conflicts has depended, quite fortu-itously, on the extent to which the conflicts had benefitted from the Cold War politics. In Angola, where the conflict was a mixture of ethnic and political differences, and where the Cold War had made considerable impact, it was possible, at least initially, to arrest the war between both sides and to conduct the UN organized general election. On the contrary, the Sudanese civil war was not influenced by the peace divi-dend brought about by the end of the Cold War, just as the war was not influenced much by the Cold War.

The conflict in Somalia presented a rather bizarre mix-ture of different factors. The crisis that brought the country to the tribunal of global attention was not really an ethnic but a clan war. Although the country benefited from the Cold War, the subsequent clan conflict itself was unassisted by the East/West ideological rivalry. The warring factions got their initial arms from the weapons that the Cold War adversaries had poured into the country in the wake of the war with Ethiopia. The fact that the clan war was not helped by the Cold War directly eliminated the "allegiance syn-drome" that would have existed between the donating power and the respective clan leaders in the country. This factor was to prove crucial when the United States launched its *Operation Restore Hope* in Somalia. It was at this stage that it was realized that no country had any leverage in Somalia that could either starve the warring factions of arms, or could force any of the clan leaders to the negotiation table. This was a technique that worked, at least to an extent, in the Angolan conflict.

POST COLD WAR ETHNIC CONFLICTS: CAUSES AND COURSE

It would be inaccurate to blame the explosion of ethnic con-flicts in the 1990s entirely on the end of the Cold War. In fact, ethno-political conflicts since the end of the Cold War are a continuation of a trend that began as early as the 1960s. It is a manifestation of the enduring tension between states that want to consolidate and expand their power, and ethnic groups that want to defend and promote their collective iden-tity and interest.[14] More often than not, ethnic tensions be-come more visible when other factors create stress between groups. For example, with the depressed economy of most African countries, with the upsurge in democratic pressures, and with an increase in the competition over scarce resources, differences that typically manifest themselves along ethnic lines have increased considerably. Despite this blurred distinction, however, it may be possible to identify some of the issues that evoked ethnic tensions in recent years. Such issues include: the pressures from economic problems, attempts at redressing previous "injustices," clamor for self-determination, and failed attempts at democratic reforms.

Pressure of Economic Problems

In a direct way, economic problems have not, at least as yet, resulted in an outbreak of any major ethnic war, although they have, in a number of cases combined with other factors to result in ethnic conflict. The link between economic pressure and ethnic conflict appears easy to establish. There is always the possibility of conflict among ethnic groups arising from competition for scarce resources. Also, where a state lacks the skilled man-power resources required to implement programs, the resulting frustration and disappointment may lead to heightened tension among various groups. As resources shrink, highly politicized groups press their demands on the state more insistently than ever.

Redressing Previous Injustice

In a number of African countries, attempts to redress injustices of the past have heightened the propensity for violence. Some ethnic groups believe that they are victims of persecution from other ethnic groups that have received implicit state endorsement. Such persistent conflicts became more pronounced in the aftermath of the Cold War. An example is the renewed tension in Mauritania between the government and the principal black groups, the Toucouleur and the Soninke. This ethnic crisis is invariably between the Arabs and the black population. Although the conflict had been on for some time, it was only in the late 1980s that it came into the open. In 1984, the Force de Liberation Africaine de Mauritanians (FLAM) was formed, and in June 1986, it published the "Manifesto of the Oppressed Black Mauritanians."

126

The manifesto denounced what it called "Mauritanian apartheid" and the "Arabization of the Mauritanian society." The tension culminated in an attempted coup in October 1987, a move which resulted in the further repression of the Mauritanian black population. FLAM also claimed that the attempted coup resulted in the dismissal of more than 500 black Non-Commission Officers (NCOs) from the army.

The Black/Arab ethnic conflict inside Mauritania has influenced the neighboring states of Mali and Senegal. The largely black state of Senegal has offered sanctuary and support for FLAM. This has damaged the relationship between Senegal and Mauritania. On the other hand, Mali has been accused of supporting the Mauritanian government. FLAM, indeed, has accused the Malian government of "genocidal racism." Two other black groups have emerged in the 1990s, the Resistance Front for Unity, Independence and Democracy in Mauritania (FRUIDEM), and the United Front for Mauritanian Armed Resistance (FURAM). Both have since launched attacks upon civilian and military targets in the country.

Clamor for Self-Determination

The clamor for self determination has become especially pronounced in the aftermath of the end of the Cold War. A number of cases have shown how politics aggravated ethnic self-determination and lead to conflict. A prominent example in this case is South Africa, especially in the run-off to the April 1994 election. To a large extent, the clamor for self determination in the country was a legacy of apartheid. In the 1970s, the apartheid regime created a number of "Homeland States" to assist in the consolidation of apartheid. Four of these "states," Transkei, Ciskei, Venda, and Bophuthatswana, were declared independent by the apartheid regime. For a long time before the April 1994 elections, the possible reaction of these states to their re-incorporation into the South African state (which the ANC had made unequivocally clear would happen) was a key issue. As the elections drew to a close, Transkei and Venda signified ready intention to join the ANC plan for re-incorporation. In Ciskei, there were initial problems, and through much of 1993 there was ethnic violence in most part of the homeland state.

The fourth of the "independent states," Bophuthatswana, experienced some problems during the early part of 1994, when there emerged what could be called a clash between the "will of the people" and the ambition of a leader. The former leader of the state, Lucas Mangope, was determined, against the wish of his people, to ensure the "independence" of the homeland by preventing its introduction into the new South Africa. This had always been expected, and the clash between the "peoples-power" and the Mangope administration came to a head, when riots engulfed Bophuthatswana, and Mangope was forcibly overthrown. Consequently, his desire for self determination for the homeland was quashed when Bophuthatswana was brought back into the South African fold.

But by far, South Africa faced the greatest ethnic problem in the KwaZulu/Natal province, where the Inkhata Freedom Party (IFP) had, since 1987, been battling with the ANC. The conflict produced upwards of 10,000 casualties and left thousand more people homeless. In short, the conflict had a dimension of a civil war and almost marred the April 1994 elections. KwaZulu was one of the six remaining self-governing homelands, and the IFP, with considerable strength in the region evoked the nationalism of the predominantly Zulu population to clamor for the independence of the Zulu state. In this desire, the IFP leader, Mangosuthu Buthelezi, succeeded for a long time in linking the struggle for this greater regional autonomy with the fate of the powerful Zulu king Zwelethini. As Gavin Cawthra pointed out, it is doubtful if half of the Zulu population supported the IFP.[15] Without any support elsewhere, however, Buthelezi exploited Zulu nationalism to threaten secession. The crisis eventually extended beyond the KwaZulu/Natal homelands of the Zulus, and areas like Witwatersrand later became affected by the ethnic conflict. The conflict in KwaZulu/Natal province also illustrated a factor that had threatened the unity of South Africa—the white extremists' support for self-determination for some of the homelands states. Indeed, for most of the apartheid period, the IFP was a beneficiary of state patronage. The white extremists also made a daring attempt to support Mangope in his fight to preserve the independence of Bophuthatswana and to ensure it was not incorporated into the new South Africa.

All these pre-election tensions were, however, resolved before the April 1994 election. Mangope was overthrown, paving way for the participation of Bophuthatswana in the election. Also, a last minute attempt to ensure the participation of the IFP in the elections succeeded when the party declared its acceptance of the pre-elections deal with other parties, especially the ANC. The IFP leader, became a cabinet minister in the Mandela administration.[16]

Although there are other pockets of areas where the clamor for self determination by ethnic groups has threatened national security, none in the post-Cold War era seems to have been most demonstrative than that in South Africa.

Failed attempt at "Democratic Reform"

Largely because of the drive for good governance and political liberalism, there has been an upsurge of ethnically motivated conflicts in Africa. Although in many cases, democratic aspirations were achieved without recourse to violence, the effort turned disastrous in some places. In the post-Cold War era, democratic aspirations resulting in ethnically underlined conflicts have shown two features. First, the antecedents to the conflicts dated back to the period before the end of the Cold War. Second, the prevailing depressed economy in many African states aggravated the conflicts.

Liberia is, perhaps, the best example of where ethnicity became ensnared in the movement for democratic reforms. There is, however, the need to qualify this assertion. The war that engulfed Liberia was not, in its origin, an ethnic war, and neither was it originally targeted at democratic reform. In fact, the government of the late President Samuel Doe, which was in power then, had metamorphosed from a military to a civilian government. Beyond these two facts, however, are a number of factors which made ethnicity and bungled attempts at democracy relevant issues in the Liberian civil war.

The conflict in Liberia escalated when Charles Taylor formed the National Patriotic Front of Liberia (NPFL), and launched an attack on the Doe government from neighboring Cote d'Ivoire. The proclaimed intention of the rebel was to remove Doe from power. Doe was accused of running an undemocratic government, and of gross human rights violations, both as military head of state, and as civilian president following his victory in an alleged rigged election. Although ethnicity had always been an underlining issue in Liberian politics, the dividing line was traditionally between the Americo-Liberians and the indigenous groups. The former, though fewer in number, dominated Liberian politics for more than a century. It would appear that the division among the indigenous Liberians, which was to play a principal role in the civil war, was greatly exasperated after Doe assumed the headship of the military government in 1980. In his desire to remain in office, he began a systematic suppression of the ethnic groups other than his own Krahn group.[17]

When the Liberian conflict broke out, the ethnic factor was quickly introduced into it. Among the first to join the rebellion against Doe were people from the Gio/Mano ethnic group. This group is believed to have suffered most from the Krahn dominated Doe regime. What however appeared to have brought ethnicity to the fore of the conflict was the massacre in July 1990 of civilians from the Gio/Mano group who were then taking sanctuary in a church in Monrovia. The massacre was perpetrated by the Krahn dominated members of the Armed Forces of Liberia (AFL). After this, the perception of the war changed, and more than any other factor, ethnicity became a key issue. This was to increase considerably in subsequent years.

After the death of Doe, ethnicity became an even stronger factor in the Liberian conflict. The remnants of the AFL still remained under General Hezekial Bowen, with the Krahn domination of its leadership still pronounced. The NPFL still derived its strongest support from among the Gio/Mano, and set up its capital in Gbarnga. Other ethnically based movements also emerged. The United Liberation Movement of Liberia (ULIMO), first emerged to challenge the NPFL, but the group later broke into two along ethnic and religious lines. The Mandingo faction under Alhaji Kromah soon went into war with the largely Christian Krahn faction under Roosevelt Johnson.

The struggle to achieve democracy and stability in Liberia turned out to be bedeviled by ethnic conflict. The West African sub-regional peace-keeping force, the ECOMOG, sent to establish peace, was unsuccessful until recently. For the greater part, its impact was felt no farther than around the capital, Monrovia.[18] Also, the United Nations Observer Mission in Liberia (UNOMIL), sent to the country in 1993, had limited impact. It took more than 30 peace accords for the conflict to be brought to some kind of conclusion with the July 1997 election.[19] However, while the conflict lasted, its ethnic element made it rather difficult to be resolved.

THE RWANDAN TRAGEDY

During the first half of 1994, Rwanda became the focus of international attention with an ethnic conflict now described as the "worst bloodletting in recent African history."[20] Within two months of its outbreak, one in every sixteen Rwandans had been killed, and more than two million inhabitants of the country had become refugees in the neighboring Zaire and Uganda. The outbreak of cholera and other diseases at the refugee camps claimed more lives and increased the long term implications of the war. It is necessary to analyze the Rwandan conflict for two reasons. First, it is the most pronounced ethnic conflict in Africa since the formal end of the Cold War. Second, the extent and the pattern of international reaction to the conflict may give some indications as to the likely response of the international community to Africa's ethnic conflicts in the post-Cold War period.

The story of the Rwandan conflict of 1994 is now so well known that it may not serve much purpose recounting it at a great length. Suffice it to say that ethnicity, the chief cause of the conflict, has always been a major factor in Rwandan politics even before its independence in 1962.[21] In fact, political parties at independence were formed along ethnic lines. Between Rwandan independence in 1962, and the 1994 crisis, the relationship between the Hutus and the Tutsis was most unstable. The crisis in the country was aggravated by the vicissitudes of colonial division, and the activities of the inheritance elites. Like practically all African states, Rwanda was an European creation. During the partition of Africa, Rwanda fell under the control of Germany, although this control was revoked after the first world war when Germany was dispossessed of all its colonial acquisitions. At independence in 1962, the tension between the Tutsi and the Hutu increased so much so that a showdown could easily be predicted. The government did recognize the need to unite the country and prevent a possible catastrophe. The Hutu dominated government, therefore, took steps to include the Tutsis in the government. To achieve this, President Juvenal Habyariamana accepted a political and military power sharing arrangement with the Tutsis. However, by 1994 the Tutsi led Rwandan Patriotic Front (RPF) had the strength to launch a sustained attack on the country. After the mass killing of Tutsi resulting from the assassination of Habyariamana, the RPF made a successful march on Kigali, the capital.

Also important in the Rwandan tragedy is the cross border impact of the conflict and what it means for similar situations in the continent. The RPF launched attack on Kigali from Uganda where there is a significant Tutsi population, and from where the movement had received considerable support over the years. The Tutsi population in Uganda had allegedly supported President Yoweri Museveni's National Resistance Movement (NMR) in its war against the Obote government. This is believed to have underlined the support Museveni gave the RPF in its bid for power in Rwanda. What this brings into focus is the issue of solidarity among the same ethnic groups separated by national boundaries, a legacy of arbitrary colonial territorial division. The sympathy provided to the black rebel movement in Mauritania by Senegal, and the support the Malian government is offering to the Arab led Mauritanian government has already been mentioned. Other examples are scattered all over the continent and they introduce a disturbing dimension into ethnic conflicts. As long as colonial boundaries in Africa continue to stay as they are, this problem will remain.

The victory of the RPF raises the question as to why a movement significantly inferior in weaponry and men could win a war against the better equipped government forces. The RPF method of warfare, compared to that of the government forces, may have accounted for this. The rebel movement exercised strict discipline uncommon among such movements. Members that violated laid down "rules" were punished severely, sometimes with death. This raised the discipline level of the forces. On the contrary, the government forces were largely undisciplined, and they focused attention on civilian targets. Thus, as the government forces were attacking civilian targets, the RPF was progressively advancing on Kigali. Another reason for the RPF's success was the extent of support received from neighboring Uganda. Besides official Ugandan support, some members of the RPF were armed with weapons initially supplied them by the Museveni rebels in the war against the Obote government.

The reaction of other African countries to the Rwandan crisis also illuminates some important lessons. The conflict glaringly showed the inability of African countries to assist neighbors in times of devastating disaster on the scale of Rwanda. The OAU has always been regarded as a lame duck, and the extent of the devastation in Rwanda did not wake the organization from its slumber. The Organization did practically nothing in Rwanda beyond the platitudinous call for an end to the crisis. Largely because of economic reasons, virtually none of the African countries could come to the aid of Rwanda. The OAU peacekeeping experience in Chad, and that of ECOWAS in Liberia cautioned against meaningful African intervention in Rwanda. A more important lesson is the attitude of South Africa to the crisis. The caution the country demonstrated in committing manpower and resources in Rwanda showed that addressing internal problems was more important to the Mandela administration than becoming continental or even regional policeman.

Finally, there is the wider issue of the involvement of countries and agencies outside Africa in the Rwandan crisis. Even before the outbreak of the war, since October 1993, the UN had sent to the country a military observer mission, the United Nations Assistance Mission in Rwanda (UNAMIR) to keep peace between the RPF and the government forces. When the war broke out, the UNAMIR stuck to its mandate of not using force. This, in a way, gave the Hutu militia a free hand to carry out the killing of the Tutsis. While conceding that numerical strength may be insufficient to prevent war, a tough stand by UNAMIR could have given the Hutu militia the impression that their activities were frowned at by the United Nations. To fold arms as it appeared to do at the beginning of the massacre lessened the credibility of the UN in its subsequent peace initiatives. To compound this problem, when the war broke out, the UN Secretary

General withdrew all but 270 of the UN soldiers. It was only after the carnage had escalated almost beyond control that the UN belatedly showed greater interest. The UN may have again unwittingly added to the initial confusion by its announcement on April 8 1994, that the RPF had left their Mulundi base and were expected to move to Kigali the following day. This report was false, but it is possible that such an announcement, coming from the UNAMIR regarded as credible, could have led the Hutu militia to step up the killings. In short, the UN role in Rwanda fell short of expectation.

The military intervention by France was as controversial as it was helpful. For understandable reasons, the RPF initially opposed the intervention, as France was believed to have sustained the deposed Hutu led regime. Whatever the possible hidden agenda behind their intention, the French peace-keepers during their short stay, established successful protection zone, to the extent that people were genuinely frightened after their departure. The Americans, too, made a late humanitarian intervention which, though initially uncoordinated, saved some lives in the refugee camps in Goma.

The situation in Rwanda is still uncertain, and it may remain so for quite some time. There was still tension on the border with Zaire for sometime, where the defeated Hutu army was reported to be regrouping and training for what its leaders called "a combined guerrilla and civil disobedience campaign modeled on the Palestinian Intifada.[22]" Indeed, there was the fear that the large arms dumps in the areas around Goma could help the 30,000 disarmed ex-Hutu soldiers there to easily re-arm. From Zaire, the Mobutu government allowed the Hutu soldiers to continue their broadcast to Rwanda from a propaganda radio station inside Zaire. It was speculated that the reason for this was Zaire's belief that the RPF in control of power in Kigali had links with rebel groups inside Zaire.[23]

FOREIGN INVOLVEMENT IN AFRICA'S POST COLD WAR ETHNIC CONFLICTS

The end of the Cold War has introduced fundamental changes to external involvement in Africa's ethnic conflicts.

For one thing, these conflicts could no longer feed on the ideological divisions that colored the global politics of the Cold War era. For another, interference in these conflicts by external powers has become unnecessary. The former Soviet Union, engulfed in an intense ethnic nationalism which finally led to its break up, could hardly afford to interfere in Africa's ethnic conflicts.

Perhaps the most important and certainly the most controversial foreign intervention in Africa's ethnic conflict in the post-Cold War era was the American involvement in the Somali inter-clan conflict. In December 1992, the United States despatched troops to Somalia in its Operation Restore Hope, to ensure the safe passage of relief materials to starving Somalis. Although the troops received an initial welcome, it was not long before the relationship turned sore. Within six months of their intervention, U.S. troops had become so embroiled in the conflict that avenues for their dignified exit were being sought. The United States eventually left Somalia with considerable casualties and a damaged reputation. Since that ill-fated intervention, the U.S. has always been cautious about getting involved in African conflicts.

What was the motivating factor for Operation Restore Hope? American involvement in Somalia could be considered as a purely humanitarian gesture, motivated by the plight of the starving Somalis. On the other hand, it could be regarded as an unabashed display of authority by a self-proclaimed Cold War victor willing to demonstrate it had the wherewithal to flex its muscles in the international arena without any constraints. Yet, American humanitarian intervention in Somalia could be interpreted as an outgoing government's desire either to score a parting glory, or create a big foreign policy commitment for its successor. Whatever motivating factor for Washington's desire to send troops to Mogadishu, American intervention did very little to bring the Somali crisis to a peaceful end.

When the war between the Hutus and the Tutsis broke out in Rwanda, the dangers and consequences of foreign involvement in African conflicts was already known. Apart from the fact that the rebel factions warned against intervention, even some African countries voted against such a response when the issue was discussed at the UN Security Council. Besides the UN and the French presence, as earlier mentioned in this chapter, there was no other military presence in Rwanda during the crisis.

A unique type of involvement in ethnic conflict was the ECOMOG deployment in the Liberian conflict. Although at the time the sub-regional peace keepers entered Liberia the conflict was not a distinctly ethnic one, it soon became so, and from 1993 onwards, ethnicity became a key issue that ECOMOG had to address in its peace keeping strategy. Of all the warring sides in the conflict, the ones that have exploited ethnicity the most were the two sides of the ULIMO, namely the Krahn and the Mandingo factions. It is, however, one of the sad realities of the Liberian conflict that these two factions divided the peace keeping efforts in the country. Due to a number of reasons, the Krahn faction had some form of "understanding" with ECOMOG. The Mandingo faction and the UNOMIL, on the other hand, had some sort of an unwritten alliance.

AFRICA'S SIMMERING CONFLICT AREAS

By the end of 1994, certain areas could be identified as having potentials for ethnic conflict. In most of the countries concerned, long standing ethnic differences are being fueled by government's neglect of the socio-economic condition of groups. Also, contributing to ethnic feud is the deliberate attempt of leaders to remain in power. To achieve this, they often employ a divide and rule tactics, and also a deliberate policy of favoring one ethnic group (usually the more populous or more influential group) over the other. Nigeria seems to be one of the countries where ethnic differences is most likely to be the dominant issue till the end of this century and well into the next. Whether this would reach the scale of the Biafran tragedy that brought the country into global attention in the late 1960s, depends on how the crisis is managed. Already, the period since 1990 has been characterized by heightened ethnic differences, especially between the minority and the major ethnic groups.

The dominant issue in Nigeria's politics since its independence in 1960 is the North/South ethnic division. The southerners, with some justification, believe that political power in the country has always resided in the north. Since the late 1980s, southern opposition to this imbalance has become more pronounced. By 1993, many people from that part of the country were determined to use the transition to civilian rule which the incumbent government of General Ibrahim Babangida promised, to overthrow the perceived feudal tyranny of the northern Hausa/Fulani oligarchy. After initial prevarications, the presidential election was held in June 1993 in which a southerner, Moshood Abiola, was victorious. However, the result of the election, widely believed to be the best organized in the country's post-independence history was nullified. After a stop-gap period of about four months, the leadership of the country again went to the Hausa/Fulani of the north when General Sanni Abacha, an Hausa, assumed power. That Abacha has held on to power against the will of many people in the south, especially among Abiola's ethnic group, the Yoruba, has further aggravated north-south ethnic tension. An indication of the indignation felt by many Yoruba people for the Abacha regime is their attempt to ostracize those Yoruba elements in the government. Although the government still clamps down on the opposition, many individuals and the media especially in the south continue their opposition.

There is another dimension to Nigeria's ethnic problem, that of minority discontent. Over the years, minority groups in the country have held the belief that they are not well represented in the political and economic scheme of things. In the last decade, spontaneous revolts by minority groups expressing dissatisfaction at their being treated as second class citizens, have come to the fore. In the ensuing clashes, thousands of people have been killed. The posture of successive Nigerian governments on this issue has not made the resolution of the minority problem easy. Where the military has not been deployed to clamp down on such expressions of disaffection, dubious efforts have been made to resolve such disputes. Thus, for Nigeria to escape what obviously looks like a possible outburst of ethnic conflict, the issues arising from the nullified 1993 elections and the concern of the minorities should be given an urgent attention.

In Ghana, an apparently trivial misunderstanding in January 1994 over the price of a guinea-fowl brought out the endemic conflict between the Konkomba and the Nanumba in the northern part of the country. A Konkomba had killed a Nanumba over disagreement on the price of a guinea fowl, and this immediately resulted in an ethnic conflict that ended in the death of thousands of people. The incident expresses the point about how an apparently minor issue can evoke deep rooted and pent-up ethnic emotion.

The incessant clashes between the Konkomba and the Nanumba are, however, rooted in the socio-political history of the two groups. The first clash was first recorded in June 1981, which resulted in the death of over a thousand people.[24] Sources traced the cause of the conflict to the increase in land and cattle grazing rents payable by the Konkomba to their Nanumba landlords. Originally from neighboring Togo, the Konkomba had crossed the border and settled in northern Ghana, on lands that traditionally belonged to the Nanumba. In the exploitative relationship that followed, the Nanumba had always claimed the right to appoint traditional chiefs for the Konkomba. These chiefs were to act as comprador agents to the Nanumba, supervising the collection of rents, and mediating local disputes.[25] Moreover, the relationship between the two groups had over the years so developed that "forced labor" was required of the Konkomba as part of their regular "tribute."

Another root of the conflicts is the alleged aid provided by the Nanumba to the cause of Ghanaian and Togolese irredentists who would like to unite Ghana's Volta region with Togo.[26] Thus, the Konkomba are seen as tools of secessionist forces, helping to destabilize Ghana's eastern borders and thus probably triggering an armed movement on lines similar to those of the Bosnian Serbs in Croatia.

Apart from heavy casualties, the ethnic conflicts in northern Ghana also created refugee situation. The 1994 conflict produced thousands of refugees who fled into Togo.[27] Part of government's efforts at resolving the conflict was the allocation of 3.4 billion Cedis relief aid to displaced persons over a three-month period. Steps were also taken to reinforce the policing of the Ghana-Togo border, because in 1981 allegations were leveled that Konkombas from Togo had crossed over the border to support their Ghanaian kinsmen when fighting broke out in that year. Additionally, parliament has suggested the passing of a legislative instrument ordering both ethnic groups to turn in their arms. But the problem here was how this could be enforced.

Burundi, like the neighboring Rwanda, has also been consumed in ethnic fighting that could further escalate if not nipped in the bud. Burundi is also composed of a Hutu/Tutsi population, and like Rwanda, the Tutsi minority have exercised dominance over the Hutu majority for decades. There has been at least three ethnic inspired fights in the country. Until 1993, when a Hutu president was elected for the first time, the Tutsi dominated the political and military power. In October 1993, the Tutsi dominated army made a failed attempt at overthrowing the government. This attempt further led to ethnic violence in which between twenty-five and a hundred thousand people were killed. With the crisis in Rwanda, Burundi, too became much more volatile, to the extent that the President of the country warned in June 1994 that the country stood on "the edge of an abyss of political and ethnic distrust".[28]

In Kenya, there is the simmering tension between the Kalenjin and the other ethnic groups in the Rift Valley Region. The Kalenjin, President Arap Moi's ethnic group, has been accused of perpetrating an alleged state endorsed persecution of the Rift Valley people. In 1992, up to 200 people were killed in the resultant unrest.[29] Again, in Kenya, the Turkana people in the north western part of the country have suffered enormous casualties as ethnic pawns in the conflict between the Toposa of South-eastern Sudan, and the Pokot people in Kenya. These warring groups have received support from their respective governments. The Sudanese government supported the Toposa in the hope that they would turn against the Sudanese rebels, while the Kenyan government provided arms to the Pokot people to win their support for President Arap Moi. A similar development is going on in Chad, where the incumbent President, Idriss Deby, has been accused of supporting his Zaghawa ethnic group against the other groups that have challenged his authority. These groups include the Hadjarai, the Kamerous, and the Gorane of the former President Hissen Habre. Finally, in Togo, the Kayes and the Kotokoho with a history of strained relationship are likely to continue in this path. In May 1992, clashes between the two groups resulted in many casualities.

Ethiopia, with 15 major ethnic groups and up to 70 languages, appears still vulnerable to some form of ethnic violence. The incumbent leader, Meles Zenawi, (a former Tigrinyan guerrilla) has been redrawing regional boundaries to forestall ethnic violence. Opposition politicians in the country are however accusing him of "divide and rule" tactics, and of trying to ensure that the southern Amharas are prevented from ruling over the Tigrinyan.[30] Under the new constitution approved in November 1994, nationalities who want self-determination and independence are now free to leave the Ethiopian state, provided this desire is supported by a referendum. This supports the government's belief that there is greater problem when these groups are forced to stay in the federation than when they are allowed to leave. However, some groups have criticized this new policy, saying it may herald the end of the Ethiopian state.

CONCLUSION

The historical evolution of the state in Africa from colonialism largely established a basis for ethnicity and ethnic conflict in the continent. It will be inaccurate to assert that the end of the Cold War made ethnic conflict an issue in Africa, or that it resulted in its proliferation. In fact, until Somalia, there had not been any major ethnic conflict of devastating consequence since the end of the Cold War. Even the Rwandan conflict had its roots deep in the Cold War period. What then is the significance of the end of the Cold War in respect of the perennial conflicts in Africa? And what are its implications for future stability and peace of the continent?

It would appear that the end of the Cold War has fueled the conditions conducive to ethnic conflict, although these conditions have not independently resulted in ethnic conflicts. All they have done so far is to aggravate the existing ethnic problems prevalent since the Cold War era. Perhaps the lesson that may be drawn is that in future years, as legacies brought about by the end of the Cold War become more glaringly manifested, more ethnically tinged conflicts may emerge. With the drastic reduction in the economic capability of African states to cope with such challenges, and with the international community unable or unwilling to cope with such problems, the outcome of these seemingly inevitable conflicts would be more devastating.

NOTES

1. Anthony Smith, "The Ethnic Source of Nationalism," *Survival*, Vol. 35, No. 1, Spring 1993, 49.
2. Engeen Rosen, *Creating Ethnicity: The Process of Ethnogenesis*, (London: Sage, 1989), 12.
3. Some of the books that have discussed this topic include: Fredrik Barth (ed.), *Ethnic Groups and Boundaries: The Social Organizations of Culture Difference*, (Boston: Little, Brown and Company, 1969); and Nathan Glazer and Daniel Moyniham (eds.), *Ethnicity: Theory and Experience*, (Cambridge: Harvard University Press, 1975).
4. A more detailed discussion of the linkage between the two concepts is provided in Winston van Horne (ed.), *Ethnicity and War*, (Madison: University of Wisconsin, 1984).
5. Donald Rothchild, "Interactive models for State-Ethnic Relations," in Francis M. Deng and William Zartman (eds.), *Conflict Resolution in Africa*, (Washington D.C.: Brooklings Institution, 1991), 194.
6. See Donald Horowitz, *Ethnic Groups in Conflict*, (Berkeley: University of California Press, 1985), 104.
7. See Donald Rothchild, *Racial Bargaining in Independent Kenya*, (New York: Oxford University Press, 1973), Chapter Five.
8. Rothchild, "Interactive Models," 194.
9. As quoted from Kathleen Newland, "Ethnic Conflicts and Refugees," *Survival*, Vol. 35, No. 1, Spring 1993, 83.
10. Robert Cooper and Mats Berdal, "Outside Intervention in Ethnic Conflicts," in *ibid.*, 133.
11. David Welsh, "Domestic Politics and Ethnic Conflict," in *ibid.*, 65.
12. Ted Gurr and Barbara Harf, *Ethnic Conflict in World's Politics*, (Boulder: Westview, 1994), 15.
13. *ibid.*
14. *ibid.*
15. Gavin Cawthra, "The New South Africa: Facing up to the Legacies of Apartheid," *Brassey Defence Yearbook, 1994*, 211.
16. Buthelezi accepted the Home Affairs Ministry.
17. For a detailed discussion on this, see Amadu Sesay, "Historical Background to the Liberian Crisis," in M. A. Vogt (ed.), *The Liberian Crisis and ECOMOG: A Bold Attempt at Regional Peacekeeping*, (Lagos: Gabumo Press, 1933).

18. For more on ECOMOG, see, Vogt, *The Liberian Crisis.*
19. For more on this, see, John Mackinlay and Abiodun Alao, *Liberia 1994: ECOMOG and UNOMIL Response to a Complex Emergency,* (Tokyo: United Nations University Press, 1995).
20. John Edlin, "Ethnic Conflict or Ethnic Manipulation," SAPEM, July 1994, 5.
21. The first clash between the two ethnic groups in Rwanda was in 1959, when the Hutus killed the minority Tutsis and drove many of them into exile in Uganda.
22. *The Guardian,* 19 December 1994.
23. *Jane's Defence Weekly,* 13 August 1994.
24. *West Africa,* 13 July, 1981, 1616.
25. *West Africa,* 20 July 1981, 1629-1631.
26. A plebiscite supervised by the United Nations in 1956 resulted in the Ewe of Trans-Volta Togoland voting to join the soon-to-be independent Ghana. Most of the support for this move came from the Ewe in the south of Togoland. The inhabitants of the north, bordering the northern region of Ghana, voted to remain in Togo. Secessionist tendencies have remained ever since.
27. *West Africa,* 14-20 March, 1994, 461.
28. *The Asian Age,* 28 May-28 June, 1994.
29. *African Event,* (8) 6, 1994.
30. *International Security Digest,* Vol. 1, No. 4, Feb. 1994.

Chapter 7

THE END OF THE COLD WAR IN AFRICA:
IMPLICATIONS FOR CONFLICT MANAGEMENT AND RESOLUTION

Adebayo Oyebade

INTRODUCTION

> Can Africa avert a future Somalia or Liberia?
> When ethnic and other forms of domestic con-
> flict spill over borders, will Africa have the ca-
> pacity and the mechanism with which to re-
> store peace and order?[1]
>   —Edmond J. Keller.

Intra-state and inter-state conflicts have throughout history constituted an integral part of the world system. The
world has constantly oscillated from one conflict to another
such that conflict poses one of the major global security dilemmas. The fall of the Berlin Wall, the disintegration of the
Soviet Union, the re-alignment of forces especially in Eastern Europe, and the world-wide movement toward democracy were indices that clearly indicated the transformation
of the present world. For many, given the collapse of the bi-

polar international political system around which much of the old world conflicts revolved, a new era of peace and tranquility was expected. Yet the global transformation to what has been popularized as a *New World Order* has not proved a trouble-free world. Serious conflicts, from Bosnia to Rwanda, demonstrate quite clearly that the emergence of the so-called New World Order has not in any way precluded the occurrence of intractable conflicts in the world.

In Africa, in particular, despite the post-Cold War changes, conflicts continue to be part of the continent's political reality. Algeria, Egypt, Tunisia, Sudan, Mozambique, Angola, Liberia, Somalia, Sierra Leone, Rwanda and Burundi, have been, and in some cases, continue to be zones of intense conflict. Conflicts of less intensity also continue to manifest in countries like Nigeria, Cameroon, Zaire, Kenya, and Lesotho, to mention a few. In some of these places, the conflicts have the potential of escalating into major crises if not properly managed. Africa, commented U.S. Assistant Secretary for African Affairs, George Moose, "is the region most heavily burdened with conflict-generated problems."[2] Indeed, many of the factors responsible for conflict during the Cold War like ethnic nationalism, religious fundamentalism, and territorial disputes, are continuing to be a source of further conflict. Other forces engendered by the collapse of the old order have also been responsible for conflicts. For instance, the demand for democracy across the continent which heralded the dawn of post-Cold War era has not been without violence.

Africa's incessant conflicts have constituted a serious danger to the security of the continent manifesting in political instability, crippled economy, social retrogression, environmental dislocation, and population displacements. The effect of conflicts especially long-lasting wars on Africa and its peoples has been devastating. This is easily measured by the collapsed economy of many states—Somalia, Ethiopia, Sudan, Mozambique, Angola—to name a few. Large-scale displacement of populations is another graphic indicator of the effect of conflicts in Africa. The problem of rising refugee cases as a result of civil wars has tended to destabilize states and whole regions even where there are stable political regimes. Where the problem has occurred in serious proportions, as in Sudan, Ethiopia, Somalia, Chad, Rwanda,

Burundi, Liberia, Zaire, Angola, and Mozambique among others,[3] it has threatened socio-political and economic stability so that recovery is an uphill task.

Since conflicts cannot be prevented in the world of ever competing interests, the ability to successfully manage them becomes very important and a necessary pre-condition for safeguarding security. Conflict in the post-Cold war period has become so endemic that a new emphasis is placed on conflict resolution and management. Thus, one of the implications of the fall of the Cold War is that it has created a new perspective from which to view conflicts and their resolution. What this chapter seeks to do is to examine the nature of post-Cold war conflicts in Africa and the future of crisis management and resolution in the continent.

CONFLICT RESOLUTION BEFORE THE END OF THE COLD WAR

African conflicts before the end of the Cold War revolved around three main issues namely, border dispute, secessionist tendency, and liberation struggle. The Organization of African Unity (OAU) duly recognized that these could be a cause for conflict in the newly independent African states and, therefore, decided to address them at the onset. To prevent inter-state border disputes, the organization resolved that inherited territories at independence remained inviolable.[4] This declaration was also calculated to discourage secession since such an action would amount to alteration of pre-ordained borders. The continued existence of colonial states was also considered a likely source of conflict in the continent. Hence, the eradication of "all forms of colonialism from Africa" was one of the important purposes of the OAU.[5] Toward this end, a liberation committee was established charged with the responsibility of co-ordinating African efforts at liberating territories still under forms of colonial rule.

These steps, however, could not prevent conflicts arising in Africa. Contested boundaries immediately gave way to intra-state conflicts as in the Algerian-Moroccan, and the Ethiopian-Somali border disputes. In later years, there would also begin re-occurring border clashes between Nigeria and Cameroon. Secessionist tendencies arising from ethnic nationalism also became manifest in some states. Both the Congo and Nigeria provide classical examples of secession cases that resulted in civil wars. Biafra's attempt, for instance, to secede from the Nigerian federation in 1967 resulted in one of the most bloody civil wars in Africa. The Southern Africa region on its part remained for a long time an area of intense conflict. The conflict was first precipitated by the liberation struggle in the supremacist states of Rhodesia (now Zimbabwe) and the Republic of South Africa, and colonial states of Namibia, Angola, and Mozambique. The state of conflict in the region further persisted when after independence Angola and Mozambique plunged headlong into civil war partly sponsored by South Africa.

The Modalities of Conflict Resolution: The OAU and the U.N.

In theory, the Organization of African Unity is the primary avenue for pacific settlement of African disputes. For this purpose, the organization set up a machinery for conflict resolution shortly after its foundation. This conflict settlement apparatus was laid down in the principle of the organization. It stipulates that:

> Member-States pledge to settle all disputes among themselves by peaceful means and, to this end, decide to establish a Commission of Mediation, Conciliation, and Arbitration...[6]

A protocol which established the commission and its activities was signed by member states of the organization on July 21, 1964. The protocol was subsequently adopted as an integral part of the charter.

However, despite their pledge to submit their disputes to the Commission of Mediation, Conciliation, and Arbitration, member states of the OAU rarely did so and the commission remained a mere decorative body. Rather than submit their disputes to the Commission, African states preferred a more flexible and direct mediation of other states under the auspices of the OAU, but not under its formal conflict resolution body. Thus, in the period before the end of the Cold War much of the organization's peace-making efforts were conducted outside the commission.

With the apparent lack of interest in the Commission of Mediation, Conciliation and Arbitration by member states of the OAU, the organization often adopted a strategy of mediation by persuasion conducted through *ad hoc* commissions. For example, to deal with the dispute between Morocco and Algeria, an extra-ordinary session of the Ministerial Council appointed an *ad hoc* commission consisting of heads of state of some African states to mediate between the two countries. For the Ethiopia-Somali crisis, the Assembly of Heads of State and Government set up a "good offices" committee consisting of some African leaders to mediate the crisis. The OAU involvement in the Congo crisis and the Nigerian Civil War also followed the same pattern as that of the Moroccan-Algerian, and Ethiopian-Somali crises. In both cases, OAU resolutions set up *ad hoc* commissions comprising of heads of states of member states to reconcile the various interests concerned in the conflicts.

From the above analysis, the pattern of the OAU involvement in African disputes is clear. In most of the major cases of conflict in which the OAU intervened, the organization's peace-making apparatus was the appointment of mediating *ad hoc* commissions consisting of heads of state of member states. This method of conflict resolution had its inherent limitations. The work of these commissions was necessarily based on persuasion since the OAU laked any legal power such as a high command, or a collective defense force to enforce its decisions. Thus the Consultative Commission on the Nigerian war could only be preoccupied with persuading Biafra to accept the OAU peace proposal which the secessionist regime consistently refused.[7]

Another crisis management approach to African conflict situation employed by the OAU, though to a limited extent, was the peacekeeping operation. In the tradition of the United Nations classical peacekeeping operation, the OAU decided in 1981 to send a multinational African force to Chad, a country in the midst of a civil war. The war was a result of bitter political wrangling between two main contenders for authority in the country, the *Gouvernement d'Union Nationale de Transition* (GUNT), led by *de facto* president, Goukouni Weddeye, and a 'rebel' group led by Hissen Habre.

A brief analysis of the OAU involvement in the conflict is important in order to understand the organization's use of peacekeeping approach to an African conflict.

The idea of an OAU peacekeeping force for Chad was hatched at the Nairobi Summit conference of the organization held in June of 1981. However, it was not until November 14, 1981, when the Paris Accord was signed in the French capital between the OAU Secretary General, Edem Kodjo, and government leader, Weddeye, that the first concrete step was taken toward the establishment of the peace keeping force. A subsequent accord later in the month gave contours to the proposed force. By the accord jointly signed by incumbent OAU Chairman, Daniel Arap Moi of Kenya, Edem Kodjo, and Weddeye, the OAU:

> reaffirms its support to the GUNT, and requests that all Member States of the OAU support this Government in its efforts to maintain peace and security in the country and abstain from interfering in the internal affairs of the country.[8]

The accord further provided a specific frame of reference for the peacekeeping mission. Its mandate was to "ensure the defence and security of the country whilst awaiting the integration of Government Forces."[9]

The peacekeeping operation was doomed to failure right from its inception. Unable to supply enough forces for the arduous task, the operation ran into serious problem of deployment. Out of a total of six African states, namely: Guinea, Benin, Togo, Senegal, Zaire, and Nigeria, who committed themselves to contributing troops to the operation, only the last three actually met their obligation. To ameliorate the situation, Nigeria had to add two more battalions.[10] Despite this, the peacekeeping force was still inadequate in strength for the purpose for which it was created. The northern part of Chad remained unguarded, resulting in rebel occupation.

The problem of deployment was further exacerbated by a poor transportation system. Transportation available to the mission was so inadequate that deployment of troops from the capital, Ndjamena, to other parts of the country proved extremely difficult. The result was that there was considerable loss of valuable time before deployment could be effected. This had adverse effect on troop efficacy.[11]

Besides the immediate problem, there were other important long term factors that contributed to the failure of the Chadian peacekeeping mission. There was the gross unpreparedness of the OAU Secretarial at Addis Ababa for logistic and financial requirements of the mission. There was also the ambiguity in the mission's terms of reference. While the OAU resolution purported to recognize and support Weddeye's GUNT as the sole authority in Chad, the peacekeeping force was not given the mandate to defend it against rival factions. Indeed, the November 28 resolution called for non-interference in Chad's internal Affairs. By a further resolution of February 11, 1982, the organization fine-tuned the function of the peacekeeping force defining it as a "neutral force" with the task of forming "an integrated Chadian Army without favoring any political faction whatsoever." This resolution also called on Weddeye and Habre to "commence negotiations for national reconciliation."[12] Thus while the government in Ndjamena saw the peacekeeping force as a defender of its authority, the mission did not feel obligated to defend it. Hence, the mission watched helplessly as Habre forces wrestled the control of Chad from Weddeye's GUNT.

In the final analysis, the OAU could not keep the peace in Chad. Its debut at crisis management through peacekeeping operation had proven to be a dismal failure.[13] That the OAU was never called upon again to perform a peacekeeping operation indicated that the organization was ill equipped to manage such a conflict management method. Indeed, the OAU's track record generally in crisis management was not particularly impressive. Its Commission of Mediation, Conciliation, and Arbitration never proved functional. It is clear that the role of the organization in solving African conflicts was not anymore than that of a "useful background to bilateral talks between disputing African state."[14]

But the OAU did not hold the monopoly of conflict resolution in Africa. As part of the larger international community, Africa often resorted to the United Nations in times of conflict. Indeed, in the period before the end of the Cold War the world body played an important role in crisis management in Africa. As a matter of fact, it was in Africa that the U.N. made its peacekeeping debut when it sent the UN

Emergency Force (UNEF) to Egypt in 1967 to diffuse the conflict between the Egyptians and the Israelis on the Suez Canal.

The second, and the last, U.N. peacekeeping operation in Africa before the end of the Cold War was that of the Congo. This peacekeeping operation is very well known because of the magnitude of its failure, and its devastating implication for African security. The Congo Crises began immediately when the former Belgian colony obtained political independence in 1960. In the face of the violent civil crisis that virtually reduced the newly independent country into a state of anarchy, its Prime Minister, Patrice Lumumba, requested for United Nations' assistance in dealing with the situation. A U.N. peacekeeping force was consequently dispatched to the country with the task of restoring order and peace. However, the Congo was to become a major theater of East-West confrontation in Africa. The U.N. peacekeeping mission soon became caught up in the ideological complexities of the conflict and emerged as an instrument in the hands of the Western powers, especially the United States.

The Congo operation left a profound lesson for conflict resolution in Africa. Its manipulation by foreign powers was a classical case of unwarranted external intervention in African affairs. The threat that external involvement in the crises posed to African security taught many Africans the dangers inherent in a U.N. peacekeeping operation in the continent. Thus, after the Congo, African conflicts were not submitted to U.N. peacekeeping operation for a long time.

POST COLD WAR PERIOD:MAJOR AREAS AND SOURCES OF CONFLICT

The post-Cold war period, even in its short history, has seen many parts of Africa in various types of domestic conflicts. There have been low-level conflicts which did not result in major conflagration. There have also been major ones, some even with profound ramifications beyond the confines of the continent. In the post-Cold War Africa, major crises have occurred in practically all regions of the continent.

Southern Africa

The end of the Cold War has brought about significant development to the Southern Africa region in terms of reduction of conflict. In 1990, Namibia achieved its independence, ending several years of liberation struggle. But the big news was the Republic of South Africa where the apartheid system became a thing of the past when in May 1994, the country inaugurated its first multiracial government. The post-apartheid development in South Africa represents a major victory for conflict resolution on the continent.

Angola

It has not all been a rosy picture for the entire Southern Africa region, however. Despite the promise of hope brought about by the end of the Cold War and the institution of majority rule in neighboring South Africa, Angola has continued on the path of a destructive war which has plagued the war-torn nation since 1975. Angola entered this course of never-ending conflict as soon as it obtained independence from Portugal when rival factions for political power resorted to war. Throughout the Cold War, the conflict in Angola was manipulated by external ideological interests which further constrained efforts at its resolution. Yet, the removal of external interests in the war as a result of the end of the Cold War has had little effect on defusing the conflict.

To be sure, hopes of a lasting peace and stability were raised on May 31, 1991, when the Bicesse Peace Accord was signed by the Angolan government and its main antagonist, the Uniao Nacional Para a Independencia Total de Angola (National Union for the Total Liberation of Angola, UNITA). This accord provided for a cease-fire, multi-party elections, and the creation of a unified national defense force. To oversee the implementation of these provisions, the UN sent a mission to Angola, the Second United Nations Angola Verification Mission (UNAVEM-2). Although a cease-fire was attained in 1992 and elections were held in September under the auspices of the United Nations, the expected era of peace did not last.

First, demobilization of existing factional army did not materialize and a unified force could not be created. Second,

the victory at the polls of incumbent President Jose Eduardo
dos Santos, and the ruling party, the Movimento Popular de
Libertacao de Angola, (Popular Movement for the Liberation of Angola, MPLA) over UNITA and its leader, Jonas
Savimbi, was unacceptable to the latter.[15] UNITA's refusal
to acknowledge the result of the election which international
observers considered free and fair sparked off renewed hostility in Angola. By early 1993, according to UN sources,
the casualties of the resumed war had risen to more than
16,000.[16]

However, a new peace offensive was launched by the
UN to bring sanity back to Angola. In early February, 1995,
the UN Security Council unanimously approved a 7,000
strong peacekeeping force for the war-torn country.[17] However, this and other peace initiatives have not succeeded in
paving the road toward a lasting peace. A peace accord signed
between the warring factions in Zambia in November 1994
only held for a while. Even the UN extension of UNAVEM-
3 has not brought peace.

Mozambique

Like Angola, Mozambique embarked on its equally devastating war after attaining independence from the Portuguese
in 1974. After the forced departure of Portugal, the Frente
de Libertacao de Mozambique, (Front for the Liberation of
Mozambique, FRELIMO), took political control of the country. A rebel faction, RENAMO, sometimes known as
Resistencia Nacional Mozambicana, (Mozambique National
Resistance MNR), subsequently emerged with no clear-cut
ideology or direction, but bent on engaging the FRELIMO
government in a violent and destructive war.

Unlike Angola, however, the changes in South Africa
seemed to have had some impact on Mozambique. Having
lost the backing of South Africa as a result of the collapse of
the apartheid system in that country, RENAMO was forced
onto the path of peace.[18] The FRELIMO forces themselves
with little resources left to continue the war were also compelled to sue for peace. Moreover, as one observer summarized it, starvation had killed the appetite for war in
Mozambique.[19] Thus, a climate of war weariness had begun

to pervade Mozambique in the dying days of the Cold War. This scenario was fit for a peace accord, the Rome Agreement, which was instituted in October 1992. By this accord, FRELIMO and RENAMO agreed to a cease-fire, the demobilization of their forces, and national election. The cease-fire was effected and demobilization subsequently commenced.[20] After some initial ambivalence, the first multi-party election in the country was held between October 27-29, 1994, with President Joaquim Chissano and his ruling FRELIMO party winning.[21] The initial doubts as to whether RENAMO would respect the election result finally gave way to optimism when its leader, Alfonso Dhlakama, promised to abide by the verdict. Mozambique was thus set on the path of recovery.

One should be cautious, however, in proclaiming the dawn of peace and stability in Mozambique. The war which the country went through was so devastating that it will take time before the political and economic will necessary for national reconstruction can be marshaled.[22]

West Africa

Since the end of the Nigerian Civil War in 1970, West Africa has remained a relatively calm sub-region in terms of the absence of major conflicts. However, this calm was shattered by the civil war in Liberia, which has had adverse repercussions on virtually all the states in the region. As the Liberian war raged on, conflict erupted in neighboring Sierra Leone between the government and a rebel force, the Revolutionary United Front (RUF). With the Liberian war and the crisis in Sierra Leone, West Africa has joined Africa's conflict areas.

Liberia

For eight years, Liberia remained a conflict zone despite all efforts at bringing the country's war to an end. Liberia became caught up in a bloody civil war on Christmas eve in 1989 when a rebel movement, the National Patriotic Front of Liberia (NPFL) led by Charles Taylor, declared war on President Samuel Doe and invaded the country from Cote d'Ivoire. Initially, the rebellion was dismissed as a minor af-

fair that would be routed out within days or weeks. As time
went on, however, the rebellion fed on the general socio-
economic disaffection in Liberia, and it became a sufficient
threat to the government. The government later took the
problem seriously and launched a retaliatory attack. By the
end of the first quarter of 1990, the country had been engulfed in flames with considerable civilian casualties.[23] At a
later stage, the rebel movement broke into two, and one of
Charles Taylor's commanders, Yommie Johnson, formed the
Independent National Patriotic Front of Liberia (INPFL).
It was this breakaway faction that later arrested and killed
former President Doe.

Attempts at resolving the Liberian Civil War proved
complex. By the end of the first quarter of 1995, up to 33
peace agreements had been signed by the warring factions
without success. All the three international organizations
with commitment to Liberia—the Economic Community of
West African States (ECOWAS), the OAU, and the UN—
had taken steps to end the war. ECOWAS was particularly
in the fore-front of the peaceful resolution of the conflict. It
established the ECOWAS monitoring Group (ECOMOG),
a peace-keeping force instituted to deal with the crisis. The
role of the OAU and the UN was largely to supplement the
ECOWAS initiative.

Of all the numerous agreements signed to bring peace
to Liberia, two are particularly important because of their
extent and promise at the time of signing. The first was the
Cotonou Agreement signed in the Beninois capital, Cotonou,
in July 1993. When the agreement was signed, there were
two major armed wings in Liberia—the NPFL and the
United Liberation Movement of Liberia (ULIMO), led by
Alhaji G.V. Kromah. There was also in Monrovia, an Interim Government of National Unity (IGNU) under Amos
Sawyer. Both the NPFL and ULIMO had their own armed
wings, and they controlled respectively about 70 percent and
20 percent of the Liberian territory. The IGNU, under the
protection of ECOWAS only controlled the capital. It was
these three sides that signed the Cotonou Agreement.

The agreement itself was a 19 article accord that centered on issues like: cease-fire, disarmament, demobilization,
repatriation of refugee, a general amnesty, and an election
set for October 1994. Two of these, the cease-fire and the

disarmament, were especially important, the success of others resting solely on them. Also, under the agreement, the ECOMOG force was to be expanded with observers from the United Nations to supervise and monitor the implementation of the cease-fire. Both the United Nations Observer Mission in Liberia (UNOMIL) and ECOWAS were also to impose military embargo on all the warring sides. On disarmament, the agreement required all the warring sides to give a detailed list of their weapons to ECOMOG, mandated to disarm all the combatants. At the time of signing, the Cotonou Agreement gave many people hope. Yet, within six months of its signing, it had become obvious that it could not deliver the promised expectation.[24]

There were several reasons why Cotonou failed. First, there was distrust between the Liberian warring factions and ECOMOG expected to act as a referee in the peace process. Second, ECOMOG and UNOMIL required to jointly oversee the cease-fire and the disarmament process saw themselves more as rivals than allies. Third, there was no economic recovery plan to guarantee the minimum peace required for the success of the cease-fire and disarmament. Finally, new armed wings that were not signatories to the initial accord emerged to destabilize the agreement.[25]

After the failure of the Cotonou Agreement, another agreement was signed in Akosombo, Ghana, to investigate why Cotonou failed and to attempt another process toward bringing peace to Liberia. The agreement was signed in October 1994, and by the end of the year, its failure was almost certain. By the time the accord was signed, some of the issues that frustrated the Cotonou accord had been further compounded reducing chances of its success. For instance, the economic situation had worsened, and more people had taken almost exclusively to banditry as a means of livelihood. There had also been an increase in the number of armed wings which further complicated the possibility of an agreeable consensus. The sub-regional peacekeeping force, despite its reinforcement with units from Uganda and Tanzania, was uncoordinated. Also the disagreement between ECOMOG and UNOMIL over assignments continued.

The agreement was signed between the NPFL, the ULIMO, and the Liberian National Transitional Government (LNTG) that succeeded IGNU. When the agreement was being signed, both the NPFL and the ULIMO had broken into factions. There had been the Roosevelt Johnson faction of ULIMO which held control of the Krahn element of the movement, and one of Charles Taylor's lieutenants, Woewuyi, had broken away with others to form another faction of the NPFL. Apart from these breakaway factions, there were other groups that had emerged in the Liberian equation. These included the Liberian Peace Council (LPC), and the Lofa Defense Council (LDC). All these bodies did not partake in the signing of the Akosombo Accord, and some of the reasons for the failure of the agreement took its root from these armed wings.

Another peace accord in Liberia was signed by the factional leaders in Accra, Ghana, on December 21, 1994. Like the Cotonou Agreement, it aroused a lot of optimism. First, it was signed by all the seven parties to the conflict. Second, one of the key players in the conflict, the recalcitrant Charles Taylor, promised that the NPFL would ensure the success of the accord. Taylor, indeed, urged his forces to prepare to disarm, promising that he would "personally ensure peace and national reconciliation, disarmament, and free and fair elections in 1995."[26] However, the agreed cease-fire that began on December 28 held only for a while. Hostilities broke out again and the conflict entered its sixth year.[27]

The Liberian crisis that defied resolution for such a long time began to see a ray of hope for solution early in 1997. The latest peace process, Abuja II, succeeded in persuading the already war weary factions to turn in their weapons to ECOMOG. By the end of January, about 80 percent of the arms had been surrendered.[28] Thereafter, with the cooperation of the factional leaders, especially Charles Taylor, Abuja II moved rapidly toward the goal of a democratic election set for May 30, 1997. However, the parliamentary and presidential elections were held successfully in July. With the emergence of Charles Taylor as president in the widely accepted presidential election, Liberia, hopefully had entered an era of lasting peace.

Sierra Leone

Liberia was two years into its war when its immediate western neighbor, Sierra Leone, also slipped into a similar violent conflict. Sierra Leone's crisis began in March 1991 when the RUF rebels launched an attack on the government. The insurgent rebel forces, led by a former army Corporal, Foday Sankoh, has since waged a most vicious war against successive Sierra Leonean governments—from that of President Joseph Saidu Momoh, to that of President Tejan Kabbah. Not even the military governments of Captain Valentine Strasser, and Brigadier Julius Maada Bio could end the war. On the contrary, the RUF progressively stepped up its guerrilla war especially in the countryside, creating a state of anarchy never before experienced in the hitherto politically stable country.[29] It is rather too early to predict if the war has, indeed, ended with the new military government headed by Major Paul Koroma, which came to power in May 1997, after a coup that overthrew the democratically elected government of Alhaji Kabbah. Rejected by the vast majority of Sierra Leoneans, and unrecognized as the legitimate government of Sierra Leone, Koroma's military junta has in a bid to counter isolation teamed up with the RUF rebels. Since the coup, the rebel forces have been reportedly joining the government forces in Freetown.[30] Indeed, the rebel leader, Foday Sankoh, was named the number two person in Koroma's government.

The conflict has, however, had a particularly devastating effect on the country in several ways. It has led to the death of thousands of people and the sending of many others into refugee camps. Many Sierra Leoneans have fled the country into neighboring states as a result of the conflict. About 185,000 people are said to have sought refuge in Guinea. A late January 1995 rebel incursion into a northern town, Kambia, sent another 30,000 people into that country as refugees. Even Liberia, already in flames, has played host to some 90,000 refugees.[31]

Foreign nationals have also not been spared in the violence that has engulfed Sierra Leone. Foreigners whose governments the RUF suspects of providing assistance to Freetown have been targets of intimidation and harassment. For instance, two British aid workers believed by the rebels to be undercover military advisers to the National Provisional Ruling Council (NPRC) were kidnapped on November 7, 1994 and held hostage. In January 1995, more foreigners were held hostage including four Britons, six Italians, and one Brazilian.[32]

Sierra Leone's already poor economy has also suffered further damage as a result of the conflict. One of the modes of operation of the RUF was to attack the country's mining industry, the mainstay of Sierra Leone's economy. In late January, 1995, the rebels attacked and seized two of the country's mines, paralyzing the production of natural rutile and bauxite for sometime.[33] The attacks on foreigners has also particularly discouraged external investment in the country necessary to buoy the economy.

The prospect for peace in Sierra Leone remains rather dim. Even if the RUF has abandoned its war against the nation, the unpopular May coup has brought fresh troubles for the West African state. The new military government of Major Koroma continues to face still opposition within and outside the country. Particularly, a Nigerian-led West African force, determined to get Koroma out of power and restore the civilian government of Alhaji Kabbah, has repeatedly bombarded Freetown. The consequent political instability has further aggravated the economic problems the country has faced for sometime. Foreign investments have almost disappeared in the country amidst the chaos. The mining industry has practically closed down with foreign mining concerns vowing not to resume operations until the volatile political situation is resolved. With the military government adamant to stay in power and poised for a long stand-off with the equally determined West African forces, peace may be a long time in coming to Sierra Leone.

Central Africa

The major conflict in Central Africa in the post-Cold War period was the devastating ethnic slaughter in Rwanda. But the same kind of conflict is slowly brewing in neighboring Burundi a situation that can easily escalate into a full-scale war.

Rwanda

The Rwandan carnage epitomized the resurgence of ethnic induced conflict in post-Cold War Africa. A country comprising mainly of two ethnic groups, the Hutu and the Tutsi, Rwanda has historically experienced violent inter-group hostilities. In the last three decades the country had witnessed a number of destructive feuds between the two groups which led to the killing of thousands and massive destabilization of populations. However, it was the catastrophic massacre of the Tutsi by the Hutu beginning in April 1994 that attracted world attention. The conflict began when the Rwandan president, Juvenal Habyariamana, died in a plane crash early in April. Accused of masterminding the death of the president, the Tutsi became a target of a well orchestrated Hutu campaign of genocide. Between April, when the pogrom started, and July, when it subsided, close to a million Tutsi were reported to have been killed by Hutu soldiers and their civilian collaborators.[34]

Although the flaming fire of war had died down in Rwanda, the embers are yet to be altogether extinguished. The animosity between the Tutsi and the Hutu is deep-seated, having its roots in the colonial history of Rwanda. The colonial powers in Africa often adopted a sectional policy that tended to favor one group over and above the other. Rwanda was such a case where Belgium promoted ethnic animosity between the Hutu and the Tutsi by favoring the Tutsi minority in education, and its elite in the colonial bureaucracy. The mutual suspicion between the two ethnic groups became further exacerbated after independence and was often exploited by power-hungry elites.

Despite the unprecedented magnitude of the Rwandan killings, the international community responded rather too late.[35] An ambitious African initiative to address the conflict was utterly lacking. Understandably, the Western world was hesitant to intervene; hence, the triumph of a carnage which did not abate until it had taken its full toll. The question is whether lasting peace could return to the country after the latest blood-bath.

The need to bring to justice the authors of the bloody conflict has been expressed, not only as a deterrent for others who might likely harbor a repeat performance, but also as a step to aid reconciliation and bring about peace. Along this line, the new Rwandan government requested the U.N. to set up a tribunal to try the perpetrators of the genocide.[36] The result was the establishment by the U.N. Security Council of the first international war crimes tribunal since the end of the Second World War. The task of the "International Tribunal" was

> the prosecution of persons responsible for genocide and other serious violations of International humanitarian law committed in the territory of Rwanda and Rwandan citizens responsible for genocide and other such violations committed in the territory of neighboring States, between 1 January 1994 and December 1994.[37]

However, it remains to be seen whether this action will prevent further violence in Rwanda.

Burundi

Like Rwanda, ethnic conflict is a dilemma in Burundi where the Hutu and the Tutsi, ever suspicious of one another, also make up the ethnic mix. The history of ethnic tensions in Burundi dated back to the immediate post-independence period. Since achieving independence in 1962, Burundi, like its northern neighbor, Rwanda, had seen series of violent conflicts between the dominant but politically subservient Hutu, and the power-wielding minority Tutsi.[38] These incessant Hutu-Tutsi conflicts often resulted in the massacre of many people and large refugee population. In 1972, a clash between the two ethnic groups resulted in the death of an estimated 200,000 people, almost all Hutus.[39] In October 1993, another Hutu-Tutsi clash caused the death of 100,000 people, the vast majority of whom were Tutsi, and the displacement of another 200,000 people who fled to neighboring countries.[40]

Since the Rwandan bloody crisis broke out in April 1994, ethnic tension has heightened considerably in Burundi. While the carnage in Rwanda captured world attention, the potentially bloody conflict quietly brewing in Burundi has remained virtually unnoticed. Before the end of 1994, increased tension between the Hutu and the Tutsi had already begun to result in the killing of many people. This in turn has unleashed a flood of refugees as people had begun to flee the country in large numbers to take refuge in neighboring states.[41] Alan Zarembo has summarized quite vividly the present situation in Burundi:

> Burundi is eroding into a state of terrorism. In the last several months, assassins have murdered at least five leaders, terrorists have exploded grenades in the capital, and armed gangs have exchanged gunfire in the suburbs and slaughtered hundreds of poor people in the countryside. Each month the death toll rises by a few hundred.[42]

As the fear of Rwanda-like bloodbath grips Burundi with an increasing threat to escalate into a full scale civil war, the only hope for abating another disaster is to punish war crimes in Rwanda. Whether an international tribunal to try war criminals in Rwanda will act as a deterrent to the volatile situation in Burundi remains to be seen. Meanwhile the country boils in ethnic tension.[43]

The Horn of Africa

The Horn had for a long time constituted a major area of conflict in Africa. For almost two decades the Ethiopian government and Eritrean secessionists waged war against each other. Conflicts had also occurred in Ogaden, Somalia, and Sudan.[44] However, the last two, Somalia and Sudan, are still currently engaged in civil strife. The Somali conflict is purely a product of post-Cold War period. Though the war in Sudan began in the Cold War period, it has remained a post-Cold War legacy.

Somalia

While the Rwandan war was a clear-cut case of ethnic strife, the war in Somalia was a manifestation of clan antagonism. With no ethnic division, Somalia is one of the very few African countries culturally homogenous. However, this seemingly important factor for unity did not prevent the outbreak of a civil war in 1992.

The crisis in Somalia was orchestrated by clan rivalry which became uncontrollable after the forced exit from power of President Siad Barre. Soon Somalia was engulfed in total chaos characterized by absence of organized government, civil lawlessness, and mass starvation. It was this situation that forced the UN Security Council to send to Mogadishu a peace-keeping force (UNOSOM I). This force, however, proved to be totally ineffective in restoring peace to Somalia, or of halting the starvation there. It was a small, under funded, ill-prepared force that was incapable of engaging in any effective military and humanitarian operation. Besides its inadequacies, the Somali warlords also contributed to its failure.

Amidst the rapidly deteriorating situation in Somalia, particularly the starvation leading to the death of thousands, the United States decided to embark on a massive humanitarian operation in that country. Mandated by the UN Security Council, the U.S. led a UN Interim Task Force (UNITAF) to mount, under the code name OPERATION RESTORE HOPE, a large-scale humanitarian operation designed to save the starving population.

Although, the U.S.-led UNITAF succeeded to a large extent in reducing starvation in Somalia, the larger issue of clan conflict was not resolved before UNITAF, satisfied that it had completed its task, handed over the country to UNOSOM II. The Somali conflict has thus so far defied resolution. There even has been renewed fighting between the warlords. Somalia thus remains a failed post-Cold War international effort at conflict resolution.[45]

Sudan

The protracted war in the Sudan expresses the manifestation of a politico-religious and ethnic conflict in Africa. The seeds of this conflict were actually sowed during the colonial period. By colonial policies of separate development and divide-and-rule, the British overlords consciously created a deep gulf between the predominantly Muslim north and the Christian south.[46] The resultant different levels of development between the two regions coupled with ethnic, cultural, and religious differences gradually gathered momentum and inevitably exploded into a violent conflict soon after independence in 1955. The war assumed greater dimension when the south, suspicious of northern domination, asked and fought for autonomy. However, the first phase of the war ended in 1972, when the Addis Ababa Accord granted local autonomy to the South.

The second phase of the war began in 1983 as a result of President Jafaar el Nimeiri's revocation of the autonomy status granted to the south by the Addis Ababa Accord. Nimeiri's attempt to impose an Islamic law, the *Shari'a*, on the south led to the resumption of hostility. Since then, a devastating war has been raging between the northern controlled government backed by a radical Islamic party, the National Islamic Front (NIF), and the southern Sudan People's Liberation Movement (SPLM). The north-south conflict became even more complex with the emergence of ethnic based factions in the south. These factions have not only been fighting the Sudanese government, they have also been at logger-heads with one another. The conflict in the south has mainly been between factions of the Sudan People's Liberation Army (SPLA) namely the SPLA-Torit and the mainstream SPLA. This is not to say that the north is politically monolithic or free of political wrangling. Here too various factions have emerged such as the National Democratic Alliance (NDA), a coalition of northern political parties in opposition to the ruling NIF. The war in Sudan is thus not a simple north-south conflict.

Though the Sudanese conflict has not attracted the attention it deserves from the international community, nevertheless, some attempts have been made to defuse it. A number of African countries, Ethiopia, Nigeria, and Kenya, for example, have hosted peace talks between the country's rival factions. Yet, so far the war has defied resolution.[47]

North Africa

Although religious nationalism has been a major source of conflict in many parts of the world, in the post-Cold War world order it has assumed an increased prominence.[48] In Africa, religious conflict arising from antagonism between dictatorial secular authority and Islamic fundamentalism is fast gaining prominence. While religious conflict has occurred within states in many parts of Africa,[49] it is in North

Africa that it has had its greatest manifestation. Algeria, Egypt, and Tunisia have in recent years experienced a most violent conflict arising from opposition of Islamic fundamentalism to state authoritarianism.

Algeria

In the last few years Algeria has been the major center in the conflict between militant Islamists and secular government that is tearing apart North African states. Militant Islamic groups in Algeria such as the Mouvement Islamique Armee (MIA), and the Front Islamique du Salut (FIS), have conducted a most violent campaign of opposition against the government and its agents, and also against foreigners. The Groupe Islamique Armee (GIA), the fanatical Islamic armed wing of the FIS has particularly been a formidable opposition to secular authority in Algeria. Dedicated to the islamization and Arabization of Algeria, the group has masterminded the killing of state officials, intellectuals, and journalists suspected of Western inclination, and foreign technocrats.[50] The state in return has committed itself to a policy of destruction of Islamic influence partly through repression of extremist groups such as the FIS and the GIA. In recent years government forces have stepped up their campaign against the Islamists. Such campaigns have resulted in great casualties in the camp of the fundamentalists. By the end of February, 1995, it was said that "more than 500 people a week were being killed."[51]

Egypt

Egypt is equally devastated by religious crisis arising from conflict between fundamentalist Islamic groups and the government. Like their counterparts in Algeria, militant Islamic groups such as *Al-Gama'a al-Islamiyaa*, and the *Jihad* have had a running bloody battle with secular authority. The campaign of terror has likewise been directed against government officials, the state security forces, foreigners, and tourists.[52] Foreign businesses and non-Islamic banks have also been targets of violence. Bombs were reportedly planted outside eight banks in Cairo in March 1994.[53] The reaction of the government of Hosni Mubarak has been ruthless repression of the Islamic elements. This has resulted in indiscriminate arrest of suspected Muslim militants and the execution of those convicted of terrorism. In April 1994, Talaat Yassin Hamman, head of *Izz al-Din al-Qassam*, the military wing of *Al-Gama'a al-Islamiyaa* was killed in a police operation in which about 98 militants were arrested.[54]

Tunisia

The case of Tunisia is not much better than that of Algeria and Egypt. Attempts at islamization of the country by Islamic movements have also been devastating, causing unrest and the death of hundreds of citizens. Although Islamic groups such as the *Al-Nahda* Islamic Party for example have been formidable, it appears the government has been able to contain them through large scale repression. For instance, the government has banned *Al-Nahda* and forced its leader, Rashid Ghannouchi, into exile. The silencing of Islamists does not, however, preclude their increasing numbers. Indeed, there is rising popularity of Islamic fundamentalism in Tunisia.

Undoubtedly, religious conflicts in North Africa constitute a most serious threat to the security of the region in many ways. The power struggle between the secular governments and the forces of radical Islam has led partly to political instability. The islamic groups base their struggle on an alleged inability of the authorities to bring about good government and economic prosperity. True, corruption is ripe among these governments propped up by Western aid against popular domestic opposition. Apart from creating political instability, religious conflict in North Africa has also led to violent killings. Islamic groups have been responsible for the murder of opponents of their cause, whether high government officials, security agents, foreign professionals, or the ordinary citizen.[55] The killings, especially of foreigners and tourists, have had a devastating effect on the economy of the states. This is glaring in Egypt where earnings from tourism has been drastically reduced.

The peace-offensive in North Africa has not been very encouraging. In Algeria, in particular, where the crisis is most serious it has been difficult to bring the two sides together for peace talks. The January 1995 proposal by opposition parties and the FIS to negotiate with the government did not come to any fruition. The authorities flatly refused any negotiation with the opposition and rejected their demand for a coalition government and fresh elections. Even more radical Islamic groups such as the GIA would do nothing with the government except cause its demise.

How could the growing problem of Islamic fundamentalism and state secularism be solved in North Africa. It is not likely that the fanatical Islamic elements will give up the fight against the secular government especially when they perceive they are fighting a holy war. It appears the way to deal with the situation is for the authoritarian governments to accommodate legitimate participation of the Islamic groups in government. Lack of political pluralism is the major factor responsible for the religious crisis in North Africa. Even a "democratic" state like Tunisia with a government installed by election has systematically eliminated opposition. In the March 1994 presidential and parliamentary elections in which Islamic parties were not allowed to participate, the incumbent president, Ben Ali, was the only official presidential candidate. In the presidential election, he won a landslide victory, 99.91 percent of the vote. The governing party, the Constitutional Democratic Rally (RCD) won 97.73 percent.[56] The belief that the accommodation of opposition would ease tension is supported by the FIS desire to negotiate with the Algerian government if the January 1992 canceled elections were restored. In the elections, the FIS recorded some success. It is also important to note that in states where islamic groups are allowed in the political process, such as Jordan and Pakistan, cases of religious conflicts are minimal.

FUTURE OF CONFLICT RESOLUTION IN AFRICA

Factors complex and varied were responsible for the failure of peaceful settlement of African disputes in the post-independence period. The Cold War structure of the international political system particularly had a profound influence on the ability of African countries to settle their own differences. The superpower rivalry that characterized the period not only fueled prevailing tensions, but also constrained regional efforts in the management of conflict. The role played by the United States and the former Soviet Union in the Congo Crisis adequately demonstrated how extra-African manipulation of an African crisis could render it unmanageable. It was also the United States' anti-communist response to Soviet presence in Southern Africa through arms build-up that prolonged the restoration of peace to that region. Thus, conflicts in the continent became distorted by extra-African considerations.

However, the contours of conflict resolution in Africa changed dramatically after the Cold War. The collapse of the old order of East-West competition in Africa has introduced a new dimension into African international relations. It is of little use, therefore, to understand African conflicts and their management through Cold War lenses. Two principal post-Cold War developments will have significant implication for conflict settlement in Africa. The first is the current Western disengagement from Africa. The second development, which is partly an effect of the first, is a growing African initiative at conflict resolution.

Western Disengagement From Africa

For the major powers of the Western world, the close of the Cold War has necessitated a re-definition of their strategic interest in the larger world. In France, Britain, and particularly in the United States, a disinterest towards involvement in foreign conflicts has begun to emerge. America's inclination to curtail involvement in Africa's conflicts seemed to have begun to take shape with U.S. attitude to the Liberian war. Although a former American "informal empire," Liberia with all its historical and sentimental linkage to the U.S. was neglected by Washington when the war broke out. Preoccupied with the Gulf War, the U.S. took no appreciable step to address the Liberian crisis.

However, it was the failure of the American-led mission in Somalia that gave content to Western inclination to limit commitments in conflict situations especially where there is no apparent compelling strategic importance. The loss of American lives in Somalia raised questions, both in official and public circles, about the cost to the United States of playing the *gendarme* in Africa, where U.S. strategic interest is no longer at stake.[57] The bitter experience of the United

States in Somalia, where some of its troops and other peace-keeping troops were brutally killed, convinced Washington of the futility of any involvement in African local conflicts. This was primarily the reason for America's slow response to the Rwandan crisis. When the United States finally responded, its involvement in the strife was limited to humanitarian relief efforts. A 7,500 strong American force was sent to Rwanda to aid in the humanitarian efforts to save thousands of refugees.

In the climate of post-Cold War Western disengagement from Africa, the French appeals for support in its intervention in the Rwanda war predictably met with disinterested response from its European partners. Even France abandoned the beleaguered African nation before any meaningful peace could return to the country and an effective solution found for the refugee problem. Fearful of being bogged down in the crisis, France withdrew its 2,500 troops from the country on August 21, 1994, its scheduled date of departure. This was despite UN appeals for delay in order to protect some 800,000 Rwandans who could possibly face annihilation.[58] The early withdrawal only indicated the limited role France intended to play in the conflict. Thus it would be naive to continue to expect extra-African military intervention in African conflicts in the post-Cold War period.

On occasions, to be sure, African conflicts with international ramifications, like the crisis in Rwanda could compel external intervention. However, such intervention would seldom be military in nature, but humanitarian. The Western powers have stated in no uncertain terms that they would be more interested in preventive diplomacy in early conflict situations. This entails helping African states to respond to early signs of conflict before graduating into a large-scale conflagration. Thus the U.S. has supported the development of an African capacity to deal with conflicts in their formative stage. It sees the OAU to be "in a unique position to defuse conflicts before they start or conduct early intervention in African conflicts."[59]

The early stage informal mediation option is really not new in U.S. crisis management history in Africa. Former Assistant Secretary for Africa in the State Department, Herman J. Cohen, acknowledged that preventive diplomacy was successfully used in early stages of conflicts related to democratization process in Africa between 1989 and 1993.[60] Even when African conflicts have gone beyond such an early stage measure, Western response would entail providing support for an African conflict resolution initiative. Thus, the United States' policy was to "help" the OAU...develop a creditable capability to plan, coordinate, and supervise efforts in conflict resolution."[61]

Indeed, the U.S. has consistently aired its support for the newly established OAU mechanism for conflict prevention and management. It has pledged both technical and financial assistance to this conflict resolution body. America's financial assistance included the provision of $3.5 million to the OAU in 1994, and an additional $5 million in 1995.[62] The funds were expected to assist in the provision of equipment and communication facilities, and training for observer and peace-keeping missions embarked upon by OAU conflict resolution mechanism. In the final analysis, therefore, the U.S. policy is to bolster Africa's crisis management capacity by increasing financial and technical aid rather than direct military intervention.

The French had also pointed to the direction of providing assistance to Africa's conflict resolution initiative when they initiated a conference in November 1994 at Biarritz, a resort town in South West France, on the formation of an African peacekeeping force. According to the French, such a force would be trained, equipped, and financed by France in conjunction with other European powers and the United States.[63] France's aim was to put squarely on Africa's shoulders the responsibility of keeping the peace in the continent, therefore absolving the West from any entanglement in African conflicts. The French President, Francois Mitterrand, has stated quite clearly that "the time has come for Africans themselves to resolve their conflicts and organize their own security."[64]

The emergence of a new order where Western powers are increasingly removing themselves from the affairs of the continent has an important implication; this is that African states will have greater flexibility in crisis resolution. With the end of the Cold War and the absence of superpower competition in Africa, no longer will African efforts at crisis management be conditioned by the pressures of a bipolar world.

Africa's New Initiatives

More than ever before, African countries have in the post-Cold War period come to appreciate the need to look more inwardly in the resolution of their conflicts. The realization that they must assume greater role in the task of settling conflicts on the continent is mainly determined by the growing reluctance of the West to intervene in intractable African conflicts. As we have seen, the Western powers are now concerned with more pressing domestic and regional problems at home that they seldom wish to be involved in foreign conflicts.

Another important factor has to do with the apparent ineffectiveness of the United Nations in dealing with disputes in the post-Cold War period. Part of the organization's problem is that it is faced with an incredible upsurge in the number of conflicts with which it must address. Some of the places for which UN peacekeeping missions have been established since the end of the Cold War include Angola, Mozambique, Somalia, Rwanda, Western Sahara, El-Salvador, Cambodia, former Yugoslavia, Southern Lebanon, Kashmir, Georgia, Tajikistan, Cuprus, Bosnia, Haiti, and Kuwait. While the post-World War II period up to 1988 saw the establishment of 13 UN peacekeeping operations, the post-Cold War period alone has seen no less.[65]

Apart from the unprecedented increase in the number of conflicts requiring UN attention, deployment of peacekeeping forces in the present age has grown considerably more complex. The mandate of peacekeeping forces in the post-Cold War period has been defined to include

> such elements as civil functions, disarming militia, providing security to the population, rescuing "failed" countries, organizing elections, launching preventive deployment, encouraging peace settlement, providing humanitarian assistance, or security for delivery of humanitarian assistance.[66]

Lacking the necessary logistic capacity and financial wherewithal to mount such an obviously expensive peace operation, it is no surprise that the UN has been unable to cope effectively with many conflicts. Angola and Somalia are clear examples of UN failure.

For the reasons above, African states are increasingly becoming aware of the necessity for African solution to crises within the continent. George Moose noted quite correctly that "there is a strong commitment on the part of African states to assume greater responsibility for conflict prevention and conflict management on the continent".[67]

It was this commitment that gave rise to a number of conflict resolution initiatives. An example is the mediatory role the Intergovernmental Authority on Drought and Development (IGADD) has played in some African conflicts such as the Somali and Sudanese wars. Established in 1986, IGADD is a sub-regional organization with members from seven states in East Africa and the Horn. Originally founded as an economic community to deal with environmental problems, the organization later took on the additional role of conflict resolution. Particularly, IGADD sought to find a peaceful end to the war in Sudan. In May 1994, the mediation committee of the organization sponsored peace talks between the warring factions with a view to ending the protracted war.

Perhaps, ECOMOG, the West African peacekeeping mission in Liberia best demonstrates Africa's conflict resolution initiative. This mission was constituted by member states of the ECOWAS as a result of their concern for the adverse regional effects the escalating conflict in Liberia was causing.[68] At the initiative of Nigeria, a country with considerable international peacekeeping experience,[69] the peacekeeping force consisting of troops from Nigeria, Ghana, Sierra Leone, Gambia, and Guinea, was sent to Liberia in August 1990. EGOMOG was thus established "for the purpose of keeping the peace, restoring law and order and ensuring that [a] cease-fire is respected."[70] Although the force barely achieved its mandate of creating "the necessary conditions for normal life to resume to the benefit of all Liberians,"[71] it has proven a bold attempt at conflict management in Africa. With far-reaching implications for future peacekeeping missions on the continent, it represents the most significant African initiative at conflict resolution in the post-Cold War period.[72]

The brunt of peacekeeping in Africa rightly falls on the shoulders of the OAU as a Pan-African organization. In fact, it has been asserted that the organization "is attempting to transform itself into a security organization—what can be referred to as a `security community.'"[73] True to this assertion, the organization has taken several initiatives, sometimes in conjunction with UN efforts, or with a sub-regional organization like ECOWAS. It has been involved in negotiations to bring peace to conflict-ridden states such as Liberia, Rwanda, and Somalia. It has also taken part in election monitoring in many parts of the continent including the first multiracial election that ushered in democracy to the former apartheid state of South Africa in April 1994.

One of the most important OAU initiatives to date is its current determined efforts to establish a mechanism for conflict prevention, management and resolution. At the June 22, 1992 meeting of the OAU Council of Ministers held in Dakar, Senegal, the organization's Secretary General, Salim Ahmed Salim, tabled proposals for the establishment of a "Mechanism for Conflict Prevention and Conflict Resolution within the organization."[74] The incumbent OAU chairman, the Senegalese president, Abdou Diouf, echoed Salim when he said at the Assembly of Heads of State and government held from June 29 to July 2, that conflict prevention and management of African disputes were OAU priorities.[75] The assembly went on to accept the establishment of the body in principle. At the next OAU summit conference held in Cairo, Egypt, in late June, 1993, the assembly finally approved the resolution on the establishment of the mechanism. Part of the resolution reads:

> The mechanism will have, as a primary objective, the anticipation and prevention of conflicts; in circumstances where conflicts have occurred it will be its responsibility to undertake peace-making and peace-building functions in order to facilitate the resolution of those conflicts. In this respect civilian and military missions of observation and monitoring of limited scope and duration may be mounted and deployed.[76]

A further step was taken toward making the mechanism a reality when on November 18, 1993, OAU foreign ministers, meeting in Addis Ababa, Ethiopia, approved the principles that would guide its establishment. The mechanism was eventually inaugurated at the 30th summit conference of the OAU held in June 1994, at Tunis, Tunisia. At this conference, nine African countries namely: Benin, Chad, Cote d'Ivoire, Egypt, Ethiopia, Mauritius, Nigeria, South Africa, and Tunisia, were appointment to the membership of the body. As a regional initiative for dealing internally with African problems, the Mechanism for Conflict Prevention, Management, and Resolution is still at its infancy. But it is expected that it will facilitate Africa's capability to effectively manage, prevent, and resolve its internal conflicts.

Also, as part of the regional efforts at conflict resolution, African states have begun to explore seriously the question of establishing a peace keeping force that could be deployed in times of crisis. In fact, the establishment of such a force was included in the resolution on the Mechanism for Conflict Prevention, Management, and Resolution adopted by the OAU at its June 1993 summit conference. Western powers, anxious to see the force in place to deal with African conflicts so that their own involvement could be reduced, have thrown their support behind it. As mentioned earlier, it was with France's encouragement that thirty-four African nations met at the November 1994 Biarritz conference to discuss the logistics of the establishment of the force. At a two-day conference held in Cairo, on January 9 and 10, 1995, to discuss the formation of the force, military and political experts from Britain, Canada, France, the United States, and Japan, joined their counterparts from fourteen African states, and representatives from the OAU and the UN.[77] A subsequent week-long meeting of twenty African states held in Harare, Zimbabwe, and attended by Britain, France, and the United States further discussed the establishment of the peacekeeping force.[78] However, progress toward the establishment of the force has been delayed by the familiar questions of logistics, command, and finance. Disagreements have surfaced over the modalities for the creation of the force and its deployment.[79] While some African states are in favor of a standing multinational force, like the African High Command advocated by Kwame Nkrumah in the early 1960s, other states think that such a force is impracticable, given the financial distress of the OAU. The co-hosts of the Harare meeting, Field Marshal Peter Inge, Chief of Defence Staff in Britain, and Mr. Moven Mahachi, Zimbabwe's Defence Minister, opposed a standing force. Instead of a standing force under the control of the OAU, Mahachi suggested that members states of the organization could have forces ready for peacekeeping duties.[80] The issues above will continue to bog down the formation of an African peace keeping force.

It is important to note also the role the new South Africa is likely to play in conflict resolution in the continent. South African leaders have themselves indicated that their country is prepared to be active in this wise. They believe that South Africa's prosperity and security are contingent upon a peaceful, conflict-free Southern Africa in particular, and of a stable continent in general. The country has thus begun to be involved in conflict resolution in the sub-region and in the continent at large. For example, under the auspices of the Southern African Development Community (SADC), Nelson Mandela played an important part in mediating the 1994 crisis in Lesotho which led to the dismantlement of the government by the country's monarch. Also, the prospect of large scale bloodshed in Kinshasa in May, 1997, between supporters of the incumbent president, Mobutu Sese Seko, and rebel leader, Laurent Kabila, who was poised to take the Zairean (now Democratic Republic of Congo) capital, prompted Mandela to initiate series of talks between the two adversaries.[81] But South Africa's involvement in conflicts in the continent has so far been largely restricted to traditional peacekeeping such as mediation. Playing an active role in peacekeeping operations involving deployment of troops is not likely to be forthcoming from Pretoria, at least in the nearest future. Although, Foreign Minister, Alfred Nzo, has stated that South Africa would be prepared to be involved in peacekeeping throughout the continent,[82] there is little indication that this will include troop deployment to keep and monitor peace in a conflict zone. This is most likely due to South Africa's inexperience in international peacekeeping operations. Although, the country is particularly suited for an active role in such peacekeeping operations given its superior military capability, it is likely that for the time being peacekeeping will be limited to mediation.

CONCLUSION

During the Cold War Africa's crisis management record was discouraging. The Cold War played its part in escalating African disputes and diminishing the ability of African states to manage internal conflicts. But the end of the Cold War has significantly altered the landscape of Africa's conflicts and the dynamics of conflict resolution. The Soviet bloc is dead and the West no longer sees Africa as a strategic prize worth coveting. The implication of the emerging unipolar world in which Africa is no longer a pawn in the chessboard of superpower confrontation is that African conflicts will be spared of external manipulation and exploitation. In other words, given the fact that the erstwhile bipolar order had a significantly destabilizing effect on African politics, the removal of East-West antagonism from the international system will considerably reduce foreign powers' escalation of African conflicts.

However, it does not mean that Africa will no longer experience conflicts some of which will lead to major crises. Apart from traditional sources of conflict in Africa such as ethnic nationalism, forces unleased by the end of the Cold War would promote new sources of tension. Democratic pressure, for instance, is one of the new forces likely to lead to conflict in Africa. Continued closed societies and the refusal of many African states to move toward democracy in the face of mounting demand for change pose a great threat to peace in the continent. Another important likely cause of conflict is the downward economic trend in many African states. The inability of these states to build up a viable economy will lead to tensions that may ultimately explode in violent internal crisis.

What is the prospect for crisis management in Africa in the post-Cold War era? An encouraging development is that with the U.N. apparently overworked and consequently ineffective, and the West retracing its steps from the continent, Africans have realized the necessity for some kind of collective security arrangements. The end of the Cold War has really galvanized Africans to begin to search for ways of settling their disputes internally. The question, however, is whether the OAU and other sub-regional organizations are sufficiently prepared and equipped to deal with conflicts. ECOMOG as a test case of Africa's peacekeeping operation has not been terribly successful although it helped to bring back peace to Liberia and to restore democracy to the country. So far, its intervention in Sierra Leone following the May, 1997 coup has not ended the crisis in the country. However, an initiative as that of ECOMOG promises hope for the future.

There is the expectation that in the post-Cold War period, Africa will, for the most part, manage its own conflicts. But in doing this, given the apparent lack of logistics and other capabilities by Africa's regional organizations especially the OAU, there is bound to be calls for Western support, particularly in terms of personnel, training, equipment, and finance. Even there will still be cases when international pressure for intervention will compel outside powers to intervene in African conflicts. In such a case, African states should set the parameters for conflict resolution. In other words, the sole responsibility for resolving conflicts in the continent rests with Africans. International response can only be in form of provision of necessary support and assistance to African initiatives. Incidentally, this is precisely the role the Western powers are willing to play in the resolution of African conflicts.

NOTES

1. Edmond Keller, "Towards a New African Order? Presidential Address to the 1992 Annual Meeting of the African Studies Association," *African Studies Review*, 36 (2), Sept. 1993, 1.
2. Quoted in the statement made by George Moose before the Subcommittee on Africa of the House Foreign Affairs Committee in Washington DC., on June 8, 1994. See George E. Moose, "U.S. Commitment to Conflict Resolution in Africa," *U.S. Department of State Dispatch*," 5 (25), June 20, 1994, 412.
3. Rwanda represents a recent massive influx of refugees into neighboring states. An estimated 2 million people were said

to have fled the country during the 1994 ethnic carnage. See *Philadelphia Inquirer*, May 15, 1994.

4. See OAU Charter, Article III (3). Also, a resolution on border dispute was adopted by the Conference of Heads of States in Cairo in July 1964. Article II of the resolution stipulates that "the borders of African states on the day of independence constitute a tangible reality."

5. See OAU Charter, Article II (d). Similar declaration is also expressed in Article III (6).

6. Article XIX of the OAU Charter. This was further reinforced by an October 26, 1965 Assembly of Heads of State and Government's Declaration on Subversive Activities. This declaration provides that "all difference between two or more member-States should be settled by bilateral or multilateral consultations, on the basis of a protocol of mediation, conciliation and arbitration as laid down in the OAU Charter."

7. For a study of the role of the OAU in the war, see Adebayo Oyebade, "The Organization of African Unity and the Nigerian Civil War, 1967-1970: A Case Study in Mediatory Diplomacy," *M.A.* thesis, University of Ife, 1985.

8. See OAU Resolution AHG/RES 102, 103 (XVIII), signed on November 28, 1981, in Nairobi, Kenya.

9. *ibid.*

10. See R. Kupolati, "The Nigerian Contingent in the Organization of African Unity Peace-Keeping Operation in Chad," in M.A. Vogt and E.E. Ekoko, (eds.), *Nigeria in International Peace-Keeping, 1960-1992*, (Lagos: Malthouse Press Ltd., 1993), 145.

11. See *ibid.*, 146.

12. RES/ST/Ctte/Chad/Res. 1, (111) of the Standing Committee on Chad, Feb. 10-11, 1982, Nairobi, Kenya.

13. For more on OAU's role in the Chadian crisis, see Amadu Sesay, "The limits of Peace-Keeping by a Regional Organization: The OAU Peace-Keeping Force in Chad," *Conflict Quarterly*, xi (1) Winter, 1991, 7-26. See also, Vogt and Ekoko, (eds.), *Nigeria in International Peace-Keeping*, 129-142, and 143-155.

14. F.S. Northedge and M.D. Donelan, *International Disputes: The Political Aspect*, (London: Europa Publications, 1971), 272-273.

15. In the parliamentary election, the MPLA won 53.7 percent of the total votes and 129 of the 220 legislative seats while UNITA won 34.1 percent and 70 seats. The presidential election also saw the MPLA candidate, President dos Santos, victorious with 49.57 percent of the votes to Savimbi's 40.07

percent. See *SIPRI Yearbook 1993: World Armaments and Disarmament,* (Oxford: University Press, 1993), 114-115.

16. Quoted in *ibid.* For recent studies on renewed fighting in Angola, see Abiodun Alao, "Angola's Second Civil War," in Robert Hall, (ed.), *The World in Conflict 1994/95,* (London: Jane's Information Group, 1995), 95-97; and Anthony W. Pereira, "The Neglected Tragedy: The Return to War in Angola, 1992-3," *The Journal of Modern African Studies,* 32 (1), 1994, 1-28.

17. Africa Report, 40 (2), Mach-April, 1995, 7.

18. For a study of RENAMO, see Alex Vines, RENAMO: *From Terrorism to Democracy in Mozambique,* (London: James Currey Publishers, 1995).

19. Tom Carver, "Starvation Kills Appetite for War," *New Statement & Society,* Oct. 2, 1992, 19.

20. *The Economist,* March 26, 1994, 45.

21. See *Facts on File,* Nov. 24, 1994, 886.

22. For a useful insight into the end of the Mozambican war, see Jim Wurst, "Mozambique Disarms," *The Bulletin of the Atomic Scientists,* Sept/Oct. 1994, 36-39,

23. By a UN estimate, the war had by the end of 1994 claimed more than 150,000 people, and about half the country's population was already living as refugees either inside the country, or in neighboring states. See *Philadelphia Inquirer,* Dec. 22, 1994.

24. For the complete agreement, see John Mackinlay and Abiodun Alao, *Liberia 1994: ECOMOG and UNOMIL Response to a Complex Emergency,* (Tokyo: United Nations University Press, 1995). 53-64.

25. The Cotonou Agreement is discussed in some details in *ibid.* Pages 22-45 particularly discuss the reasons for the failure of the agreement.

26. *African New Weekly,* Jan. 20, 1995.

27. *New York Times,* March 20, 1995.

28. *Africa Confidential,* March 28, 1997, 4.

29. For a detailed study of the RUF, see Paul Richards, *Fighting for the Rain Forest: War, Youth and Resources in Sierra Leone,* (Portsmouth: Heinemann, 1996). See also *New York Times,* Feb. 17, 1995, and *The Economist,* Jan. 14, 1995, 40.

30. *New York Times,* May 30, 1997.

31. *Africa Report,* March-April, 1995, 5-6.

32. *ibid.,* 5.

33. *ibid.*

34. *UN Chronicle*, 31 (4), Dec. 1994, 8.

35. See *National Catholic Reporter*, July 1, 1994, 28.

36. In rejecting a broad-based amnesty for the perpetrators of the Rwandan carnage as an argument for national reconciliation, the country's Prime Minister, Faustin Twagimarungu, argued that such would only encourage the culture of impunity in Rwanda. The Prime Minister called for accountability as a form of deterrence. See "Rwanda: Accountability for War Crimes and Genocide," (Washington, D.C.: United States Institute of Peace, 1995), 15.

37. See UN Security Council Resolution 955.

38. The worst of these clashes occurred in 1965, 1969, 1972, 1988, and 1991. See "Rwanda: Accountability for War Crimes," 20.

39. *ibid.*

40. *ibid.*

41. *African News Weekly*, April 14, 1995.

42. Alan Zarembo, "Standing on the Brink, *Africa Report*, 40 (2), March-April, 1995, 26. The deteriorating state of affairs is also provided in *New York Times*, March 25, April 2, 4, and 7, 1995.

43. See *Newsweek*, April 10, 1995, 32-39.

44. Geopolitically, Sudan has been variously situated in the Middle East, sub-Saharan Africa, Central Africa, and the Horn of Africa. This chapter will adopt the last affiliation.

45. For more on the UN mission in Somalia, see Ramesh Thakur, "From Peacekeeping to Peace Enforcement: the UN Operation in Somalia," *The Journal of Modern African Studies*, 32 (3), 1994, 387-410.

46. A brief analysis of the historical background to the Sudanese war is provided in Mohamed Abbas Mohamedali, "Independent Africa and Ethno-Regional Conflicts: The Case of Sudan," *UFAHAMU: Journal of the African Activist Association*, 22 (1&2), Winter/Spring, 1994, 108-118; and Kenneth Okeny, "Historical Basis of Southern Sudan's Demand for Self-Determination," in *ibid.*

47. For various essays on prospects for peace, see United States Institute of Peace, *Sudan: The Forgotten Tragedy, Essays by Francis M. Deng, Kamal Osman Salih, Ali Abdalla Abbas, Peter Nyot Kok, Taisier Mohamed Ahmed Ali, and Bona Malwal,* (Washington, D.C.,: U.S. Institute of Peace, 1994).

48. See for a discussion of the importance of religious national-
ism in the post-Cold War world, Mark Juergensmeyer, *The New Cold War: Religious Nationalism in Confronting the Secular State*, (Berkeley: University of California Press, 1993); and J ames Wyllie, "Islamic Revivalism" in Hall, (ed.), *The World in Conflict,* 11-15.

49. Nigeria is an example of a state where there has been on-and-
off, and most often, violent clashes between Christians and Muslims. The most serious of these were the incessant *Maitatsine* riots between 1980 and 1985 when fundamentalist Muslim elements in northern Nigeria killed many Christians and burnt down churches. For discussions on the *Maitatsine* movement and its uprising in northern Nigeria, see the fol lowing: Hamman-Tukur Saad, "Urban Blight and Religious Uprising in Northern Nigeria," *Habitat-International,* 12 (2), 1988, 111-128; and Niels Kastfelt, "Rumours of Maitatsine: A Note on Political Culture in Northern Nigeria," *African Affairs,* 88 (350), Jan. 1989, 83-90.

50. According to a secret Algerian Army report, about 35,000 people were killed in fighting between government troops a nd Islamists in the first ten months of 1994. See *African News Weekly,* Jan. 10, 1995.

51. *Africa Report,* 40, (2), March-April, 1995, 11. See also *New York Times,* March 21, and 26, 1995.

52. The *Jihad* was responsible for the assassination of the former Egyptian president, Anwar Sadat in 1981. The attack on Prime Minister Sedki in November 1993 was also the work of the militants of this group. See Wyllie, "Islamic Revivalism," 12.

53. *ibid.*

54. *ibid.*

55. The pattern of Islamic groups' killings has demonstrated the wide range of their target. In Algeria, teenage school girls have been reported killed because they did not wear veils. See Wyllie, "Islamic Revivalism," 12. More than 30,000 people have reportedly been killed in the Algerian conflict since it began in 1992 after the annulment of the election that would have pronounced the FIS victorious. See *Africa Report,* 40, (2), March-April, 1995, 11.

56. See *Facts on File,* June 9, 1994, 419, for a brief report of the election.

57. The American experience in Somalia has persuaded some Congressional members to argue for US non-involvement in

the so-called Third World. See *New York Times*, March 5, 1995.

58. See *Washington Post*, Aug. 22, 1994. The large scale massacre of the Rwandan fracticidal warfare had prompted France to create a so-called "safe zone" in southwestern Rwanda in order to protect thousands of refugees and prevent further slaughter.

59. Moose. "U.S. Commitment to Conflict Resolution in Africa," 412.

60. See Herman Cohen, "Africa's Forgotten Successes," *Foreign Service Journal*, Oct. 1993, 23.

61. Moose, "U.S. Commitment to Conflict Resolution in Africa," 412.

62. *ibid.* See also "Address to the Zimbabwe Staff College, Harare, Zimbabwe, October 22, 1994," by U.S. Deputy Secretary Talbott, *U.S. Department of State Dispatch*, 5 (45), Nov. 7, 1994, 739.

63. *Washington Post*, Nov. 10, 1994.

64. *ibid.*

65. See Robert B. Oakley, Indar Jit Rikhye, and Kenneth M. Jensen, (eds.), "The Professionalization of Peacekeeping: A Study Group Report," (Washington, D.C.: United States Institute of Peace, 1993), 5-6.

66. *ibid.*, 8.

67. Quoted from the opening statement by Assistant Secretary George Moose, at a press briefing in Washington, DC, Oct. 31, 1994. See the full statement in *U.S. Department of State Dispatch*, 5 (45), November 7, 1994.

68. For details on this, see Osisioma B.C. Nwolise, "The Internationalisation of the Liberian Crisis and its Effects on West Africa," in Margaret A. Vogt, (ed.), *The Liberian Crisis and ECOMOG: A Bold Attempt at Regional Peace Keeping*, (Lagos: Gabumo Publishing Co. Ltd., 1992), 55-72.

69. See Vogt and Ekoko, (eds.), *Nigeria in International Peace-Keeping*.

70. Final Communiqué of the First Session of ECOWAS Standing Mediation Committee, held in Banjul, Gambia, August 6-7, 1990.

71. *ibid.*

72. A comprehensive discussion of ECOMOG is provided in Vogt, (ed.), *The Liberian Crisis and ECOMOG*. See also John Inegbedion, "The ECOWAS Intervention in Liberia: Toward

Regional Conflict Management in Post-Cold War Africa?" (Research paper for the Academic Committee on the United Nations System and the American Society of International Law Summer Workshop on International Organizations, Dartmouth College, Hanover, New Hampshire, July 1922.

73. Richard S. Mukisa, "Toward a Peaceful Resolution of Africa's Colonial Boundaries," *Africa Today*, 44, (1), Jan-March, 1977, 11.

74. See Organization of African Unity, *Resolving Conflicts in Africa: Proposals for Action*, (Addis Ababa: OAU Press and In formation Series (I), 1992).

75. "OAU: Dakar Summit Meeting," *Keesing's Record of World Events*, 38, (7-8), 1992, 38992.

76. AHG/Decl. 3, (XXXIX), Rev. 1, "Declaration of the Assembly of Heads of State and Government on the Establishment Within the OAU of a Mechanism for Conflict Prevention, Management, and Resolution," 29th Ordinary Session of the Assembly of Heads of State and Government, June 28-30, 1993, Cairo.

77. *Africa Research Bulletin*, Jan. 1st-31st, 1995, 11707. The participating African countries were: Egypt, Botswana, Burkina Faso, the Central African Republic, Nigeria, Senegal, South Africa, Tanzania, Togo, Tunisia, Ethiopia, Kenya, Mali, and Zimbabwe.

78. *ibid.*

79. See for example, the report on the Biarritz conference in *Washington Post*, Nov. 10, 1994. The issues and problems involved in the creation of a pan-African defense force are discussed in S.O. Agbi, *The OAU and African Diplomacy, 1963-1979*, (Ibadan: Impact Publishers, 1986), 114-131.

80. *Africa Research Bulletin*, Jan. 1st-31st, 1995, 11707.

81. For a report on one of the talks, see *The Weekly Review*, May 9, 1997, 27-28.

82. See Helmoed-Romer Heitman, "New South African Defence Force Takes Shape," in Hall, (ed.), *The World In Conflict*, 89.

CHAPTER 8

BEYOND THE COLD WAR:
PAN-EUROPEANISM AND THE CHALLENGE
OF AFRICAN UNITY

Ayele Bekerie

INTRODUCTION

What started as the political hurricane of 1989 ultimately became a global shake up. The formal removal of the ideological pretenses of the Eastern and Western European blocs resulted in the dismantlement of the Berlin Wall and the redrawing of spheres of influences with new regions emerging in the world scene. In Africa, one of the post-Cold War changes is the elimination of the formal and legal system of apartheid in South Africa.

Indeed, the end of the Cold War has brought about the birth of a new world, one which is quickly taking shape. The East-West ideological rivalry that reduced the African people into that proverbial grass on which the Cold War elephants carried out their mock fights has ended. The relevant question to ask then is this: will the emerging new world be shaped to further undermine Africa's efforts at finding solutions relevant to its conditions and realities? Given such post-Cold War development as pan-European unity, Africa may be in danger of being further marginalized in the new global configuration. While Europeans are fervently struggling to resolve their ideological differences and are campaigning

for a United Europe, Africans are confronted with contradictions from within and from without that seem to grow
deeper and deeper making their resolution more complex
and more difficult. It is the contention of this chapter that
the centerpiece of African security in the post-Cold War
world is pan-African unity. The aim of the chapter is to examine the prospect for the unity of the continent in the face
of the consolidation of pan-Europeanism.

THE PROCESS OF EUROPEAN UNITY

It is useful, first, to examine the process of Europe's march
to economic and political unity. This process is, perhaps, the
most talked about and debated idea and praxis in contemporary European politics. West Europeans, that is, the twelve-
member European Economic community (EEC) are care-
fully defining the ground rules for the inevitable economic
union which was originally projected to have been a reality
by 1992. This Pan-European movement has continually been
orchestrated and backed by a wide range of European and
American intellectuals and political leaders. Even before the
disintegration of the Soviet Union, former Soviet leader,
Mikhail Gorbachev had spoken of "our common European
home."[1] This feeling was aptly summarized by Zbiginew
Brezinski, a former U.S. National Security Adviser. Brezinski
called for the establishment of:

> a policy founded upon the grand concept of a
> trans-European commonwealth with the Eu-
> ropean Community at its core, but embracing
> Central Europe and being open also to even-
> tual association with the Soviet Union.[2]

A number of steps have been taken to promote Pan-European unity. The most significant of these is the consolidation and expansion of Pan-European institutions. Some of
the institutions being used to promote the collective economic, political, cultural, and social interests of Europe are
the EEC, the European Parliament, the 35-member Helsinki
Conference on European Security and Cooperation, the European Free Trade Association of the Scandinavian Countries, the European Space Agency (which holds half the

world's commercial satellite business), and North Atlantic Treaty Organization (NATO). Perhaps, the most central Pan-European institution at this junction of European history is the EEC. It is actively guiding the democratization process in Central Europe and the transition to market economy there.[3] The transition in Central Europe from state economy and one-party political system to market economy and multiparty system is aided by this institution. For instance, it allocated $900 million to Poland and Hungary to assist them in the pursuit of free-market economy. Also, a second Marshall Plan is being put together, or in the process of being implemented by the EEC, the United States, and Europe, to aid Central Europe and, to some extent, the former USSR. Such measures have not only helped Central Europe in the march towards a market economy, but also have aided the region in the adoption of multiparty system.

The role of the United States in the process of Pan-European Unity is quite substantial. U.S. political leaders have already held several summits with European leaders— bilaterally or regionally. The former U.S. Secretary of State, James Baker, made trips to Western and Central Europe and the former USSR more times than his immediate predecessors. According to Baker, the United States and Canada share Europe's neighborhood.[4] European leaders have also flocked to Washington in search of advice and assistance. The new leaders in Central Europe, particularly in Poland and Czechoslovakia, have even given speeches to members of Congress. The United States foreign aid policy has been so restructured that a significant portion of available assistance is allocated to Central Europe to the detriment of other regions, such as Africa. For instance, even the number of Peace Corps volunteers working in Africa has been slashed in order to meet the increasing demand from Central Europe. In short, the changes in Central Europe appears to generate more political, financial, and economic backings from the United States than similar changes in Namibia, Angola, and Mozambique. It is sufficient to compare the $500,000 United States aid to Namibia to the $300 million to Poland and Hungary in fiscal year 1990.[5] As Brezinski concurs, "American support for European integration [is] consistent with the fostering of even more intimate trans-Atlantic ties."[6]

Brezinski, indeed, associates the security of the new Europe with a firm United States-Europe linkage.

THE END OF THE COLD WAR AND PROSPECTS FOR PAN-AFRICANISM

Undoubtedly, the end of the Cold War is good news for Africa. The continent's visions, ideals, feelings, political aspirations, economic objectives and socio-cultural growth have, to a large extent, ceased to be secondary to East/West ideological discourse. Political leaders like Jonas Savimbi, Mengistu Haile-Mariam, and Siad Barre fizzled away with the end of the Cold War. The developments that rocked several African countries from Ethiopia to South Africa, from Cote d'Ivoire to Mozambique clearly indicate the end of the era of Cold War politics. In Ethiopia, as an example, Mengistu could not count anymore on the Soviets to back his repressive regime, hence his unceremonious removal from power in 1991.

The strengthening of the gains of the end of the Cold War is, perhaps, the greatest challenge facing Africa. It seems that the way for Africa to stay in touch with history's rapidly moving tide lies in the attainment of lasting unity and peace. It is important to accelerate the pace of regional cooperation, and only this can guarantee continental security. This contention was once echoed in an editorial:

> Nelson Mandela, a universal symbol of freedom, has also exposed a major challenge for Africans on the continent and abroad. The world's nations are clustering themselves around political ideologies, religious, ethnic groups, and geographical locations....Africans throughout the world must recognize that their place has not been reserved in any of these other alliances. To move forward in the next century—and eventually cooperate meaningfully with other groups—Africans must first coalesce with each other. The time is here when Africans facing environmental, development and health crisis in both Africa and abroad must

pull their resources, skills and talents for their
very survival.[7]

Yet in Africa, there is no concrete movement for pan-Africanism to match the drive for European unity. Although, pan-Africanism is a concept with a long history dating back to Marcus Garvey, W.E.B. DuBois, George Padmore, and Kwame Nkrumah, it has remained a mere intellectual exercise. To guarantee Africa's security in the emerging new world order, the continent needs to transform the intellectual idea of Pan-Africanism to political, economic and military reality. African leaders, like their counterparts in Europe, must vigorously pursue the unity of the continent in all areas, especially economic and political. The end of the Cold War and the open campaign for Pan-European Unity should find its challenge in African open campaign for Pan-African Unity.

It must be recognized, however, that some of the changes occurring in many parts of Africa augur well for pan-Africanism. For instance, the democratization movement in Africa is a good ingredient for the attainment of pan-African unity. The democratic movement that engulfed Central Europe has its equivalence in Africa, particularly in Southern Africa. The April 1994 election that made Nelson Mandela the first democratically elected president of the former apartheid state ushered a new dawn and hope for Africa as a whole. While South Africa is a good example of where fundamental political change has occurred, what took place in Namibia is as revolutionary and remarkable as the events in East German or Czechoslovakia. Namibia is implementing one of the most democratic constitutions in Africa, featuring an independent judiciary, guarantees for freedom of speech and the press, a bill of human rights, and legally enforceable obligation to uplift disadvantaged sections of the population. Namibia and South Africa have thus laid down foundations that may encourage other African states to take the democratic path.

South Africa could also lead the way to the much needed economic integration in Africa. South Africa has a highly sophisticated infrastructure capable of supporting a major industrial economy. The South African economy can economically unite the whole continent of Africa in the interest of African people. If black South Africans gain real economic power in terms of substantial control over the means of production and distribution then they would be poised to influence the economic well being of the continent. Thus the emergence of South Africa as a central element in the economic dynamics of Africa may chart new and progressive course for the continent in terms of economic unity.[8]

There is also an indication that Africans have begun to look more inwardly to manage their conflicts rather than relying exclusively on external intervention. Undoubtedly, the most significant indication of this is the successful deployment of a regional peace-keeping force, (ECOMOG), to Liberia, in August of 1991. Thanks to ECOMOG for its persistent and determined intervention in Liberia's civil war, a lasting peace is taking hold in that war ravaged nation. The warring factions have signed peace agreements which are being implemented with the supervision of ECOMOG, the United Nations, and the Organization of African Unity. In fact, the positive role of ECOMOG in Liberia encouraged the Economic Community of West African States (ECOWAS) to sign a treaty in July 1993 in Cotonou, Benin, which provides for the safeguard of regional security, peace, and stability. Despite its shortcomings, ECOMOG remains a rudiment of regional cooperation in conflict resolution. As Adama Gaye eloquently puts it:

> the ECOWAS peace-keeping effort, long ignored, sometimes criticized and frequently considered illusory, could in fact provide the basis for an authentically African doctrine of peace.[9]

However, this West African initiative needs to be developed on a larger scale involving the whole continent. It is the responsibility of the OAU and its members to find ways to expand the ECOMOG model throughout Africa. For instance, a serious African conflict resolution initiative should be set in motion to address such persistent conflict areas as the Horn. Indeed, no region is in more turmoil, particularly in terms of tragic wars and large number of population dislocation, than the Horn. Thousands of people have lost their lives to wars in Ethiopia, Somalia and the Sudan. At this juncture, millions of people are on the verge of death from starvation in the northern part of Ethiopia. The political, economic, and social upheavals of the region are coming to a climax, but the end result is yet to be determined. The military authoritarian rulers of these countries have exhausted all their political cards and an OAU sustained effort must be immediately set in motion. Such efforts must also be applied to the other numerous conflict areas in Africa.

CONCLUSION

With the end of the Cold War era, there was the expectation in some circles that enormous amounts of human energy would be freed from the grip of the ideological struggle. Some even speculated about the notion of peace dividends. True, despite the new conflicts and tensions accompanying nationalism, democratization, and the demand for economic prosperity in many parts of the world, the end of the Cold War has ushered in new political possibilities. One of the new challenges is the drive towards pan-Europeanism.

At stake in the new global order is African security. Although NATO has transformed itself into a maker of peace even beyond the boundaries of Western Europe, its military projection remains a clear threat to the independence and security of countries in Asia and Africa. Since almost all the former colonial powers of Africa are members of NATO,[10] it becomes difficult for African countries to implement security policies contrary to the neo-colonial interests of the former colonial powers. The attempted coup in the Comoros and the swift intervention of France to crush it is a clear indication of the undisputable presence of France, both politically and economically, in the so-called Francophone Africa. If Africa is to consolidate the gains accompanying the end of the Cold War, the answer, it seems, lies in a Pan-African security system that would encompass among other features, economic integration and cooperation, and a collective conflict resolution apparatus.

NOTES

1. See *The Atlanta Journal and Constitution,* March 18, 1990, H1 and H4.
2. Zbiginew Brezinski, "For Eastern Europe: A $25 Billion Aid Package," *New York Times,* March 7, 1990, A-15.
3. *New York Times,* Dec. 10, 1989, 16.
4. *ibid.,* Dec. 13, 1989, 10.
5. *Washington Post,* March 29, 1990, A-21.
6. *New York Times,* March 7, 1990, A-15.
7. See *Michigan Chronicle,* Feb. 24, 1990, 6-A.
8. For the expression of such an opinion, see Francis A. Kornegay, "Africa in the New World Order," *Africa Report,* 38 (1), Jan/Feb. 1993, 16.
9. Quoted in *West Africa,* 9-15 Oct. 1995, 1559-1560.
10. France decided to rejoin the NATO military structure after 30 years of independent military strategy. See *New York Times,* Dec. 6, 1995. A1.

Chapter 9

CONCLUSION:
A SHORT PEEP INTO A LONG FUTURE

Adebayo Oyebade and Abiodun Alao

INTRODUCTION

For most part of the last three decades, Africa remained largely in the footnotes of global security considerations. On the few occasions that it strayed into the main text, it was either to discuss the super-power connection or to draw global attention to "human suffering" born out of on-going wars. Of course, there were countries in some geographical regions that occasionally made inroads into global headlines such as Angola, on account of its protracted civil war; South Africa because of its racial problem; and the Horn of Africa, given the enormity of the conflict there. However, the circumstantial eruption of attention in these cases did not translate into the placement of Africa into the force of global security calculations. For most of the years following the independence of African states, global security attention was focused on areas like the Middle East, Europe, Latin America, and to a much lesser extent, Asia. The "relegation" of Africa in this regard has resulted in a number of consequences, one of which is that early studies on African security centered almost exclusively on the impact of the then prevailing Cold War on the continent. It is true that in this process the inherited constraints brought about by colonialism are often discussed. Yet, the larger political, economic, and social policies which African countries pursued immediately after their independence, and which to a large extent underlined the nature of their security concerns, were not placed under any wider global or even continental framework. Inferences and conclusions were only drawn from conflict case studies. Thus, where platitudinous UN/OAU resolutions were not used to seek "solutions" to African security problems, cosmetic explanations were advanced to rationalize most of the conflicts as Cold War extensions.

But the end of the Cold War has resulted in the need to reconsider African, and, indeed, global security. In a way, the fundamental changes which the end of the Cold War brought to the study of security show the inadequacy of global analysis of security in the last three or four decades. A cursory look at global security analysis during the Cold War period would reflect a dependence on a monocausal explanation, the ideological rivalry between the East and West. The Cold War mentality particularly pervaded African security thinking and analysis. But with the unexpected collapse of the Soviet Union and the end of the Cold War, most of the studies that had based their analysis on, and had woven projections and calculations almost exclusively around Cold War consideration suddenly realized the ephemeral nature of this operational framework. This has now resulted in global and regional searches for more enduring tools of explanation. In short, what the current reconsideration of security reflects is that while a global phenomenon as profound as the Cold War may offer some background upon which to make analysis and offer projections, no single explanation should be inflated as to become the only tool to analyze all global security issues. This concluding chapter will serve a triple purpose. First, it will overview African security perception prior to the end of the Cold War. Second, it will examine the impact of the passing of this historical epoch in African security analysis. Lastly, the chapter will discuss the issues that will likely predominate, and dictate the terms of African security in the future.

AFRICAN SECURITY DURING THE "OLD ORDER:" AN OVERVIEW

Africa's perception of security during the Cold War can only be appreciated against the background of the historical evolution of the continent and the global order prevailing at the time. The historical evolution owes a lot to the colonial experience that preceded the entrance of African states into global politics. The limitations colonialism imposed on post-independent Africa are now so well documented that it suffices here to only summarize the relevant components. Inherent in colonialism were the legacies which sowed the seeds of how Africa was to become relevant to international security questions. Economically, the basically exploitative nature of colonialism left at least three direct consequences for African security. First, it developed trading links with countries in Western Europe to the detriment of intra-African economic cooperation. This deprived African countries of economic and social ties with one another, a situation that was to increase the propensity for inter-state tension after their independence. Second, colonialism made African states, after their independence, highly vulnerable to manipulation by their former colonial masters. Interference and domination which they possibly would have rejected were accepted because of the leverage the erstwhile colonial masters had and still have over their economies. Third, as a result of the economic structure bequeathed to post colonial Africa, the ability of African states to maneuver in matters of their defense and security became severely curtailed. What to purchase and where to purchase became matters to be decided in European capitals.

Politically, colonialism also introduced a number of problems. A major one in this regard was the creation of a neo-colonial elite class which took over in most of the new states immediately after independence. The activities of these "inheritance elites" had quite profound effects. First, they took particular pleasure in perpetuating the dependence already inherited from colonialism. Possibly because of their inability to grasp the intricacies of their new offices, or because of personal political and economic gains, most of the emergent leaders became more committed to perpetrating themselves in office than to advancing the interests of their new nations. The colonial links they pursued further entangled their countries' economies in an unequal partnership with the former colonial overlord.

Another problem, the creation of artificial boundaries, remains one of the most controversial legacies of colonialism, and one which also left lasting effects on African security. In practical terms, the haphazard demarcation of African boundaries without regard for ethnic or religious differences created two inter-twined problems. First, it resulted in inter-group tensions within the state which, in some cases, gave rise to secession attempts by groups uncomfortable under the prevailing state structure. Second, it created a number of disputes between African states as regards their boundaries with their neighbors. These two problems littered African security throughout the Cold War period, with renewed versions of them transcending into the post-Cold War period.

The global political arena at the time Africa made its entrance into the international scene was not a particularly harmonious one. The preceding decade saw the Cold War just beginning, and for the next four decades, the heat, tension, and fluctuating politics of this ideological conflict were to determine the context and content of security and warfare in the world. For Africa, the end of World War II did not only occasion the emergence of two new "super-powers" and the subsequent introduction of ideological rivalry between these two groups, it also resulted in the reduction of the strength and relevance of the colonial powers that had, thanks to colonialism, dominated African affairs before the advent of the war. A direct consequence of this which is often ignored is that the emergence of these super-powers increased the number of forces African countries had to contend with in their political and economic considerations. By virtue of their colonial inheritance, the trade and economic contacts of African countries had been with their erstwhile colonial masters. But with the emergence of the Cold War and the subsequent polarization of the world into two camps, African countries had to start establishing some form of links with either or both of the new super powers. The difficulties of this could be much more appreciated, given the fact that these emergent super powers were countries with which Africa had no direct historical relationship during the colonial period. Given the fact that most of the issues that were to determine the major security questions in the world occurred before Africa's emergence on the world stage, the continent's relevance to global security became severely limited.

END OF THE COLD WAR: IMPLICATIONS FOR AFRICAN SECURITY

The concentration of global attention on the impact of the Cold War on Europe has obscured the arguable point that the changes introduced by the end of that era had been present in Africa well before *Perestroika* and *Glasnost* became the propelling Soviet ideology of reform. By the early 1980s, the Cold War was already on its way out in the continent. A number of developments seem to reflect this. First, some of the states that had hitherto shunned the path of "free-economy" had begun to reconsider this stand. Examples of this include Mozambique, and to an extent, Ethiopia. Second, popular demands for democracy had begun, either in the form of opposition to human rights violations, or outright attempt to de-throne "sit-tight" leaders. Thus, all that the changes in Eastern Europe did was to further fuel reform momentum in Africa, and to put an existing phenomenon under the dominant Cold War explanation that all global security issues of the period were adjusted to fit.

A basic point that should be noted about the Cold War rivalry is that throughout its duration, nowhere in Africa was it a cause of conflict per-se. African conflicts have always had their own peculiar causes, independent of Cold War politics. Thus, all that the Cold War did was to exacerbate existing conflicts in the continent. This was especially true in those regions where the Cold War belligerent had specific strategic and ideological interests like in the Horn, and in southern Africa.

The implication of the end of the Cold War for African security has expectedly, been profound.[1] While the Cold War has created new demands, it has equally brought about new challenges in conflict resolution. In what appears to be rather surprising, the end of the Cold War has not translated into a reduction of local conflicts in the continent. It has, on the contrary, exacerbated them. At the end of the Cold War, there

195

were still on-going conflicts in Angola, Burundi, Somalia, and Sudan. The Liberian civil war started just about the time the Cold War was ending. Rwanda, too, soon went up in flames, while, more recently, the civil war in Sierra-Leone has come to the fore of global attention, resulting in the dispatch of a United Nations mediatory team in February 1995. Other countries like Ghana, Mauritania, Senegal, Zaire, Kenya, Nigeria, Cameroon, South Africa and Mozambique, either have internal strife or are high risk countries of conflict.

Some of the issues made more profound by the end of the Cold War include: the emergence of "people's power," courtesy of the democratization movement in the continent; wide ranging concern for the continent's economic plight; diminished emphasis on the military as an instrument of political power; new attention on environmental issues; renewed concern for ethnic differences; and the demand for new conflict management procedures. What all these show is that while many of Africa's long-standing security problems still remain, the end of the Cold War also brought dividends with challenges. For example, the upsurge in the clamor for democracy on the continent means that the process of taking security-related decisions would now have to undergo necessary debate in appropriate quarters. Unlike in the past when security related decisions were taken by a selected group of privileged individuals, the parliament, the media, labor movements, and other recognized pressure groups would now affect decision-making. The extent to which these groups are ready for this new role is yet to be seen. The widening of the scope of the security debate apart, the new dawn that could come from the democratization of African politics is expected to produce other dividends. They include an end to such things as military rule, massive acquisition of weapons for internal suppression, violation of human rights, and suppression of ethnic minorities within nations.

The need to expand the concept of security beyond the guarantee of the territorial integrity has equally become obvious. What constitutes the security of a state or a region, is now seen as involving a myriad of internal factors far beyond the narrow confines of external aggression. The economic component of security is, for developing countries, perhaps, the most important. With virtually all the countries on the continent pursuing some form of imposed economic adjustment policies, and with a significant percentage of the population living below the poverty line, the role that economy could play in the post-Cold War era appears obvious, more so when civil protest against the conditions imposed by the IMF and the World Bank to adjust African economic problems have created internal security problems. Political and economic problems apart, ultra nationalism, political fragmentation, religious fundamentalism and ethnic cleavages are also gathering momentum in the continent.

On another global consideration, it seems clear that the legacies the end of the Cold War brought to the Western world have made African problems of remote concern to Europe and the United States. This position was well articulated by *Le Monde*:

> ...our priorities are elsewhere in Europe. At a time when our brothers on the other side of the iron curtain...desperately need us, why continue favouring African regimes...why not spend elsewhere the fund we spend there in vain.[2]

The expression of the feeling by the West that it has limited roles to play in post-Cold War Africa has, in fact, already begun to manifest itself. The United States has reduced drastically its aid package to Africa. America's economic assistance to Africa between 1960 and 1980, the height of the Cold War, was $6 billion.[3] Since the New World Order no longer justifies such assistance, America's aid to the continent has gone down considerably. Also, France, which for decades propped up the local currencies of its former colonies, has signaled its intention to withdraw assistance. The British Overseas Development Administration annual report for 1994 equally shows a drastic drop in bilateral aid for countries in Africa by £60 million from the previous year.[4]

Africans themselves do not necessarily see the withdrawal of the West from the continent as negative. As a matter of fact, it is largely viewed as a blessing in disguise. This perception is aptly put by Nobel laureate, Wole Soyinka:

> The 'Satanic Kingdom' of the West and the 'Evil
> Empire' of the East are locked in a seemingly
> unbreakable embrace...The honeymoon is be-
> ing consummated before the eyes of the world
> [and] we must come to realize we no longer
> exist for them. I, for one, do not regret this.
> On the contrary, I consider this the greatest
> development incentive that ever came our way
> since the end of slavery.[5]

True, the Western powers' waning interest in Africa has,
among other things, resulted in the willingness of Africans
to take more interest in the affairs of the continent. While
these may not have yet resulted in the articulation and a
sustained pursuance of any coherent policy, some directions
have been charted. For instance, African initiative at conflict
resolution is encouraging.

The end of the Cold War has also coincided with another major development with enormous security undertones
in Africa. This is the attainment of majority rule in South
Africa. For more than three decades, the apartheid policy
which the white minority government in South Africa used
to perpetrate itself in power brought enormous security implications for that country and beyond. Inside the country,
armed revolutionary wings emerged with the assistance of
neighboring countries to fight for majority rule. In retaliation, the South African government created an effective military force to suppress the activities of the liberation movements and to inflict direct and indirect damages on the neighboring states. The struggle for and against the preservation
of apartheid in the region was to dominate regional attention for three decades. With the attainment of majority rule,
however, new challenges with far-reaching implications faced
the country and the continent. Fundamental issues like re-
structuring the legacies of apartheid, establishing new regional policy directions, handling the extreme tendencies of
white extremists, recreating a new national armed forces,
and managing internal ethnic problems, became potential
issues with wider continental implications.

AFRICAN SECURITY: ISSUES FOR THE FUTURE

The preceding chapters have attempted to identify and discuss some of the issues that have come to the fore of African security consideration in the wake of the end of the Cold War. It is, of course, the case that not all the issues are discussed for obvious lack of space. However, from the limited discussion presented, it is undeniable that the end of the Cold War has launched Africa on a new course of opportunity, challenge, and endeavor. While the legacies of colonialism and the Cold War that characterized the first three decades of their independence still remain in a diffused form, African countries now have to contend with a new set of legacies. For these countries, therefore, a fundamental restructuring of perception of security becomes imperative.

Some of the legacies brought to the fore by the end of the Cold War are not new. In fact, most have appeared on the continent in one form or the other for three decades. What has happened, however, is that the end of the Cold War has injected, in most cases, a particular coloration to these issues such that they have now assumed renewed importance. What then are the issues that will predominate and dictate the terms of African security in the future? And what are the prospects for lasting regional peace and stability?

Before considering the above questions, the point must be made about the drought of information necessary for present understanding of issues. It is thus sufficient to caution against the optimism of making any reliable prediction. Also, events in Africa often move at speeds too fast for prediction to be easily or accurately made. What is likely today may, due to unforeseeable circumstances, take a different dimension thereby invalidating any prediction. What is thus attempted here is nothing more than a use of present events to consider some of the issues that are likely to dominate security considerations in Africa during the rest of the century. Having sounded this note of caution, it could be said that four principal issues will dominate the arena of African security and ultimately determine its course. These are the liberalization of the political process, management and resolution of conflicts, implementation of economic reforms, and

concern for the environment including the effects of growing refugee population.

The democratization of the political system will undoubtedly continue to be at the fore-front of African security for the remainder of this century. This has particular
relevance to security consideration in the continent in a number of ways. First, the demand for democratic forms of governments has not been heeded in some countries still under
military dictatorship or non-democratic civilian administrations. In such countries, unheeded calls for democratization
could bring about violent tension. Nigeria provides a good
example where a botched political transition program instituted by the erstwhile president, General Ibrahim Babangida,
resulted in violent crisis that nearly pushed the country to
the rough edges of another civil war. The continued existence of military dictatorship in Nigeria, accompanied by the
use of coercive state apparatus to suppress demands for democracy, has been a source of never ending tension in the
country. The current military administration of General
Sanni Abacha has not, as yet, emerged with a creditable
agenda to return the country to democratic rule.

The still-born democracy and new-born autocracy in
Nigeria can be considered somewhat of an extreme example
of a security problem arising out of demand for democracy.
However, a number of African states which prided themselves as "democratic" have not escaped political crises capable of degenerating into civil strife. Some incumbent leaders allowed elections supposedly to fulfil demands for democracy merely out of external pressure and threat from
foreign donors. These stage-managed elections invariably
ensured that the incumbent governments returned to power
under the facade of democracy. The rigging of elections and
other electoral malpractice that usually accompany such
exercise plus government's repression of opposition have not
given way for peace, stability, and national security. If autocratic governments continue to suppress opposition, a likelihood of armed revolt cannot be ruled out. Support for this
type of revolt could come from neighboring countries, especially if such neighbors have democratic form of government. This will automatically extend the dimension of the
conflict to result in strained relations between neighbors.
Countries that are likely to be the fore of attention in this

call for democratic reform are Kenya and Cameroon. Thus, the way African states handle the key issue of political reform will determine whether the continent will achieve peace and stability necessary for safeguarding security.

The post-Cold War era has not seen a decline in African conflicts. Ethnic tensions have traditionally been a major source of conflict in the continent as demonstrated, for instance, by Katanga and Biafra. The devastating ethnic induced warfare in Rwanda has shown quite clearly that ethnicity, as a source of conflict, is still very much part of Africa's problems. Rwanda exploded in ethnic conflict in April 1994 in a carnage that resulted in the massacre of half a million people and the displacement of another two million, creating unprecedented refugee problem for neighboring countries. The relationship between the Hutus and Tutsi remains precarious, and civil tension continues in the country. Although efforts at resolving the conflict still continue, relations between these two ethnic groups are likely to be unstable for quite some time to come.

There are a number of other African countries with potentials for ethnic conflict. Indeed, because they are a product of artificial creation, practically no African state is immune to ethnic tension. Even a homogenous state like Somalia erupted in clan warfare in 1993. It cannot be guaranteed that Rwanda's genocidal war will not spread to neighboring Burundi, with its Tutsi and Hutu population, and where ethnic tension has also been rife.[6]

In the years to come, ethnic problems are likely to combine with a number of other factors to cause security problems in many African countries. Nigeria's failed attempt at re-democratization has partly led to the politicization of ethnicity. With the annulment of the June 12, 1993 presidential election widely believed to have been won by Chief Moshood Abiola, a politician from the Yoruba ethnic group, the Yoruba people in the federation have particularly felt themselves marginalized in the country's political life. This has resulted in deep inter-group animosity and distrust that bordered on ethnic conflict.[7]

The root of African conflicts is not limited to ethnic rivalry, however. Other sources of conflict include religious tension and border disputes. These, too, are likely to pose a threat to national security in the post-Cold War period. The escalation of religious nationalism has particularly been a major source of conflict in states like the Sudan and Algeria. Although cases of disputed boundaries have lessened considerably in comparison to the preceding decades, they have, however, not entirely disappeared from the list of African conflicts. The demise of the Cold War has thus not removed the problem of interstate conflict propelled by disputed boundaries. Indeed, the potential for bloody interstate conflict arising from border disputes continues to exist. The tendency of border disputes to create deep conflict becomes high if the disputed territory is potentially rich in natural or mineral resources. The dispute between Nigeria and Cameroon over the Bakassi Peninsula is still a cause of deep animosity between the two countries.

As far as conflict is concerned on the continent, it is the extent and seriousness to which African countries are willing to face the perennial problem that matters. In the past, in the era of super power rivalry in Africa, regional approach to crisis resolution was not always successful, as testified to by the Congo crisis and the Nigerian civil war.[8] But the end of the Cold War has undoubtedly created an opportunity for conflict resolution within the African framework. It is hoped that African leaders will take their destiny into their own hands. Although, Africa failed to prove it had the political wherewithal to deal with the crises in Somalia and Rwanda, it remains too early to determine whether the continent will be able to marshall the will to solve its own problems in the future.

For a number of understandable reasons, the African economic situation continues to dominate any discussion of the continent's future especially about its security. It is certain that the debt problem confronting most African countries and the general hardship created by the economic problem present a most immediate and significant threat to their security. The debt problem and the attendant conditionalities of the lending financial institutions have the tendency of eroding some of the gains accomplished in the struggle for democratic reforms. The fulfillment of the conditionalities imposed by these financial institutions are likely to encourage, unwittingly, autocratic regimes. The irony of it is that these autocratic governments in many cases created the economic problems many African countries presently face.

Since it does not appear that many of these countries are overcoming their economic problems, and since the conditions imposed for the payment of debts are not being relaxed in any significant way, the propensity for autocracy and the possible resurgence of all its attendant ramifications increase.

For some of the countries in Africa, the peace brought about by the end of the Cold War has translated into a reduction in their defense expenditure. Already, countries like Mozambique and South Africa are currently thinking of reducing emphasis on militarism, and the diversion of resources to other areas of social and economic life. It is also true that what is needed by some of the countries for their post-war reconstruction is far too much for what the economy can shoulder. Perhaps the best example in this regards is Mozambique. The poorest country in Africa, the financial resources Mozambique requires to bring about the most basic level of reconstruction far exceed what the nation can generate internally. Much the same problem applies to Liberia, Angola, and a number of other countries where protracted wars are presently undergoing mediatory efforts. The relevance of this to security is evident in the inability of any future government to provide basic amenities thus breeding a situation that can result in mass revolt.

Finally, in recent years environmental problems have graduated from the hitherto position of neglect to that of prominence. The management of some environmental problems would continue to face African states for quite some time to come. For instance, the environmental implications of militarization are so enormous that no government can afford to take them for granted. Escalating refugee cases have also tended to exercerbate environmental problems. Other environmental problems like water and air pollution, destruction of natural resources including extensive deforestation, and destruction of wildlife would also continue to threaten African security for the remaining part of the century.[9] The economic difficulties presently confronting most of the countries in the continent will further aggravate environmental problems.

NOTES

1. For a concise discussion of the implication of the end of the cold war for African security, see, Abiodun Alao, *African Conflict: The Future Without the Cold War*, (London: Brassey Pub lishers, 1983).
2. Quoted from *Time Magazine*, September 7 1992, 31.
3. *Congressional Quarterly Weekly Report*, vol. 50. no. 2, May 16, 1992.
4. *African Business*, March 1995, 16.
5. Quoted in *United States Institute of Peace Journal*, vol. vi. no 5, Oct. 1992, 3.
6. See reports of escalating ethnic unrest in Burundi in *Philadelphia Inquirer*, Aug. 13, 1994.
7. Rumors of impending war between the Yoruba and the Hausa/ Fulani was commonplace throughout 1995. For instance *Tempo* of 18 August, 1994, reported the Hausa/Fulani preparation for war through importation of large cachet of arms shipped through Kano Airport.
8. For the dismal role of the OAU in the Nigerian Civil War, see for instance, Adebayo Oyebade, "The Organization of African Unity and the Nigerian Civil War, 1967-1970: A Case Study in Mediatory Diplomacy," MA thesis, University of Ife, 1985.
9. For a discussion of some of the environmental problems being faced by African countries, see Norman Myers, *Ultimate Security: The Environmental Basis of Political Stability*, (New York: W.W. Norton and Company, 1993).

CONTRIBUTORS

Abiodun Alao is a lecturer in the Department of War Studies, King's College, University of London. He has held teaching and research positions at the Obafemi Awolowo University, Ile-Ife, Nigeria, and at the Center for Defence Studies, King's College, London. He is the author of *African Conflicts: The Future Without the Cold War*, London: Brassey Publishers, 1993; and *Brothers at War: Dissidence and Rebellion in Southern Africa*, London: British Academic Press, 1994. He has contributed chapters to edited books and has also published articles in various journals among which is *Jane's Intelligence Review*. He holds a Ph.D. in War Studies from King's College, University of London.

Ayele Bekerie is an Assistant Professor in the Department of African American Studies, Temple University. He was educated at Addis Ababa University in Ethiopia, Cornell University, and at Temple University where he obtained his Ph.D. in African American Studies. He is currently a Visiting Professor in the Africana Studies and Research Center at Cornell. He has published articles in academic journals such as *Journal of Black Studies*. He is the author of *Ethiopic: An African Writing Systems, its History and Principles*, (NJ: Red Sea Press, 1997).

Victor Oguejiofor Okafor is an Assistant Professor of African American Studies at Eastern Michigan University, Ypsilanti, Michigan. Previously he served as Director of African American Studies at the North Carolina State University in Raleigh. He holds a Ph.D. in African American Studies from Temple University, and an M.A. in Public Affairs from Indiana University. His research and writing focus on the theoretical and methodological foundation for

Black Studies (Africology); Afrocentric theory, analysis and synthesis; African and African American Political and Public Policy issues; and African Civilization. He has published scholarly articles in journals including *the Western Journal of Black Studies* and *Journal of Black Studies.*

Funmi Olonisakin is a Research Associate at the Center for Defence Studies, King's College, University of London. She has done research in regional security in West Africa and has conducted a number of field trips to the region. She holds a Ph.D. from the Department of War Studies, University of London. She has published articles on West African security.

Adebayo Oyebade is an Assistant Professor in the Department of History at Lane College, Jackson, Tennessee. Formerly he was a lecturer in African history at Ogun State University, Nigeria. He holds a Ph.D. in history from Temple University, Philadelphia, and has been a recipient of scholarly awards including the Fulbright, and Ford Foundation Research grant. He has contributed chapters to books on African history and has published articles in learned journals including *African Eonomic History*, and *Journal of Black Studies.* His current research focuses on ethnicity, conflict resolution and management, democratization process, and political liberalization in Africa in the post-Cold War order.

Ahmadu Sesay is a professor of International Relations at the Obafemi Awolowo University, Ile-Ife, Nigeria. He has written several articles on African security and international Relations. Some of his published books on the subject include, *Africa and Europe: from Partition to Inter-dependence or Dependence*, London: Croom Helm, 1984; *The Future of Regionalism in Africa*, (Co-edited), London: Macmillan; and *The OAU After Twenty Years*, (Co-authored) Boulders Colorado: Westview.

Sheriffdeen A. Tella is Coordinator of the Department of Banking and Finance at Ogun State University in Nigeria, where he also teaches courses in monetary economics and economic development. He was a Fulbright research scholar at the Department of Economics, University of Nebraska,

Lincoln, in the 1992-93 academic session. He has written articles for professional journals like *Research for Development*, and *Savings and Development*. He has also contributed a chapter to an edited collection on business performance. He holds a Ph.D. from the University of Ibadan.

BIBLIOGRAPHY

Adedeji, Adebayo. (ed). *Indigenization of African Economies.* (New York: Africana Publishing Company, 1981).

_____. et al. (eds.). *The Challenge of African Economic Recovery and Development.* (Portlaand: Frank Cass, 1991).

Adekanye, J.B. "Structural Adjustment, Democratization and Rising Ethnic Tensions in Africa." *Development and Change.* 26 (2), April 1995, 355-74.

Adepoju, Aderanti. *The Impact of Structural Adjustment on the Population of Africa.* (Portsmouth: Heinemann, 1993).

African Center for Monetary Studies and Association of African Central Banks. *Instruments of Economic Policy in Africa.* (Portsmouth: Heinemann, 1992).

Ake, Claude. *A Political Economy of Africa.* (New York: Longman Publishing Company, 1981).

_____. "Rethinking African Democracy." *Journal of Democracy.* 2 (2), Winter 1991.

Akinrinade, Olushola. "Threats to Security and Stability in Nigeria: Perception and Reality." *Geneve-Afrique,* 26 (2).

Alagappa, Muthiah. *The National Security of Developing States: Lessons from Thailand.* (Dover: Auburn House Publishing Company, 1987).

Al-Mashat, Abdul-Monen M. *National Security in the Third World.* (Boulder: Westview Press, 1985).

Alao, Abiodun. *African Conflicts: The Future Without the Cold War.* (London: Centre for Defence Studies, University of London, 1993).

Ambrose, Brendalyn P. *Democratization and the Protection of Human Rights in Africa: Problems and Prospects.* (Westport: Praeger, 1995).

Anderson, Hillary. *Mozambique: War Against the People.* (New York: St Martins Press, 1992).

Anglin, D., Timothy Shaw, and C. Widstand. (eds). *Conflict and Change in Southern Africa.* (Washington D.C.: University Press of America, 1978).

Anyang'Nyong'o, Peter. (ed.). *Popular Struggles for Democracy in Africa,* (New Jersey: Zed Books, 1987).

Arlinghaus, Bruce, E. (ed.). "Military Development in Africa: The
    Political and Economic Risk of Arms." *African Security
    Issue: Sovereignty, Stability and Solidarity*, (Boulder:
    Westview Press, 1984).

Asante, Molefi Kete. "A Six-State Structure for Africa." *African
    Concord*. 17 September, 1987.

Ashbire, David and Richard Allen. (eds.). *National Security:
    Political, Military and Economic Strategies in the
    Decade Ahead*. (New York: Praeger, 1963).

Ashley, Richard. *The Political Economy of War and Peace*. (New
    York: Nicholas Publishing Company, 1980).

Asiwaju, A.I. and P.O. Adeniyi. (eds.). *Borderlands in Africa: A
    Multidisciplinary and Comparative Focus on Nigeria and
    West Africa*. (Lagos: University of Lagos Press, 1990).

Ate, Bassey E. and Bola A. Akinterinwa. (eds.). *Nigeria and Its
    Immediate Neighbors: Constraints and Prospects of Sub-
    Regional Security in the 1990s*. (Lagos: The Nigerian
    Institute of International Affairs and Pumark Nigeria,
    Limited, 1992).

Austen, Ralph. *African Economic History: Internal Development
    and External Dependency*. (Portsmouth: Heinemann,
    1987).

Ayoob, Mohammed. "Security in the Third World: The Worm
    About to Turn?" *International Affairs*. 60 (1), Winter
    1983/4.

_____. *Regional Security in the Third World: Case Studies From
    Southeast Asia and the Middle East*, (London: Croom
    Helm, 1986).

_____. *The Third World Security Predicament*. (Boulder: Lynne
    Rienner Publishers, 1995).

Axelson, Diana E. "Philosophical Justifications for Contemporary
    African Social and Political Values and Strategies," in
    Richard A. Wright. (ed.). *African Philosophy*, (Lanham:
    University Press of America, 1984.)

Azar, Edward. "Peace Amidst Development: A Conceptual Agenda
    for Conflict and Peace Research." *International Interac-
    tions*. 6 (2), 1979.

Azar, Edward, and Chung-in Moon. (eds). *National Security in
    the Third World: The Management of Internal and
    External Threats*. (Aldershot: Edward Elgar Publishing
    Limited, 1988).

Babangida, Badamasi I. "National Interest is National Security."
    Nigerian Journal of Political Science. 5 (1-2), 1987.
Babu, Abdur Rahman. "Africa Urged to Adopt Social Economies."
    West Africa. 11-17, November, 1991.
Barber, James and John Barratt. South Africa's Foreign Policy:
    The Search for Status and Security, 1945-1988.
    (Cambridge: Cambridge University Press, 1990).
Barth, Fredrik. (ed.). *Ethnic Groups and Boundaries: The Social
    Organizations of Culture Difference.* (Boston: Little,
    Brown and Company, 1969).
Bayart, Jean-Francois. *The State in Africa: The Politics of the
    Belly.* (London: Longman, 1993).
Benoit, Emile. *Defense and Economic Growth in Developing
    Countries.* (Lexington Books, 1973).
Berberoglu, Berch. *The Political Economy of Development.*
    (Albany: State University of New York Press, 1992).
Berkowitz, Morton and P.G. (eds.). *American National Security.*
    (New York: The Free Press, 1963).
Berman, Bruce J. and Colin Leys. *African Capitalists in African
    Development.* (Boulder: Lynne Rienner Publishers, 1994).
Berridge, G.R. *South Africa, the Colonial Powers and African
    Defense.* (New York: St Martin's Press, 1993).
Bertram, Christoph (ed.). *Third World Conflict and International
    Security.* (Hamden: Archon Books, 1982).
Binsbergen, Wim van. "Aspects of Democracy and Democratiza-
    tion in Zambia and Botswana: Exploring African Politi-
    cal Culture at the Grassroots." *Journal of Contemporary
    African Studies.* 13 (1), Jan. 1995.
Black, Jan, K. *Development in Theory and Practice.* (Boulder:
    Westview Press, 1991).
Bock, P.G. and Morton Berkowitz. "The Emerging Field of Na-
    tional Security." *World Politics.* (19) 1, 1966.
Bozeman, A.B. *Conflict in Africa: Concepts and Realities.*
    (Princeton: Princeton University Press, 1976).
Brown, Harold. *Thinking About National Security.* (Boulder:
    Westview Press, 1983).
Bryant, Coralie and Louise G. White. *Managing Development in
    the Third World.* (Boulder: Westview Press, Inc., 1982).
Buijtenhuijs, R. and E. Rijnierse. *Democratization in sub-Saharan
    Africa, 1989-1992: An Overview of the Literature.* (Leiden:
    African Studies Centre Research Reports no. 51, 1993).

Bull, H. "The Third World and International Society." *Yearbook of World Affairs*, 1979.

Buzan, Barry. *People, States, and Fear: The National Security Problem in International Relations.* (Sussex: Wheatsheaf Books, 1983).

Callaghy, T.M. "Africa's Debt Crisis." *International Affairs.* (38) 1, Summer 1984.

Calvert, P.A.R. *The Foreign Policy of New States.* (Brighton: Wheatsheaf Books, 1986).

Calvocoressi, P. *Independent Africa and the World.* (Essex: Longman, 1985).

Carey, Roger and Trevor C. Salmon. *International Security in the Modern World.* (New York: St Martin's Press, 1992).

Cawthra, Carvin. "The New South Africa: Facing up to the Legacies of Apartheid." *Brassey Defence Yearbook.* 1994.

Chabal, Patrick. *Power in Africa: An Essay in Political Interpretation.* (New York: Martin's Press, 1992).

Chanainwa, D. "African Initiatives and Resistance in Southern Africa," in A.A. Boahen. (ed.). *General History of Africa: Africa Under Colonial Domination, 1880-1935,* Vol. II. (California: Heinemann Educational Books, Ltd. 1985).

Chazan, Naomi. "Africa's Democratic Challenge." *World Policy Journal.* 9 (2), 1992.

_____. John W. Harbeson, and Donald Rothchild. *Civil Society and the State in Africa.* (Boulder: Lynne Rienner Publishers, 1993).

Chenery, H.B. and L.Taylor. "Development Patterns: Among Countries and Over Time." *Review of Economics and Statistics.* 50 (4)., Nov. 1968, 391-416.

Cheru, Fantu. *The Silent Revolution in Africa: Debt, Development, and Democracy.* (London: Zed Books, 1989).

Cheysson, C. "Europe and the Third World After Lome." *World Today.* June 1975.

Chibber, Ajay. and Stanley Fischer. *Economic Reform in Sub-Saharan Africa.* (Washington, DC: World Bank Press, 1991).

Chipasula, James and Alifeyo Chilivumbo. (eds.). *South Africa's Dilemma in the Post-Apartheid Era.* (Lanham: University Press of America, 1993).

Cliffe, Lionel. *The Transition to Independence in Namibia.* (Boulder: Lynne Rienner, 1994).

Cock, Jacklyn. (ed.). *Society at War: The Militarization of South Africa.* (New York: Martin's Press, 1989).

_____ and Eddie Koch. (eds.). *Going Green: People, Politics and the Environment in South Africa.* (Cape Town: Oxford University Press, 1991).

Cohen, Raymond. *Threat Perception in International Relations.* (Madison: University of Wisconsin, 1979).

Cohen, Ronald. et. al. (eds.). *Human Rights and Governance in Africa.* (Gainesville: University Press of Florida, 1993).

Commander, Simon. (ed.). *Structural Adjustment and Agriculture: Theory and Practice in Africa and Latin America.* (Portsmouth: Heinnemann, 1989).

Cornia, Giovanni Andrea. et al. (eds.). *Africa's Recovery in the 1990's: From Stagnation and Adjustment to Human Development.* (New York: St Martin's Press, 1993.)

Crocker, Chester. *High Noon in Southern Africa: Making Peace in a Rough Neighborhood.* (New York: W.W. Norton and Company, 1992).

Daly, M.W. and Ahmod Skaingu, (eds.). *Civil War in Sudan.* (New York: St Martin's Press, 1993).

Damus, Lloyd. "Systems Reliability and National Insecurity." *Peace Research Reviews.* 7, November 1977.

Davidson, Basil. *The Black Man's Burden: Africa and the Curse of the Nation-State.* (New York: Times Books/Random House, 1992).

Delgado, C.L. and S. Jammeh. (eds.). *The Political Economy of Senegal Under Structural Adjustment.* (New York: Praeger, 1991).

Deng, Francis M. and William I. Zartman. (eds.). *Conflict Resolution in Africa.* (Washington: The Brookings Institution, 1991).

Denton, Frank H. *Some Regularities in International Conflict, 1820-1949.* (Santa Monica: Rand Corporation, 1965).

Dewaal . and R. Omaar. "The Genocide in Rwanda and the International Report." *Current History.* 94 (591), April 1995, 156-161.

Diop, Cheikh Anta. *Civilization or Barbarism: An Authentic Anthropology.* (Brooklyn: Lawrence Hill Books, 1991).

Duncan, Alex. and John Howell. (eds.). *Structural Adjustment and the African Farmer.* (Portsmouth: Heinemann Publishers, 1992).

ECA. *African Alternative Framework for Structural Adjustment Programme for Socio-economic Recovery.* (Addis Ababa: 1989).

ECA/OAU. *Africa's Economic and Social Crisis.* (A Report submitted to the Special Session of the United Nation's General Assembly, Addis Ababa; March 31, 1986).

Elias, O.T. "The Charter of the OAU." *American Journal of International Law.* April 1965.

Emerson, R. and M. Lilson. *The Political Awakening of Africa.* (Englewood Cliffs: Prentice-Hall, 1965).

Emmerij, Louis. *New Technologies and Enterprises Development in Africa.* (Paris: OECD, 1992).

Ergas, Zeki. *The Catharsis and the Healing: South Africa in the 1990s.* (London: Janus Publishing Company, 1994).

Esman, Milton J. and Shibley Telhami. (eds.). *International Organizations and Ethnic Conflict.* (Ithaca: Cornell University Press, 1995).

Etherington, Norman. *Peace, Politics and Violence in the New South Africa.* (London: Hans Zell, 1992).

Falola, Toyin and Julius Ihonvbere. *The Rise and Fall of Nigeria's Second Republic, 1979-84.* (London: Zed Press, 1985).

_____, A. Ajayi, A. Alao, and B. Babawale. *The Military Factor in Nigeria, 1966-1985.* (Lewiston: Edwin Mellen Press, 1994).

Fatton, Robert Jr. *Predatory Rule: State and Civil Society in Africa.* (Boulder: Lynne Rienner Publishers, 1992).

Feuchtwanger, E.J. and P. Nailor. (eds.). *The Soviet Union and the Third World.* (London: Macmillan Press, 1981).

Finnegan, William. *A Complicated War: The Harrowing of Mozambique. Los Angeles: University of California Press,* 1992).

Forrest, Tom. *Politics and Economic Development in Nigeria.* (Boulder: Westview Press, 1993).

Frimpong-Ansah, J.H. and Barbara Ingham. *Saving for Economic Recovery in Africa.* (Portsmouth: Heinemann Publishers, 1992).

Frank, A. G. "Arms Economy and Warfare in the Third World." *Third World Quarterly.* July 1983.

Fukui, Katsuyoshi and John Markakis. (eds.). *Ethnicity and Conflict in the Horn of Africa.* (London: James Currey, 1994).

Gallagher, Mark. *Rent-Seeking and Economic Growth in Africa.* (Boulder: Westview Press, 1991).

Gambari, Ibrahim A. *Theory and Reality in Foreign Policy Making: Nigeria After the Second Republic.* (New Jersey: Humanities Press International, 1989).

Garba, Joseph Nanven. *Fractured History: Elite Shifts and Policy Changes in Nigeria.* (Princeton: Sungai Books, 1995).

Gauhar, Altaf. "The Hidden Cost of the Arms Race." *South.* July, 1982.

Gavshon, A. *Crisis in Africa: Battleground of East and West.* (Harmondsworth: Penguin, 1978).

Gebremedhin, Naigzy. "The Environmental Dimension of Security in the Horn of Africa: The Case of Somalia." *Life and Peace Research.* 5 (1), 1991.

Gibbon, Peter. et al. (eds.). *Authoritarianism, Democracy and Adjustment: The Politics of Economic Reform in Africa.* (Uppsala: The Scandinavian Institute of African Studies, 1992). Seminar Proceeding No. 26.

Giblin, James. *The Politics of Environmental Control in Northeastern Tanzania.* (Philadelphia: University of Pennsylvania press, 1992).

Gladwin, Christina H. (ed.). *Structural Adjustment and African Women Farmers.* (Gainesville: University of Florida Press, 1991).

Gleick, Peter. "Water and Conflict." *International Security.* 18 (1), Summer 1993.

Glickman, Harvey. (ed.). *Political Leaders of Contemporary Africa South of the Sahara.* (Westport: Greenwood Press, 1992).

Goheen, R.F. "Problems of Proliferation: U.S. Policy and the Third World." *World Politics.* Jan. 1983.

Goldblat, J. (ed.). *Non-Proliferation: The Why and the Wherefore.* (London: Taylor & Francis, 1985).

Gorman, Robert. *Refugee Aid and Development.* (Westport: Greenwood Press, 1993).

Grove, J.D. (ed.). *Global Inequality: Political and Socio-Economic Perspectives.* (Boulder: Westview Press, 1979).

Gordon, April A. and Donald L. Gordon. *Understanding Contemporary Africa.* (Boulder: Lynne Rienner Publishers, 1992).

Grosh, Barbara and R.S. Mukandala. *State-Owned Enterprises in Africa.* (Boulder: Lynne Rienner Publishers, 1994).

Gruhn, I.V. "The Lome Convention: Inching Towards Interdependence." *International Organization.* 30, 1976.

Gurdon, Charles. *The Horn of Africa.* (New York: St Martin's Press, 1994).

Gurr, Ted and Barbara Harf. *Ethnic Conflict in World's Politics.* (Boulder: Westview, 1994).

Gutteridge, Williams. (ed.). *South Africa: From Apartheid to National Unity, 1981-94.* (Aldershot: Dartmouth Publishing Company, 1995).

Halter, Marilyn. *Between Race and Ethnicity.* (Champaign: University of Illinois Press, 1993).

Hamilton, David. *Technology, Man and the Environment.* (New York: Charles Scribner's Sons, 1973).

Handel, Michael. *Weak States in International System.* (New Jersey: Fracas, 1981).

Hanlon, Joseph. (ed.). *South Africa: The Sanctions Report: Documents and Statistics.* (Portsmouth: Heinemann, 1990).

_____.Apartheid's Second Front: *South Africa's War Against its Neighbours.* (New York: Viking Penguin, 1986).

Hansen, Holger B. and Michael Twaddle. *Changing Uganda: The Dilemmas of Structural Adjustment and Revolutionary Change.* (Athens: Ohio University Press, 1992). revolutionary?

Hatchard, John. *Individual Freedoms and State Security in the Africa Context.* (Athens: Ohio University Press, 1993).

Helleiner, G.K. "The IMF, the World Bank and Africa's Adjustment and External Debt Problem: An Unofficial View." *World Development.* 20 (6), 1992, 779-792.

Herbst, Jeffrey. *U.S. Economic Policy Toward Africa.* (New York: U.S. Council on Foreign Relations, 1993).

Hirsch, John L. and Robert Oakley. *Somalia and Operation Restore Hope: Reflections on Peacekeeping and Peacemaking.* (Washington D.C.: United States Institute of Peace Press, 1995).

Holsti, K.J. *International Politics.* (New Jersey: Prentice Hall, 1972).

Horowitz, Donald. *Ethnic Groups in Conflict.* (Berkeley: University of California Press, 1973).

Hunwick, John O. (ed.). *Religion and National Integration in Africa.* (Evanston: Northwestern University Press, 1992).

Jackson, John G. *Introduction to African Civilization.* (New York: University Books, 1970).

Jaeger, William K. *The Effects of Economic Policies on African Agriculture.* (Washington, DC: World Bank, 1992).

James, Valentine U. *Resource Management in Developing Countries: Africa's Ecological and Economic Problems.* (New York: Bergin and Garvey Publishers, 1991).

Job, Brian L. (ed.). *The Insecurity Dilemma: National Security of Third World Studies.* (Boulder: Lynne Rienner Publishers, 1992).

Juergensmeyer, Mark. *The New Cold War: Religious Nationalism in Confronting the Secular State.* (Berkeley: University of California Press, 1993).

Kaldor, Nicholas. *Strategic Factors in Economic Development.* (Ithaca: Cornell University Press, 1967).

Kalyalya, Denny et al. (eds.). *Aid and Development in Southern Africa: Evaluating a Participatory Learning Process.* (Trenton: Africa World Press, 1988).

Karenga, Maulana. *Introduction to Black Studies.* (Los Angeles: University of Sankore Press, 1988).

Keller, Edmond. "Towards a New African Order? Presidential Address to the 1992 Annual Meeting of the African Studies Association." *African Studies Review,* 36 (2), Sept. 1993.

Keller, Edmond and Donald Rothchild, *Africa in the New International Order: Rethinking State Sovereingty and Regional Security.* (Boulder & London: Lynne Rienner, 1996).

Khan, Moshin. "The Macroeconomic Effects of Fund-Supported Adjustment Program." *IMF Staff Papers.* 37 (2), 1990, 195-231.

Kibreab, Gaim. *African Refugees: Reflections on the African Refugee Problem.* (Trenton: Africa World Press, 1985).

_____. *Reflections on the African Refugee Problem: A Critical Analysis of Some Basic Assumptions.* (Uppsala: The Scandinavian Institute of African Studies, 1983).

Kiros, Tedros. "Moral Philosophy and Development: The Human Condition in Africa." *Monograph in International Studies, African Studies, No. 61.* (Athens: Ohio University, 1992).

Kornegay, Francis A. "Africa in the New World Order." *Africa Report.* 38 (1), Jan./Feb. 1993, 14-17.

Knorr, Klaus. (ed.). *Historical Dimensions of National Security Problems* (Manhattan: University Press of Kansas, 1976).

_____. and Frank Trager, (eds). *Economic Issues and National Security.* (Lawrence: The Regents Press of Kansas, 1977).

Kolodziej, Edward A. and Robert E. Harkavy. (eds.). *Security Policies of Developing Countries.* (Lexington: Lexington Books, 1982).

Kpundeh, Sahr. (ed.). *Democratization in Africa: African Views, African Voices.* (Washington D.C.: National Academy Press, 1992).

Lasswell, Harold. *National Security and Individual Freedom.* (New York: McGraw-Hill, 1950).

Lehman, Howard. *Indebted Development: Strategic Bargaining and Economic Adjustment in the Third World.* (New York: St Martin's and Macmillan. 1993).

LeMarchand, Rene. *Burundi: Ethnocide as Discourse and Practice.* (New York: Cambridge University Press, 1994).

Little, Ian M.D. *Economic Development: Theory, Policy and International Relations.* (New York: Basic Books, 1982).

Louw, Michael. *National Security.* (Pretoria: Institute for Strategic Studies, 1978).

Low, Allan. *Agricultural Development in Southern Africa: Farm House hold-Economics and the Food Crisis.* (Portsmouth: Heinemann, 1989).

Luckham, R. "Dilemmas of Military Disengagement and Democratization in Africa." *IDS Bulletin.* 26 (2), April 1995, 49-61.

Mackinlay, John and Abiodun Alao. *Liberia 1994: ECOMOG and UNOMIL Response to a Complex Emergency.* (Tokyo: United Nations University Press, 1995).

Mare, Gerhard. *Ethnicity and Politics in South Africa.* (Atlantic Highlands: Zed Books. 1993).

Markovitz, Irving Leonard. (ed.). *Studies in Power and Class in Africa.* (New York: Oxford University Press, 1987).

Marte, Fred. *Political Cycles in International Relations: The Cold Warnd Africa, 1945-1990.* (Amsterdam: Vu University Press, 1994).

Martin, James. *A Political History of the Civil War in Angola, 1947-1990.* (New Brunswick: Transaction, 1992).

Martin, Matthew. *The Crumbling Facade of African Debt Negotiations.* (New York: St. Martins Press, 1992).

Martin, Michael. "Corporate Interest and Military Rule." *Canadian Journal of African Studies.* 17 (2), 1973, 267-285.

Marx, Anthony W. *Lesson of Struggle: South African Internal Opposition, 1960-1990.* (New York: Oxford University Press, 1992).

Massdorp, Gavin and Alan Whiteside. *Towards a Post-Apartheid Future.* (New York: St Martin's Press, 1992).

Mazrui, Ali A. *The African Condition: A Political Diagnosis.* (London: Cambridge University Press, 1980).

McAleese, Dermotet. et al. *Africa and the European Community after 1992.* (Washington DC,: World Bank, 1993).

McCarthy-Arnolds, Eileen. et al. (eds.). *Africa, Human rights and the Global System: The Political Economy of Human Rights in A Changing World.* (Westport: Greenwood Press, 1994).

McGowan, Pat and Charles Kegley. (eds.). *Threats, Weapons, and Foreign Policy.* (Berverly Hills: Sage Publications, 1980).

McNamara, Robert. *The Essence of Security.* (New York: Harper and Row, 1968).

Moose, George E. "U.S. Commitment to Conflict Resolution in Africa." *U.S. Department of State Dispatch,* 5 (25), June 20, 1994.

Mortimer, Michael. *Adapting to Drought: Farmers, Famines, and Desertification in West Africa.* (Cambridge: Cambridge University Press, 1989).

Museveni, Yoweri. *What is Africa's Problem?* (Kampala: NRM Publications, 1992).

Nafziger, Wayne E. *The Debt Crisis in Africa.* (Baltimore: The John Hopkins University Press, 1993).

Naldi, Gino. (ed.). *Documents of the Organization of African Unity.* (New York: Mansell Publishers, 1993).

Neocosmos, Michael. *The Agrarian Question in Southern Africa and Accumulation from Below: Economics and Politics in the Struggle for Democracy.* (Uppsala: The Scandinavian Institute of African Studies, 1993), Research Report No. 93.

Newbury, Catharine. "Introduction: Paradoxes of Democratization in Africa." *African Studies Review.* 37 (1), April 1994.

_____. *The Cohesion of Oppression and Ethnicity in Rwanda, 1860-1960.* (New York: Columbia University Press, 1993).

Newland, Kathleen. "Ethnic Conflicts and Refugees." *Survival,* 35 (1), Spring 1993.

Nkrumah, Kwame. *Africa Must Unite.* (New York: Praeger, 1963).

Nweke, Aforka. "African Perception of Global Disarmament and Prospects for Denuclearization of the Continent." *Nigerian Journal of International Affairs.* 8 (1), 1982.

Nyang'oro, Julius E. "Reform Politics and the Democratization Process in Africa." *African Studies Review.* 37 (1), April 1994.

_____ and Timothy M. Shaw. (eds.). *Beyond Structural Adjustment in Africa: The Political Economy of Sustainable and Democratic Development.* (New York: Praeger, 1992).

Nyong'o, Peter. (ed.). *30 Years of Independence in Africa.* (Oxford: African Books Collective, 1992).

_____. (ed). *Arms and Daggers in the Heart of Africa: Studies in Internal Conflict.* (Kenya: Academy Science Publishers, 1994).

Obasanjo, Olusegun. (ed.). *Challenges of Leadership In African Development.* (New York: Crane Russack, 1990)

_____.and Hans d'Orville. (eds.). *The Leadership Challenge of Economic Reforms in Africa.* (New York: Crane Russack, 1991).

O'Connor, Anthony M. *Poverty in Africa: A Geographical Approach.* (London: Belhaven Press, 1991).

Oden, Bertil and Haroub Othman. (eds.). *Regional Cooperation in Southern Africa: A Post-Apartheid Perspective.* (Uppsala: The Scandinavian Institute of African Studies, 1989). Seminar Proceedings No. 22.

Ogunsanwo, Alaba. *The Transformation of Nigeria: Scenarios and Metaphors.* (Lagos: University of Lagos Press, 1991).

Ohaegbulam, Festus Ugboaja. *Towards an Understanding of the African Experience: From Historical and Contemporary Perspectives.* (New York: University Press of America, 1990).

Okechie-Offoha, Marcellina and Matthew N.O. Sadiku. (eds.). *Eth nic and Cultural Diversity in Nigeria.* (Trenton: Africa World Press, 1996).

Okwudiba, Nnoli. (ed.). *Dead-End to Nigerian Development: An Investigation on the Social and Economic and Political Crisis in Nigeria.* (London: ABC for CODESRIA, 1993).

Olukoshi, Adebayo. (ed.). *The Politics of Structural Adjustment in Nigeria.* (Portsmouth: Heinemann, 1993).

Olusanya, Gabriel O. and R.A. Akindele. (eds.) *The Structure and Process of Foreign Policy Making and Implementation in Nigeria, 1060-1990.* (Lagos: Nigerian Institute of International Affairs, 1990).

Onimode, Bade. *A Political Economy of the African Crisis.* (London: Zed Books Ltd., 1988).

_____. "The Bretton Woods Institutions and Africa's Development." *Development: Journal of Society for International Development.* 1, 1992, 62-67.

Ottaway, M. *South Africa: The Struggle for a New World Order.* (Washington, DC: Brookings Institute, 1993).

Oyebade, Adebayo. "The Dilemma of Conflict Resolution: A Re-Assessment of the Role of the OAU in the Nigerian Civil War." *Ogun Journal of Arts.* 2 (1), 1989.

Oyugi, Walter O. et al. (eds.). *Democratic Theory and Practice in Africa.* (Portsmouth: Heinemann, 1988).

Palmer, Ingrid. *Gender and Population in the Adjustment of African Economies.* (Geneva: ILO, 1991).

Pearce, Robert. (ed.). *Then the Wind Changed in Africa.* (New York: St Martin's Press, 1993).

Prendergast, John. *Peace, Development and the People of the Horn of Africa.* (Washington, DC: Bread for the World Institute, 1992).

Raokes, Philip. *Modernizing Hunger: Famine, Food Surplus and Farm Policy in the EEC and Africa.* (Portsmouth: Heinemann, 1988).

Raskin, Marcus. *The Politics of National Security.* (New Brunswick: Transaction Books, 1979).

Ratner, Stephen R. *The New U.N. Peacekeeping.* (New York: St. Martin's Press, 1995).

Reichart, John F. and Steven R. Sturm. *American Defense Policy.* (Baltimore: John Hopkins Press, 1982).

Richards, Paul. *Fighting for the Rain Forest: War, Youth and Resources in Sierra Leone.* (Portsmout: Heinemann, 1996).

Richardson, Lewis. *Arms and Insecurity.* (Pittsburgh: Boxwood Press, 1960).

Rivage-Seul, D.M. and M.K. Rivage-Seul. *A Kinder and Gentler Tyranny: Illusions of a New World Order.* (Westport: Praeger, 1995).

Roberts, Adam. *Nations in Arms: The Theory and Practice of Territorial Defense.* (New York: Praeger, 1976).

Robinson, Pearl T. "Democratization: Understanding the Relationship between Regime Change and the Culture of Politics." *African Studies Review.* 37 (1), April 1994.

Rosen, Engeen. *Creating Ethnicity: The Process of Ethnogenesis.* (London: Sage, 1989).

Rothchild, Donald S. (ed.). *Africa in World Politics: Post-Cold War Challenges.* (Boulder: Westview Press, 1995).

Ruedy, John. *Modern Algeria.* (Bloomington: Indiana University Press, 1992).

Sandberg, Eve. (ed.). *The Changing Politics of Non-Governmental Organizations and African States.* (Westport: Praeger, 1994).

Sandbrook, Richard. *The Politics of Africa's Economic Recovery.* (New York: Cambridge University Press, 1993).

Saro-Wiwa, Ken. *Genocide in Nigeria: The Ogoni Tragedy.* (Oxford: African Books Collective, 1992).

SCF/ODI. *Prospects for Africa: A Special Report by Save the Children Fund and Overseas Development Institute.* (London: Hodder and Strughton, 1988).

Schraeder, Peter. (ed.). *Intervention Into the 1990s: U.S. Foreign Policy in the Third World.* (Boulder: Lynne Rienner Publishers, 1992).

Scott, Gerald E. "Transfers, Economic Structure, and Vulnerability of the African Economy." *Journal of Developing Areas.* 26, 1992, 213-238.

Seidman, Ann and Frederick Anang, (eds.). *Twenty First Century Africa: Towards a New Vision of Self-Sustainable Development.* (Trenton: Africa World Press, 1992).

Shaw, John and Edward Clay. (eds.). *World Food Aid: Experiences of Recipients and Donors.* (Portsmouth: Heinemann, 1994).

Shaw, Timothy M. *Reformism and Revisionism in Africa's Political Economy in the 1990s.* (New York: St. Martin's Press, 1993).

Shepherd, George W. and Karamo N.M. Sonko. (eds). *Economic Justice in Africa: Adjustment and Sustainable Development.* (Westport: Greenwood Press, 1994).

Sindima, Harvey J. *Africa's Agenda: The Legacy of Liberalism and Colonialism in the Crisis of African Values.* (Westport: Greenwood Press, 1995).

Sklar, Richard L. and C.S. Whitaker. *African Politics and Problems in Development.* (Boulder: Lynne Rienner Publishers, 1991).

Smith, Anthony. "The Ethnic Source of Nationalism." *Survival,* 35 (1), Spring 1993.

Sparks, Donald L. and December Green. *Namibia: The Nation after Independence.* (Boulder: Westview Press, 1992).

Stedman, Stephen J. *South Africa: The Political Economy of Transformation.* (Boulder: Lynne Rienner Publishers, 1994).

_____. *Peacemaking in Civil War: International Mediation in Zimbabwe, 1974-1980.* (Boulder: Lynne Rienner Publishers, 1991).

Stewart, Frances. et al. *Alternative Development Strategies in Sub-Saharan Africa.* (New York: Martins Press, 1992).

Strack, Dieter and Siegfried Schönherr. (eds.). *Debt Survey of Developing Countries.* (Boulder: Westview Press, 1990).

Stewart, Frances. et al. (eds.). *Alternative Development Strategies in Sub-Sahara Africa.* (New York: St. Martin's Press, 1992).

Suhrke, Astri and Lela N. Garner. (eds.). *Ethnic Conflict in International Relations.* (New York: Praeger Publishers, 1977).

Swearingen, Will D. and Abdellatif Bencherifa. *North African Environment at Risk.* (Boulder: Westview Press, 1995).

Tella, Sheriffdeen A. "Basic Needs Development Concept: A Complement in Development Package." *Research for Development.* 5 (1), NISER, Nigeria, 1988.

Thakur, Ramesh. "From Peacekeeping to Peace enforcement: the UN Operation in Somalia." *The Journal of Modern African Studies,* 32 (3), 1994.

Thomas, Caroline. *In Search of Security: The Third World in International Relations.* (Boulder: Lynne Rienner Publishers, 1978).

Thompson, Joseph E. *American Policy and African Famine: The Nigeria-Biafra War, 1966-1970.* (New York: Greenwood Press, 1990).

Thompson, Leonard Monteath. *South African Politics.* (New Haven: Yale University Press, 1982).

Thompson, Scott. *National Security in the 1980s: From Weakness to Strength.* (San Francisco: Institute for Contemporary Studies, 1980).

Tordoff, William. *Government and Politics in Africa.* (Bloomington: Indiana University Press, 1993).

Trout, Thomas and James E. Harf. (eds.). *National Security Affairs.* (New Brunswick: Transaction Books, 1983).

Turok, Ben. (ed.). *Alternative Development Strategies for Africa. Volume Three: Debt and Democracy.* (London: Institute for African Alternatives, 1991).

UNCTAD. *Restructuring of World Industries: New Dimension for Trade and Cooperatives.* (New York: United Nations, 1978).

UNIDO. *World Industries Since 1960: Progress and Prospects.* (New York: United Nations, 1979).

Vasquez John A. et al. *Beyond Confrontation: Learning Conflict Resolution in the Post-Cold War Era.* (Ann Arbor: University of Michigan Press, 1955).

Villa-Vicencio, Charles. *A Theory of Reconstruction: Nation Building and Human Rights.* (New York: Cambridge University Press, 1992).

Vines, Alex. *RENAMO: Terrorism in Mozambique.* (Bloomington: University of Indiana Press, 1991).

_____. *RENAMO: From Terrorism to Democracy in Mozambique.* (London: James Currey Publication, 1995).

Vogel, Ronald J. *Financing Health Care in Sub-Saharan Africa.* (Westport: Greenwood Press, 1993).

Vogt, M.A. (ed.). *The Liberian Crisis and ECOMOG: A Bold Attempt at Regional Peacekeeping.* (Lagos: Gabumo Press, 1993).

Vogt, M.A. and E.E. Ekoko. (eds.). *Nigeria in International Peace-Keeping, 1960-1992.* (Lagos: Malthouse Press, Ltd., 1993).

Weeks, John. *Development Strategy and the Economy of Sierra Leone.* (New York: St. Martins Press, 1992).

Weller, M. (ed.). *Regional Peace-Keeping and International Enforcement: The Liberian Crisis.* (Cambridge University Press, 1994).

Whitaker, Jennifer. *How Can Africa Survive.* (New York: Harper and Row Publishers, 1988).

Widner, Jennifer W. (ed.). *Economic Change and Political Liberalization in Sub-Saharan Africa.* (Baltimore: John Hopkins University Press, 1994).

Wiseman, John A. 1990. *Democracy in Black Africa: Survival and Revival.* (New York: Paragon House).

Woodward, Peter and Murray Forsyth. (eds.). *Conflict and Peace in the Horn of Africa: Federalism and its Alternatives.* (Aldershot: Dartmouth Publishing Company, 1994).

Wordsworth, Filo J. "The Evolution of the Bamako Convention: An African Perspective." *Colorado Journal of International Environmental Law and Policy.* 4, (2), Summer 1993.

World Bank. *World Development Report 1992: World Bank and the Environment.* (Washington, DC: World Bank, 1992).

Zartman, William I. (ed.). *Europe and Africa: The New Phase.* (Boulder: Lynne Reinner Publishers, 1992).

_____. (ed.). *Collapsed States: The disintegration and Restoration of Legitimate Authority.* (Boulder: Lynne Rienner, 1995).

Zartman, William I. and William Mark Habeeb. *Polity and Society in Contemporary North Africa.* (Boulder: Westview Press, 1993).

INDEX

The global political changes that we have seen in the last few years have shown quite clearly that the Cold War has, indeed, ceased to be the dynamic factor in international relations. In Africa, the march toward a new world order is fraught with old problems and emerging ones: extreme ethno-religious nationalism still underscores intra-African conflicts; the continent is sunk more than ever before in the deep abyss of economic stagnation; catastrophic wars are still going on; environmental degradation is increasingly becoming a major problem, and in some states, the search for a democratic political system has turned into civil violence which threatens the very foundation of national sovereignty. These are fundamental problems that collectively pose a threat to the security of the continent.

Although it is widely recognized that Africa's security problems are acute, it has never been a subject of much intellectual inquiry. This lack of scholarly discourse of the many dimensions of the problem of African security is the major consideration for this book. The approach to the question of security in this book differs markedly from the traditional approach that gives primacy to the threat of military aggression as sole factor in state security. A departure must be made from this dominant preoccupation in a new global order that has seen profound changes. The authors then place primacy on the complex problems of ethno-religious nationalism, economic stagnation, catastrophic civil wars, environmental degradation and the prospects for democratic structures in considering Africa's security issues after the Cold War.

Adebayo Oyebade teaches in the History Department at Lane College in Jackson, Tennessee. Formerly he was a lecturer in African history at Ogun State University, Nigeria.

Abiodun Alao is a lecturer in the department of War Studies, King's College, University of London. He has held teaching and research positions at the Obafemi Awolowo Univeristy, Ile-Ife, Nigeria, and at the Center for Defense Studies, King's College, University of London.

0-86543-651-7 $21.95

52195

9 780865 436510

Africa World Press, Inc.

P.O. Box 1892   P.O. Box 48

Trenton, NJ 08607   Asmara, ERITREA